Business and Politics in Peru

Business and Politics in Peru

The State and the National Bourgeoisie

Francisco Durand

Westview Press

BOULDER • SAN FRANCISCO • OXFORD

This Westview softcover edition is printed on acid-free paper and bound in library-quality, coated covers that carry the highest rating of the National Association of State Textbook Administrators, in consultation with the Association of American Publishers and the Book Manufacturers' Institute.

Copyright © 1994 by Westview Press, Inc.

Published in the United States of America by Westview Press, Inc., 5500 Central Avenue, Boulder, Colorado 80301-2877, and in the United Kingdom by Westview Press, 36 Lonsdale Road, Summertown, Oxford OX2 7EW

A CIP catalog record for this book is available from the Library of Congress.
ISBN 0-8133-8472-9

Printed and bound in the United States of America

The paper used in this publication meets the requirements
of the American National Standard for Permanence of Paper
for Printed Library Materials Z39.48-1984.

10   9   8   7   6   5   4   3   2   1

Contents

Tables

Acknowledgments

Several individuals and institutions have contributed to the completion of this book and deserve to be mentioned.

I would particularly like to express my appreciation to the Center for Latin American Studies at the University of California, Berkeley. The Center, with its interdisciplinary emphasis and fluid dialogue among students, professors and guest scholars, proved to be a stimulating and supportive environment. Financial support from the Ford Foundation gave me the opportunity to complete my research in Lima.

Three Berkeley scholars must be specially thanked. David Collier offered helpful and constant advice in terms of content and style and strongly stimulated my interest in comparative politics. Tulio Halperin provided me with a framework of historical analysis on Latin America as a whole which proved to be extremely helpful. Alejandro Saragoza contributed with his continuous support through years of intensive reading and research and helped me to understand the peculiarities and characteristics of the Mexican business community by sharing his knowledge of the famed Grupo Monterrey.

At the Pontificia Universidad Católica del Perú, many friends and colleagues supported and encouraged my research. First of all, I must mention Alberto Flores Galindo, a bright Peruvian scholar who fought bravely but unsuccessfully against cancer. I render tribute to this friend and colleague who struggled to continue working and thinking about Peru's deep social and political problems to the very last. Rolando Ames, Inés García, Luis Miguel Glave, Javier Iguíñiz, Orlando Plaza, Gonzalo Portocarrero and Guillermo Rochabrum encouraged me to keep working and deepening my thoughts on the Peruvian labyrinth of power with their constructive criticism. At Centro de Estudios y Promoción del Desarrollo-DESCO, I would like to mention Carmen Rosa Balbi, Eduardo Ballón, Raul Gonzáles, Juan Larco, Henry Pease, Marcial Rubio and Abelardo Sánchez León for stimulating the study of the country's erratic and surprising political changes. At *Actualidad Económica del Perú*, Humberto Campodónico and Alberto Graña enabled me to accurately follow economic policies and trends.

I am also grateful to many business leaders and high state officials (including three Ministers and three Vice Ministers) whom I interviewed for several hours with open questions on confidential matters. In several cases, their identity must remain anonymous due to the political sensitivity of the information provided. In our numerous in-depth conversations key opinions frequently had to remain off the record. One individual, an entrepreneur, can be mentioned. From our first meeting at a business conference in 1978, Edgardo Palza, for fifteen years manager of the Peruvian Institute of Business Administration and for a further three years manager of the Confederation of Private Entrepreneurs, became a reliable source of sound information and insightful analysis on the business sector and its often intricate and variable relations with the state.

I would like to acknowledge Manuel Estela, for many years an economist at the Central Reserve Bank of Peru and from 1991 to November 1992 head of the Tax Office (SUNAT). He was the inspirer of the most profound tax administration reform of recent decades. Estela convinced me to become a consultant at SUNAT, where I had the chance to learn, from the inside, the workings of the state and assess the importance of tax issues to understand the relation between business and politics. Although I have become a prisoner of state secrets, what I have learned has helped me to confirm that, generally speaking, I was on the right track.

A final word of gratitude to my wife, Tula, and my two daughters, Ursula and Alessandra, for considering this book a family matter.

Francisco Durand

1

Introduction

The incorporation of emerging social actors in the political system, and their participation in the power game, has been one of the key issues in Latin American politics during the twentieth century. This itself has been a period of profound social and economic transformation brought about by industrialization and urbanization. Much has been written about the politicization of blue collar workers, peasants (*campesinos*), informal urban dwellers and the middle class, but there have been fewer in-depth studies and more controversy regarding the role of the national bourgeoisie.

In the post-World War II period, the national bourgeoisie was initially viewed by different schools of thought (modernization and dependency theory) as playing a leading role in the transition to modernization. However, this argument was quickly dropped as the evidence increasingly pointed away from this interpretation. The national bourgeoisie could not keep up its heroic role as economic and political modernizer, as analysts initially described the business class. Thus, the national bourgeoisie became the "ugly duckling" of Latin American politics, a class that did not correspond to the expectations of prejudiced observers. Fritz Wils, one of the first to notice the pessimistic outlook that pervaded the analysis of business people, correctly stated that an overextended set of theoretical expectations led to the disillusionment that the industrialists were the driving force of economic modernization (Wils 1979: 25). Even more alarming than this initial misinterpretation of the situation was the lack of intellectual attention which followed (Acuña 1985: 2).

Until very recently the national bourgeoisie was a political actor not only misunderstood but, worst of all, understudied. In the late 1970s and 1980s, however, the early paradigms began to lose ground and a realist approach tended to predominate, with a number of studies starting to emerge in several countries. The active role played by the business sector in key regional events, the political transition from militarism to civilian democracy, and the policy transition from economic protectionism to free trade policies, forced analysts to review the old paradigms about the political role of the businessmen.

In the transition to democracy, a gradual, troublesome and yet incomplete process of regime change, business people made sure that political parties guaranteed their economic interests because the civilian political class urgently needed business support to isolate the authoritarian coalition led by the military. The political transition also forced the national bourgeoisie to focus on its general interests as soon as new constitutions were adopted and profound changes in a number of policy areas took place: These changes demanded class cohesion and common stances on key constitutional and legal problems. An innovative form of collective bargaining between interest groups and the state (known as *concertación*, concerted action) was adopted during this period of democratic consolidation, in order to facilitate communication between civil society (interest groups) and the state.

In addition to the political transition, the adoption of a new set of liberal-exporting macroeconomic policies taken in a context of severe economic recession, prompted collective business action. The Great Depression of the 1980s forced governments to pay more attention to business demands and to stimulate investment which was badly needed to stabilize the economy. Business people became politically important to policy-makers interested in changing the rules of the game and to administrations besieged by economic problems. It must be noted that the business sector did not always collectively support these changes. In the midst of the economic recession and policy transition a number of opportunities to speculate arose, opportunities that were often more attractive than productive investments. Furthermore, the recession and the economic policy changes frequently divided business interests and affected class cohesion. Those class fractions negatively affected by the recession and/or hit by free trade and stabilization policies (predominantly industrialists), tended to oppose policy changes and demanded state protection. Those fractions who benefited from policy changes (or who were powerful or competitive enough to remain unaffected by the recessionary trends) disagreed with the industrialists and supported government actions. The business sector as a whole, however, also exerted collective pressure on a number of policy areas such as the modification of labor laws, privatization of state-owned firms, reformation of bureaucracy and reduction of the welfare system. These actions were often coordinated and channeled through trade associations. Collective action was also considered necessary to fight proposals that threatened business interests whenever populist and/or socialist forces gained momentary political influence, another factor that prompted class cohesion and forced businessmen to consider collective and not the individualistic behavior common in normal times.

It is worth noting that in this period the business elites, particularly the *grupos*, the most powerful class fraction, found effective, silent, and less visible ways to maintain and improve their access to the state. Informal mechanisms used by the *grupos* however, were not the sole, nor predominant form of political action in all cases.

Several business peak associations (also known as comprehensive associations or umbrella organizations)[1], were formed or reactivated in a number of countries (Costa Rica, Dominican Republic, Guatemala, Honduras, Mexico, Nicaragua, Panama and Peru). In others, the peak association became well organized and enjoyed greater political recognition (Bolivia, Chile and Venezuela).[2] Moreover, national entrepreneurs now felt more inclined to directly and openly intervene in politics, another important dimension of the politicization process. Trade associations demanded a greater share of power and, in many cases, business leaders decided to participate in party politics either by supporting new right political movements or traditional parties.

Analyses of these developments can be found in recent studies of several countries and reveal the region's surge of business political activism. In Peru political analysts talk about the "awakening" of the national bourgeoisie (Castillo 1988: 195; Rospigliosi 1991); in Chile its vigor to participate in "the battle over ideas" (Campero 1988: 262-263); in Ecuador its "consolidation" (CEDIS 1988: 31). In Brazil, probably the most spectacular case, analysts have debated the "strengthening as a political actor" of the national bourgeoisie and, even more so, its "hegemony" (Diniz and Boschi 1988: 307 and 310; Cueva 1988: 66; Touraine 1984: 16). In Mexico several analysts have often made remarks about its "new political will" (Casar 1988: 211). In Nicaragua a most interesting case, the national bourgeoisie became a key political player to defeat the Sandinistas and articulate an alternative political coalition. The national bourgeoisie certainly cannot continue to be ignored as a political actor (Castillo Aramburú 1987: 97-120; Spalding 1992).

In this context Peru is, without a doubt, a fascinating case. It shares the basic traits of business political activism found generally in the region, but has special elements due to a political climate defined by extreme uncertainty, a continuing economic recession and unusually intense and ceaseless forms of social and political violence. Peru is one of the few countries in which the relations between the national bourgeoisie and the state in the 1980s suffered constant changes and occasionally violent confrontations. The industrialists and the *grupos*, for example, participated as partners in a governing coalition headed by Alan García in 1985. Two years later, relations were broken when the government suddenly attempted to nationalize the banking system, a proposal that was stopped by the mobilization of the private sector led by Mario Vargas Llosa, leader of the new right. In 1990, Alberto Fujimori was elected president and, despite the fact that most business people supported his opponent, Vargas Llosa, they, particularly the *grupos* and the exporters, were able to restore relations with the state. In Peru, the national bourgeoisie operates in a highly unstable and politically uncertain climate, characterized by high levels of violence and the destabilizing influence of the economic crisis.[3] Peru, not surprisingly, has often been described by analysts as a "worst case scenario," as a "disaster" area (Palmer 1990). The intense political and socio-economic conflict in Peru has, in turn, accelerated the political transformation of the national bourgeoisie.

This process, however, has its limits and must be carefully assessed. The political changes studied in this book are measured more in terms of the national bourgeoisie's ability to have access to the state in a time of crisis; in terms of its organizational gains that enable it to act collectively through a peak association; and, finally, in terms of an innovative way to express and politically defend its collective interests through the party system. These modifications cannot be seen as a return to the old paradigms of early analyses (modernization and Marxist theory) which viewed the national bourgeoisie as a conquering class, as the driving force of Latin American modernization. This book does not discuss a transformation of the national bourgeoisie into a "leading," "ruling," or "hegemonic" class. It points out specific organizational and political developments from a realist perspective, which implies the recognition of changes as compared to a preceding period; it attempts a cold assessment of the national bourgeoisie's political capability viewed as a process that is yet unfinished. The social recognition of its economic importance and the ideological consensus that other bourgeoisies enjoy in developed nations as economic forces, that is, its integration to society, is still not accomplished in the Latin American case.

The Interpretative Framework

A detailed analysis of the literature published this century on the national bourgeoisie in Latin America reveals, with few exceptions, a number of characteristics that are worth mentioning. First of all, the literature is mostly concerned with the idea of entrepreneurs as forces of economic change, as agents of economic modernization. Secondly, it is usually focused only on the leading business segments (the landed oligarchy, the industrialists, the *grupos*, multinational corporations).

Thirdly, it is usually based on secondary sources and, occasionally, on interviews. This book shifts the focus from the economic to the political developments of the Peruvian national bourgeoisie; it emphasizes its formation as a collective political actor and its participation in governing coalitions. The analysis is not limited to one business fraction. Rather, it studies the internal differentiation of the business sector as a whole (strong and weak fractions of different economic sectors) from an organizational and political viewpoint. Finally, while this analysis strongly derives from primary sources (in-depth interviews and observation of entrepreneurial events such as congresses and conferences), it also relies on the extensive consultation of secondary material (governmental reports and documents, journals and newsletters published by business trade associations).

The approach here views the relationship between economic and political power (the bourgeoisie and the state) as complex and variable. The national bourgeoisie controls key economic material resources but it is not the only agent in the economic system (the state and foreign capital are the two other economic agents to be considered). The national bourgeoisie's ability to have access to political power is conditioned by economic factors, demonstrated by the fact that the most powerful fraction usually has easier and more constant access to the highest offices to defend specific interests. But its individual and collective ability to defend general interests is conditioned, mediated, by political variables. Business people have to develop an ability to act cohesively, overcome internal divisions, form organizations that formally and permanently unite the different business segments and influence both the state, other institutions (the armed forces, political parties) and society. These forms of organization and actions are, in turn, influenced by the rules of the political system. Both sets of factors, economic and political, are thus complexly combined and have to be adequately examined. The changing, variable nature of the relationship between business and politics is conditioned by the ups and downs of the economic cycle and the variable circumstances of the political process: regime changes, the shifting balance of forces in society as a whole and within political institutions (the executive, the Congress, the party system), and public policy changes that define (redefine) the role of the state in society. An analysis of the national bourgeoisie as a political actor since the late 1960s to the early 1990s reveals changing patterns of bourgeois/state relations that express this complex and variable relationship. A detailed and careful analysis of these patterns is critical to understanding the modalities and the extent of influence of business in Peruvian governmental politics. The approach adopted must also be defined as realist because it does not start with an assumption of what the business people ought to be. The analysis does not have particular expectations of entrepreneurs as economic and/or political agents. A realist view discusses the national bourgeoisie as it actually is.

Defining Concepts

A definition of the main concepts used in this book is necessary before continuing further. The national bourgeoisie is understood to be the class that owns the property and controls the management of firms whose capital belongs either completely or almost completely to citizens and whose higher decision-making centers are controlled by nationals who live in the country.[4] This class is, at the same time, divided into several fractions (segments) that share the characteristics mentioned above, but do however have specific differences.

Fractions of the national bourgeoisie are distinguished according to size (big or medium-sized capital) and location within the economic structure (capital specialized in agroexporting activities operating in the external market and/or urban industrial activities operating in the domestic market.) At the top of the pyramid are the *grupos*, the most powerful contemporary economic agents who are characterized by a diversified investment portfolio. The *grupos* have investments in several economic activities and usually exert a tight control over the financial system. Below them are the weaker fractions that, unlike the *grupos*, have specific sectoral locations and less economic power. Whether in the urban-industrial area or the primary-exporting export area, these fractions limit their investments to one sole economic sector. They are defined as "sectoral fractions" because their actual location defines a particular set of interests. This distinction is crucial to the analysis. Traditionally, the national bourgeoisie has been identified with the industrialists, that is, a sectoral fraction with a well defined location within the economy. As noted above, the *grupos*' main characteristic is their control of powerful firms across several economic sectors.[5] Therefore, the industrialists and the *grupos* comprise structurally distinct fractions of the same class and must not be confused.[6]

Becoming a political actor implies a complex process of class formation in which the national bourgeoisie, due to a combination of endogenous (leadership) and exogenous factors (changing factors such as an economic recession, a political crisis), seeks to act more effectively in the political arena. By effectively mobilizing its economic resources and organizing collectively to influence political outcomes, the national bourgeoisie can project its political power in a way which is much more effective than in previous periods. The question of class cohesion is important as it emerges as a factor usually in times of crisis, in times when a particular set of factors forces business people (usually concerned with the defense of individual and, at most, sectoral interests), to mobilize all their resources in order to achieve common goals. The national bourgeoisie's experience as a political actor entails building up a peak association that represents the business sector as a whole, developing class leadership (in trade associations and/or political parties) and, based on those factors mentioned above, participating in political coalitions.

Following Guillermo O'Donnell's definition, governing coalitions can be understood as alliances which impose policies conforming to the orientation and demands of its components through the institutional system of the state (O'Donnell 1978: 25).[7] The two major policy orientations in Latin America are the nationalist-developmentalist and the liberal-exporting ones. The first policy orientation favors import substitution industrialization through market protection, demand stimulation and *dirigiste* policies that reinforce the social and economic role of the state. National-developmentalist policies have predominated in Latin America since the 1950s and have been supported principally by industrialists, developers and governmental contractors. The second policy orientation favors export activities (traditional and non-traditional) and productive specialization based on comparative advantages through free trade, deregulation and privatization policies. Liberal-exporting policies have successfully challenged nationalist-developmentalist policies as the new paradigm of the 1980s and the 1990s. It articulates the interests of exporters and bankers and it is strongly supported by international financial organizations and governments of developed countries, whose concern has focused on Latin America's ability to pay the external debt. The *grupos*, who were originally formed when the industrialization process was stimulated by nationalist-developmentalist policies, were able, through investment diversification, to survive and successfully adapt themselves to the new policy orientation.

The Organization of the Book

This book has been divided into eight chapters. The analysis of the way in which different schools of thought have conceptualized the relation between business and politics is studied in Chapter 2. A critical assessment of the most influential schools of thought (elitism, pluralism and Marxism), vis-à-vis the national bourgeoisie, helps to focus on an approach that views the relationship between the national bourgeoisie and the state as being influenced by both economic (control of economic resources) and political factors and as a variable, changing phenomenon.

A detailed and updated "map" of the economic power structure in contemporary Peru is presented in Chapter 3. It identifies the main economic fractions into which the private sector is divided and the way in which the whole power structure has changed since the mid 1960s to the early 1990s. In terms of property types, it assesses the changing balance of power between private (national and foreign) and public property. Regarding economic sectors, the shifts in importance between the urban-industrial economic activities and the export-oriented economic activities are analyzed. In terms of the key dominant fractions, it considers how the leading economic position passes from the hands of the landed exporting oligarchy to the hands of the new economic power groups. The process of structural change within the national bourgeoisie in the post-oligarchic period, when the landed elite has lost its power and a recomposition of the power structure takes place, is examined in Chapter 4. It assesses the different explanations about the recomposition of the national bourgeoisie relying on a long-term, comprehensive perspective of social change. The arguments that the industrialists or the miners became the heir of the oligarchy are dismissed; it argues about the emergence of the *grupos* as the most powerful class fraction, whose ascension to power becomes evident in the mid-1980s.

The organizational structure of the national bourgeoisie since the 1970s is studied in Chapter 5. It shows how the different fractions were organized as political actors in diverse ways and had different levels of access to the centers of the decision-making process. While the *grupos* privileged the firm and informal mechanisms of access to political power centers, the weaker fractions emphasized action through trade associations and formal bargaining channels. It also discusses the importance of internal unity and the role played by business peak associations in ensuring the possibility of a collective mobilization of business interests. The emergence of an organization of this type signals a key moment when the bourgeoisie becomes capable of collectively defending the general interest and of neutralizing the efforts of the state to take advantage of internal divisions and lack of organizational cohesion.

Chapters 6 and 7 study the logic of business coalition behavior, that is, the patterns of participation in governing coalitions. The 1980s and early 1990s constitute a period where deep political and policy transformations take place and where the national bourgeoisie develops its collective ability to increase its influence on policy decisions and the political process as a whole. Chapter 6 studies the development of Belaunde's liberal-exporting coalition initiated in 1980, this being the first democratic government after twelve years of military rule.

Belaunde was replaced by García in 1985. He changed Peru's policy direction and organized a dominant coalition with a national-developmentalist orientation. In the first case, the coalition counted on the presence of the *grupos* and the exporters, while in the second, the *grupos* remained as an important partner but the exporters were replaced by industrialists and internally-oriented fractions. There was, then, a qualitative organizational change that took place. In 1984, the different business fractions formed a peak association to defend the general interest and started to develop a capability for collective action which changed the system of interest representation and the pattern of relations. The state is now obliged to deal with a new business organization that represents the business sector as a whole and demands participation in the decision-making process.

A period of intense conflict between the state and the national bourgeoisie initiated by García's attempt to nationalize the banking system in July 1987 is analyzed in Chapter 7. The nationalization attempt was the end of the governing coalition inaugurated by García who broke relations with the *grupos* which were the fraction in control of the banking system. This rupture, however, led to the confrontation between the business sector as a whole, now organized under a single, comprehensive association, and García's government. In this conflict, the national bourgeoisie won a political battle against García who was unable to carry on with the plan for the nationalization. The consolidation of the business organization followed the politicization of business leaders who backed the formation of a new right political movement. This Chapter is brought to a close with a brief analysis of the formation of a new liberal-exporting governing coalition led by Fujimori in 1990 and the political role played by the bourgeoisie in the critical events of April 5, 1992, when Fujimori decided to close the Congress.

The conclusions about the political "making" of the national bourgeoisie and the evaluation of the legacy of the changes that took place in the 1980s, the decade of business politicization are summarized in Chapter 8. It considers the importance of these changes (formation and consolidation of a comprehensive association, political activism of business leaders), and critically assesses the limits of the role played by the national bourgeoisie in politics.

Notes

1. Peak associations are third-order business associations composed of several lower-order associations which represent specific economic sectors (com-

merce, banking, mining, agriculture, etc.) Peak associations, that is, an umbrella organization of trade associations, enjoy public recognition as representatives of the business sector as a whole.

2. Basic information about peak associations in Latin America can be found in CIEDLA (1984). A book edited by Dos Santos (1987) provides complementary information on Argentina (p. 210), Colombia (pp. 252 and 266) and Venezuela (p. 68). Another book edited by Garrido (1988) offers information about other countries: Brazil (p. 311), Chile (p. 249), Mexico (p. 215), Nicaragua (p. 114) and Peru (pp. 190 and 275). For additional information about FEDECAMARAS, Venezuela's business peak association, which is one of the best organized in the region, see Moncada (1985), Salgado (1987) and Becker (1991). There are also some detailed analyses on business peak associations for several countries: Peru (Durand 1987), Brazil (Weyland 1992), Mexico (Luna and Garrido 1992) and Nicaragua (Spalding 1992).

3. See McClintock "Comments on Chapter 9/Daniel Shydlowsky" in Hartlyn and Morley (1986: 361-362) and Iguiñiz (1989).

4. This definition corresponds to that of O'Donnell (1978a: 2). See also Portes (1985: 3).

5. The *grupos* are few in number but economically powerful. This definition coincides with that of Hazari (1966), Strachan (1976), Leff (1986), Dahse (1983), Silva Colmenares (1983), Anaya (1989) and Malpica (1989). It differs from that of Stolovich, Rodríguez and Bértola (1988: 33), who define the *grupos* more broadly, including smaller groups. Despite their links with foreign capital, the *grupos* have to be considered as part of the national bourgeoisie. Their association with foreign capital does not imply a loss of control on property and/or management.

6. The concept of fraction refers to structurally different segments of this class. The concept of faction is different and must not be confused with the former one, since it refers to "wings" within a class or a class fraction identifiable by sharing a common political stance. A pro-coup, authoritarian faction, for example, might exist within the *grupos*, the miners, etc.

7. The concept of governing coalitions is similar to that of ruling or dominant coalitions as a type of alliance of the propertied classes articulated by the state. See Collier (1979: 402) and Malloy (1988: 238). On the logic of coalition formation based on a realist approach on business and politics, see Kenworthy (1970b).

2

The National Bourgeoisie as a Political Actor

The political role of the national bourgeoisie can best be understood by analyzing the process through which it becomes a political actor (class formation) and by studying the variable and complex relationship it holds with the state (forms of mediation).

The approach adopted here on social classes and the state assumes that there is not an overall conditioning economic factor that can explain the relationship between the bourgeoisie and the state. Economic power helps to establish a special relationship with the state but it is not the sole factor. Certainly an economic power differential partially explains an asymmetry of access to the state, both between social classes (workers and capitalists) and within the business class (strong and weak fractions). The class (or the class fraction) that controls key economic resources is in a better position to have quicker and easier access to the decision-making process and to establish a privileged relationship with the state. But the formation of a political actor and its complex mediations with the state also depends on political factors such as class leadership and organizational ability. These, in turn, depend on the type of political regime (democratic, dictatorial) and the type of political system (political culture, party system and governmental system) in which the bourgeoisie operates. The bourgeoisie's process of class formation as a political actor and its mediations with the state are conditioned by both economic and political factors.

When using this dynamic approach, which focuses on social classes as political players, it becomes particularly important in studying "latecomers," countries where the emergence of the bourgeoisie has recently occurred. The native bourgeoisie emerged as a class both economically and politically speaking only during the twentieth century. It must be noted that this class was not only young but weak, because it never exerted full economic hegemony. Its "making" was certainly conditioned by economic factors (themselves weak compared to other economic agents, the state and foreign capital), but this did not automatically lead to political weakness or its political subordination to stronger economic agents. Furthermore, the condition of economic weakness should not be viewed as fixed and invariable. The relative economic power differential among several economic agents (public firms, multinational corporations and national investors) changes over time. In addition, political strengthening under certain conditions enables the national bourgeoisie to overcome or compensate for such economic weakness. Although the national bourgeoisie is generally held back by such weakness in its relationship with the state, the balance of power can change in its favor when the other economic agents have less dynamism and when it can develop the ability to penetrate the state, consolidate its organizations, achieve internal unity and mobilize itself collectively whenever general interests are at stake. When the achievements of the national bourgeoisie become politically effective, more regularly influencing policy outcomes according to its own interests, then it is possible to speak about its transformation into a primary political actor.

Class Formation and the Mediation Between Economic and Political Power

Different schools of thought (pluralism, Marxism and elitism) and several contemporary analysts have widely and intensely discussed the relation between economic and political power. At the heart of the discussion is the fact that in modern, market-oriented societies, the state is formally independent from economic power. This poses the question of the relation between those who control economic resources (the bourgeois class or business sector) and the political class that runs public institutions.[1]

How close or distant is the relationship between the two power centers vis-à-vis other social classes and groups? What factors influence this relationship? Is sheer economic power a necessary and sufficient condition for a class to influence the decision-making process according to its economic interests? Are there other variables influencing this relationship? How constant and permanent is the influence of business on politics and the state? These are the key questions being discussed by leading theorists, questions that are, generally speaking, also valid questions in Latin America.

The pluralist school claims that a democratic society grants to individuals and groups with different power resources the right to organize and exert public pressure on government to defend their interests. This school takes for granted the belief that all interest groups have equal access to public institutions. From a pluralist perspective, the bourgeoisie is one among several interest groups and its control of economic resources does not imply "special access" to government (Acuña 1985: 20-21). The analytical emphasis of this school of thought lies in the study of the formation of public interest groups, the individual characteristics of their members, and the way all groups participate in the decision-making process in competition with each other. In this process, the government plays an impartial, mediating role between competing groups. Among the arguments made by critics of this school, those of Charles Lindblom and Eric E. Schattschneider are important to consider. Lindblom has correctly pointed out the need to break with the "unthinking habit" of treating all interest groups as if they all appeared on the same plane. To support his argument, he states that the business sector has a special relationship with government due to its control of crucial societal resources (Lindblom 1977: 193-198). Schattschneider agrees with Lindblom's approach but places the emphasis of his critique on the fact that the pluralist school exaggerates the importance of interest groups and underestimates the importance of party politics. In addition, Schattschneider argues that the relationship between business and politics is not always public and formally channeled through trade associations. Individual access to the state and informal mechanisms are an important element to understanding the interconnection between business and politics (Schattschneider 1956: 40).[2]

Arguments from other schools of thought, Marxism and elitism for example, contradict this pluralist paradigm. In a similar vein to Lindblom and Schattschneider, they claim that there is a closer relationship between those who have a privileged position in society (the bourgeois class, select minorities in general) and political power.

Marx's theory of the state is important, but it must be remembered that it was based only on an analysis of particular historical situations of nineteenth-century Western Europe and as such does not constitute an organized, fully developed theory.[3] In its instrumentalist version based on *The Communist Manifesto*, Marxism asserts that the state plays a role in which its decisions are subordinated to the economic hegemony of the bourgeois class.[4] The state acts as the "instrument" of the bourgeois class and public policies clearly reflect those interests. The structuralist version, however, avoids such a simplistic vision. Based on the *XVIII Brumaire of Louis Bonaparte*, this version offers a more complex view of the state. In a particular situation, the state assumed a "relatively autonomous" position from the dominant classes when bourgeois fractions were deeply divided and their political representatives unable to agree. The analysis of a key critical juncture (the French revolution of

1848), shows a situation where the state acted separately from specific agrarian and industrial-financial bourgeois fractions, but still managed to defend the general interests of capitalist society. Although Marx's contribution to dominant class analysis is important (identifying different fractions and their political representatives, emphasizing internal class divisions), the bourgeoisie remains an abstract entity. Bourgeois actions are seen as only concerned with economic motivations. There are no empirical references to this class itself and its formation as a political actor, but rather to its "representatives." In Marxism, the economic logic of capitalism pervades the analysis; the bourgeoisie's specific forms of political action do not need to be specified because their interests are clearly expressed in public policies or, in a more specific analysis, are reduced to its "representatives."

Elitism offers an alternative explanation to pluralism and Marxism. In this perspective, economic power holders are neither omnipotent (as in instrumentalism) nor impotent (as in pluralism) (Mills 1956). Vilfredo Pareto (1935) and Gaetano Mosca (1939), the founders of this school of thought, claim that the state is controlled by a privileged minority. The elite (Pareto) or political class (Mosca), always serves the particular interest of power holders but the power elite does not necessarily stem from economic factors. In this perspective, the state is not the instrument of one class, the bourgeoisie. Economic power is one of many factors that explains why a privileged minority uses the state for its own benefit. Thus, the political elite in control of the state can be as influential or powerful as the economic elite, and both enjoy the privileges of their success. Elitist thinkers emphasize the notion of an elite or political class that dominates the rest of society (conceived of as "the masses") rather than looking at the connection among elites (business elites and the political class) that interests us here. The political class and the entrepreneurs are part of the elite, but the nature of their relationship remains unspecified.[5] Nevertheless, the notion of an elite in the sense of a select minority, that is, a leadership group within a class rather than a social class in itself, is a useful analytical concept. It helps to identify those who play a crucial role both among the bourgeoisie and in government.[6]

The contemporary debate on economic and political power relations developed by Lindblom, Alberto Martinelli and Antonio M. Chiesi, Anthony Giddens and Adam Przeworski has enhanced the argument of this book. Lindblom states that relations between social classes and the state are asymmetrical. Economic resources, as well as the organizational capabilities of the business sector, imply a power differential compared to other social classes and groups. The business sector's control of key resources helps them to be politically more effective and enables them to establish a "special relationship" with government (Lindblom 1977: 193-198). It must be pointed out, however, that asymmetry, in terms of access to the state, can exist not only among classes, but also within the bourgeoisie itself. This is because some bourgeois fractions are economically more powerful than others. While Lindblom does not attempt to analyze this problem specifically, it can be deduced from his premises. In other words, more economically powerful bourgeois fractions enjoy a "special relationship" with the state, vis-à-vis weaker fractions.

Another important argument concerning the drifting nature of economic factors is developed by Martinelli and Chiesi. They carefully consider, from a dynamic perspective, that specific analysis of the bourgeoisie must take into account the fact that economic power changes with time. Factors such as wars and revolutions, economic depressions and booms, bring about sudden changes in the sources of wealth and thus tend to make the relationship with the state more variable. Both authors also emphasize the importance of political factors as an analytical element which conditions the complex relationship between business and politics (Martinelli and Chiesi 1989: 109-110).

Giddens and Przeworski point out that economic and political power relations are both complex and dynamic and that this relation cannot be understood without an analysis of the interplay between the two. Giddens's concept of mediation, a useful analytical tool, is defined as the "modes in which possession of economic resources can be, and are mobilized to pursue political ends, and vice versa" (Stanworth and Giddens 1975: xi). This mediation, in turn, has an impact on the decision-making process. Specific situations which reveal the effect of this power, according to Giddens, can be summarized as follows: (a) the bourgeoisie's ability to prevent decisions being taken against specific interests (a non-decision), (b) its ability to make or participate in decisions, and (c) its ability to exert pressure so as to annul a decision already taken.

Rather than seeing the bourgeoisie as embedded in the state (instrumentalism), or as a select minority whose relationship with the state is not clarified (elitism), or is separated from it (pluralism), what matters is the complex and dynamic political connection between a social class that controls key resources and the state.[7] This is a key theoretical statement and it must be complemented with the analysis of political factors from a class formation perspective, that is, to understand how specific modes to mobilize economic resources for political purposes come to be developed.

Przeworski has noted that social classes do not appear politically only as epiphenomena of objective economic interests. Before the mediations with the state take place, the bourgeoisie assumes a particular organizational form that makes it, politically speaking, an actor (an effective political force). This process is affected by political variables. For him, "the classes that move history [are] those that appear as political forces" and are not "those defined as places in the relations of production" (Przeworski 1977: 348-349). The organizational process is conditioned by the rules of the game operating in the political system.

Bourgeois power, then, rests also on its political capabilities. The bourgeoisie has a political advantage because, in comparison to other social groups and classes, it mobilizes economic resources that are crucial to the reproduction of society. But these resources have to be politically effective, or functional to specific institutional settings. The power of the bourgeoisie has to be politically constituted. As a class, it has to be formed through a trial and error process which helps the bourgeoisie to find the most effective way to mobilize individual and collective resources. The question then, is not only whether a class controls certain resources, but how well it is politically organized and how effectively it deploys resources for political purposes.

Latin America: A "Conquering Bourgeoisie"?

Latin America poses a theoretical problem because of the difficulty in understanding the region's "historical peculiarities."[8] In this setting, the analyst has to be particularly cautious. Although theory claims universal validity, it has also been conditioned by concrete historical developments that took place in Western Europe. The analytical risk of transferring assumptions based on Western experience, as Wils and others have pointed out, has always been present in studies of the Latin American bourgeoisie (Wils 1979: 166; Conaghan 1988a). When theory "travels" to Latin America, it carries with it both particular (historical) and universal (heuristic) contents. Careful use of a theoretical framework involves making the distinction between the heuristic function of a concept and the historical load that it carries.[9]

Latin American historical peculiarities are related to the timing of industrialization and to the nature of its dominant classes. When Latin America was still ruled by landlords, and the economy centered around *haciendas*, mines and plantations, other Western countries were already industrialized and rapidly conquering the region's market with manufactured goods (Waisman 1982: 80). When the path toward industrialization was paved in the first decades of the twentieth century, foreign investors were a powerful and active stimulator of economic modernization. In this context, the native business class appeared late, was economically weak,[10] technologically dependent and, therefore, did not exert full economic hegemony. Alain Touraine correctly points out that a disarticulated elite is typical of the Latin American "dependent societies" (1987: 23-25). It must be noted that industrialization in the region was also induced by the state, this having been attributed by some authors to the fact that a strong national bourgeoisie was absent (Waisman 1982: 81; Canak 1984: 402).

These latecomers and weak native economic agents became a puzzle to various authors who expected them to play a similar role as their European counterparts when the process of modernization was set in motion. Schools of thought as different as modernization and dependency theory were trapped in the mirror image of other historical experience. For Marxist scholars concerned with the question of imperialism, the first nationalist-populist revolutions that fostered industrialization (the Mexican revolution of 1910-1917, Brazil in the 1930s with Getulio Vargas, Argentina in the 1940s with Juan Perón), were identified as processes led by a national bourgeoisie. Industrialists were supposed to be the vanguard of social and economic change, able to conquer political power and impose protectionist state policies. In the late 1960s and early 1970s, this optimistic vision of a "bourgeois revolution" was replaced by a pessimistic one when foreign capital penetrated the region's domestic market and seemed to displace the national bourgeoisie. The image of the conquering, nationalistic bourgeoisie was substituted then for a different, negative vision. In André Gunder Frank's terminology the national bourgeoisie was converted into a "lumpen bourgeoisie," a native elite incapable of acting independently (1972: 23-25). Along the same lines, John Weeks's argument in his study of Peru's 1968 military revolution (a country that experienced a late anti-oligarchical, nationalistic and pro-industrializing revolution), follows the same cycle. Weeks first attributes the national bourgeoisie with a capacity to conquer power and shape economic policies. The Peruvian industrialists, according to this version: "once in power...instituted a land reform which eliminated landed property...and also carried out a number of complementary nationalizations."[11] Later events such as the adoption of liberal-exporting economic policies in the late 1970s and 1980s, in contrast signaled "the admission of the defeat and surrender of the national bourgeoisie to the overwhelming dominance of foreign capital."

The modernization school was concerned with other questions (the positive side of industrialization) and raised arguments about the circulation of elites and the transition from tradition to modernity. They also passed, in a similar vein to dependency theory, from optimism to pessimism. In the 1950s, John J. Johnson thought that internal factors such as the emergence of new elites, the industrialists and the middle

class provided the foundation of democratic stability and continued economic growth in the region.[12] This optimism about modernization led
Johnson to remark that "the acceptance of industrialization as national
policy...made the owners of industrial and commercial enterprises a
highly effective force both as a constructive and as a veto group" (1966:
14). Later versions of this school used the image of a closed elite, the
landed oligarchy, being rapidly replaced by a new open and dynamic
elite, the industrialists, an image that helped to justify U.S. policy decisions toward Latin America. The Cuban revolution of 1959 prompted
the U.S. government to promote modernization efforts based on the idea
that industrialists, together with foreign capital (now increasingly interested in the process of industrialization), were the new emerging elite
and key partners of the "Alliance for Progress" (ALPRO).[13] In accordance with ALPRO plans, John D. Harbrom argued that economic and
social stability was based upon the influence of the new "progressive
industrial elite" (1965: 45). However, the heroic image of the new breed
of entrepreneurs as the agent of a stable democracy soon faded as the
Latin America political pendulum moved to authoritarianism in the
1970s. The enthusiasm about the new elite also languished with the
region's economic slowdown, and the adoption of liberal-exporting
policies to correct the path to modernization. Modernization studies
then took a pessimistic outlook. The idea of the "historical mission" of
the emerging bourgeoisie, influenced by the Western paradigm, was
replaced by studies that displayed an ethnocentric bias by focusing on
the lack of entrepreneurial cultural values (its "absent qualities") or the
deviant behavior of inefficient entrepreneurs.[14]

Major errors of interpretation expressed on the part of analysts from
different schools of thought can be seen in the initial exaggeration (a
"conquering bourgeoisie," a "highly effective force") and the disillusionment that followed (a "lumpen bourgeoisie," dominated by foreign capital, a class with "absent qualities" and no political influence). These
errors were due to the analysts' inability to understand the region's
peculiar path to modernization. In addition to the ethnocentric bias,
both schools of thought emphasize the role of the national bourgeoisie as
economic agents rather than as political players; thus, they pay scant
attention to its formation as a political actor.

A critical reaction to these approaches came from different authors,
particularly from Fernando Henrique Cardoso and Enzo Faletto (1979:
14). Cardoso and Faletto developed a more realistic vision by closely
studying the political incorporation of the national bourgeoisie into
dominant coalitions, where the analysis of negotiation and compromise
were much more significant than the mere "domination" or "hegemony"
of one business fraction (the industrialists during the populist phase of

development; foreign capital during the phase of "internationalization of the domestic market").[15]

Along similar lines, other authors, such as Eldon Kenworthy and Peter Evans, emphasized the need to study the political role of business people in the process of political change and coalitional formation. Kenworthy based his studies on the Argentinian case. His detailed analysis of the formation of Perón's governing coalition helped to clarify the non-hegemonic role played by industrialists in Argentinian politics (Kenworthy 1970a). Kenworthy's "coalition approach" moved away from theories that emphasized "what was to happen, not what is happening or who is making it happen." He reversed the emphasis by asking "in whose existing interest is a particular change, who are likely allies and enemies, and what resources they have to bring this change about" (Kenworthy 1970b). Evans, in turn, pointed out in his studies of Brazil's "triple alliance" (foreign capital, the state and the national bourgeoisie), that "industrialization was a project built on compromise and not on bourgeois domination." Like Kenworthy, Evans contributed to refocusing the analysis on more realistic grounds (1979: 39). This line of thought exerted an important influence on the analysis of the dynamics between economic and political power in Latin America. It stimulated the revision of arguments about the rise and fall of "national bourgeois governments," (Vargas in Brazil, Perón in Argentina, and Velasco in Peru), and the components of the governing coalitions in the "bureaucratic-authoritarian" regimes of the 1970s. The transition to democracy in the 1980s, as pointed out in Chapter 1, showed that the national bourgeoisie was not "missing in action," but actively participating in this political transition, a fact that could be explained only with a previous analysis of its role in politics.

The influence of a pessimistic outlook, however, still pervades much of the contemporary analysis of the national bourgeoisie due to the increasing influence of economic "neo-liberalism," an updated version of the modernization school. This school, headed by Hernando de Soto, has revived the critique of the native business elites as "mercantilists." While criticizing the "rent-seeking" behavior of the national bourgeoisie, Soto presents an idealized image of informal entrepreneurs, without much analysis of the national bourgeoisie itself. Soto and others have emphasized again the vision of what the national bourgeoisie ought to be instead of comprehending it as it is.[16] This is another reason why a realist approach to business people is particularly useful.

Now that the issue of theory and history has been clarified and the need for a realist approach on business and politics has been laid out, a detailed look at other aspects of the main research questions is necessary. Questions such as the internal differentiation of dominant class structures (big business and other less powerful sectoral class fractions), the national bourgeoisie's structural economic weakness, and its organizational (associational) patterns and logic of political mobilization will be analyzed in order to set more specific theoretical guidelines.

Internal Differentiation of the Bourgeois Class

The internal differentiation of the dominant class serves as a map of business power and helps to specify changes that have been taking place in the twentieth century. The first distinction is the one between foreign and national fractions. The second distinction is to identify different fractions within the national bourgeoisie.

National and Foreign Bourgeoisie

At the beginning of the century, a national firm was unquestionably different from a foreign one. National capital and foreign capital were totally separate entities operating in the same economic structure, each exerting full control of property and management, without any association. This clear difference remained approximately until the 1950s. Following this period, foreign and national capital tended to associate in different ways. A first mode of association takes place when foreign capital controls both a firm's property and its management, but incorporates national capital as a subordinate minor partner. A second mode of association is the merging of national and foreign capital in ways that do not imply the subordination of national capital. This occurs in several ways: Foreign capital controls a minor portion of the shares, provides financial and/or technological support, or provides access to markets. Despite the association, national capital still controls both property and management. This distinction is crucial since national capitalists in the second mode can still be considered as members of the national bourgeoisie because a total subordination to foreign capital has not taken place. National and foreign capital can be associated, but this association does not necessarily imply that national capital has surrendered itself to foreign interests (a "puppet of imperialism" according to a Marxist definition), lacks any sense of autonomy.

The Sectoral Fractions and the Grupos

Another controversial issue is the internal differentiation of the national bourgeoisie (according to power differentials and diverse sectoral location in the economic structure). A conventional approach developed in the 1960s emphasized the sectoral distinction of capital (manufacturing versus export sector) as central to the analysis. Markos Mamalakis's sectoral clash theory, for example, assumes the existence of a clash of interests between class fractions in clearly defined economic sectors: world market-oriented extractive-exporting capital and national market-oriented industrial capital (Mamalakis 1969; Story 1978). The problem, however, is that the sectoral approach does not properly classify the fractions of the national bourgeoisie today.

If the current Latin American property structure is observed, it can be concluded that dominant class fractions cannot be clearly correlated with economic sectors in all cases.[17] This is because economic conglomerates, such as the *grupos*, are found in several economic activities at the same time; thus, they have global interests rather than sectoral ones. The study on *grupos* challenges Mamalakis's theory because the diversified investment portfolio of the *grupos* invalidates the sectoral approach identification.[18]

This is not to deny the importance of the distinction between sectoral capitals but to question its validity as the only criterion of differentiation. What has taken place is a process of investment diversification that has created multi-enterprise organizations that no longer have a sectoral identity but rather a more global strategy of accumulation. The *grupos* have diverse sectoral origins because they include individuals who were formerly industrialists, miners, bankers or merchants, but who today do not have a clear-cut sectoral identification. Recent developments in the more advanced layers of the Latin American national bourgeoisie indicate that the sectoral distinction is relevant only for a capital whose investment is concentrated in one economic activity (usually correlated with particular markets, external or domestic). This capital develops a sectoral rationale in defending its interests.

The upper sector of national capitalists, which have constituted themselves as *grupos*, does not necessarily follow such sectoral identity since a fusion between banking and industrial capital has taken place. Although a careful mapping remains to be done for each country, it is possible to assert that the *grupos* in most countries have the ability to move capital from one economic sector to the other, according to modifications of the profit rate, reinforcing the diversified nature of this modern form of firm. The *grupos'* flexibility to move capital is facilitated by their control of the banking system. Additionally, they also tend to combine an increasing amount of business from the external and domestic markets. The evolution of this "new bourgeoisie" is crucial to the understanding of the modern dominant classes in Latin America. Its emergence has thus blurred the old dividing lines between economic sectors. The *grupos*, therefore, cannot be classified as "industrialists" or "exporters." It must be noted that the *grupos* tend to associate themselves more and more with foreign capital, but without losing control over property or management. What must be kept in mind is that distinctions based on sectoral/market identification and those based on a simplistic foreign/national capital differentiation do not properly apply today.

The Economic Weakness of the National Bourgeoisie

If the power (relative control of economic resources) of the national bourgeoisie is compared to the power of both foreign capital and the state (particularly in countries where public firms are still economically significant), it can be asserted that the national bourgeoisie is economically weak. However, as William Canak states, there is a need for the "careful mapping of class structure" because "without this mapping the deeper meaning of the 'weakness' assertion is left vague" (Canak 1984: 7). More careful distinctions of power resources within the national bourgeoisie (among different fractions), help in understanding the real meaning of this question.[19]

As explained above, capitals of distinct "sizes" are found within the national bourgeoisie: One fraction (the *grupos*), is stronger than others (the sectoral fractions). The power differential between the sectoral fractions and the *grupos* is that the former are "strong" in one economic sector (one branch of the manufacturing industry, for example) but not in the economy as a whole.[20] The *grupos*, in this sense, are the strongest fraction within the "weak" national bourgeoisie. It must be pointed out that the relative strength of the *grupos*, compared to foreign and public firms, is based on the fact that wealth is concentrated in a particular way. The *grupos* control conglomerates composed of several firms that, taken together, constitute a respectable expression of economic power.

Another element to be taken into account is that changes in the economic structure modify the relative weight of the different forms of capital (national private capital, foreign capital, public firms). The evolution of these changes can be briefly summarized as follows. At the turn of the century, the power structure changed due to the dynamism of the export-oriented model. These changes, however, occurred within the realm of the private sector, and so tended to favor foreign capital and national capital in the export sector. Later on, under the auspices of the import substitution model, the correlation changed dramatically. Public firms developed in several sectors while multinationals and *grupos* flourished in the manufacturing industry and the urban sector. Today, the process of liberalization and privatization which has been set in motion is inaugurating another period (Glade 1991). The correlation is again changing in favor of the private sector as a whole (national and foreign), exporters in general and the *grupos* (who adapt themselves more easily to policy changes and can take advantage of the process of privatization). The weakness assertion, then, does not have a great deal of analytical validity unless both the internal differentiation of the national bourgeoisie and the modifications of the power structure between different forms of property and economic sectors are taken into account.

Bourgeois Politics in Cuba and Nicaragua

Two different cases, Cuba and Nicaragua, illustrate the fact that although the national bourgeoisie is a relatively weak economic agent, its possibilities of defending short-term and long-term interests are deeply affected by political factors.

Divided and unorganized social actors are easy prey for powerful and aggressive enemies. In contrast, united and organized social actors, that is players capable of defending not only specific but general interests and arrange political coalitions, can win political victories and defeat powerful opponents. The study of the behavior of the national bourgeoisie in two different revolutionary situations (Cuba in 1959 and Nicaragua in 1979) helps to illustrate the point.

In Cuba, according to Alfredo Padula Jr. and Jorge I. Domínguez, the predominance of conflicts among bourgeois interest groups and a narrow perspective of business interests doomed the Cuban private sector at the time of the revolution. When Fidel Castro issued the Agrarian Reform Act of 1959, cattle ranchers did not coordinate with sugar growers. At the same time, the act was fervently supported by industrialists, bankers, textile manufacturers, etc., "none of whom were capable of the coordinated activity needed to defend those who had been hit so hard and so soon" (Domínguez 1982: 195). In Cuba, the political game among economic elites amounted to a total lack of coordination between foreign and private capital and among the different fractions of the national bourgeoisie. This was the best possible scenario for Castro and his revolutionary forces. As Domínguez bitterly argues, the anticapitalist revolution easily unfolded in Cuba because the private sector lacked unity and cohesion and was thus totally incapable of coordinating its own defense when the attack on the private sector started:

> Let the Cuban government take over the plantations; it was not the industrialists' business to oppose it. Let the Cuban government intervene in the running of the U.S.-owned public utilities; it reduced rates and lowered

overhead costs. Let the Cuban government challenge the United States; it gave more business to Cuban-owned private enterprises.... Interest groups sought solely to defend themselves and found themselves alone (1982: 195).

In the case of Cuba in 1959, the political situation of the business sector was critical because of internal divisions and political isolation. Thus, differences of bourgeois political capabilities, a factor rarely analyzed, proves to be crucial in the analysis of anti-capitalist revolutions.

Take the case of the second socialist revolution that occurred 20 years later, in Nicaragua. There, the business sector actively participated in the boycott against the dictator Somoza and formed part of the rebels' first government in 1979. In the 1980s, as soon as the revolution took a radical, anti-private sector course, businessmen shifted positions and became active members of the opposition. As a key force, the national bourgeoisie, already organized into a business peak association success-fully coordinated as much as possible with foreign forces (the U.S.), and other social groups and institutions (the Catholic Church), to isolate the government (Spalding 1992: 27; Castillo 1988: 114-119). In 1990, the Sandinistas lost the elections and Violeta Chamorro, with the decisive support of the Nicaraguan private sector, pushed them out of power. In sum, coordination, organization and alliances were critical factors in reversing the anti-capitalist trend in Nicaragua. Economically, the Nicaraguan bourgeoisie was weaker than its Cuban counterpart despite the 20-year difference, but it was politically stronger, united, better organized, adequately funded and allied to powerful forces.

Political Organization

Having studied the importance of political factors in two cases, it is now convenient to turn to the analysis of bourgeois political organiza-tions. The organizational forms that channel the activity of the national bourgeoisie (and its distinct fractions), are centered around firms, trade associations and political parties. The predominance of one organiza-tional form over the others depends on the type of economic resources controlled by the national bourgeoisie and the nature of the political system.

Economic resources influence organizational patterns in the follow-ing way. The stronger the business fraction, the greater the importance of the firm as a permanent organizational channel to contact and have access to the state. Strong business fractions tend to establish a pattern of mediation with political power which is direct. Contacts are estab-lished on a private, discrete basis and access does not have to pass through trade associations and/or political parties. The most powerful economic firms are more easily "recognized" by state officials and given special treatment. As Lindblom argues, big business (in this case the *grupos*), enjoy the tremendous advantage of having "extraordinary sources of funds" and "organizations at the ready" (the corporation) which enables them to be powerful competitors in the political game (1977: 194). This game is not apparent to outside observers and its secret nature is necessary because it implies discrimination in terms of access to the state.[21]

In contrast, economically weaker fractions are more prone to be ignored by state officials. Their firms are less politically important at a national level and do not count with the numerous human and material resources which would assure a direct, privileged and permanent relationship with the state. This is very much the case of the sectoral fractions, who play the game by relying more on trade associations than on firms; that is, by emphasizing the sectoral significance of their firms. In this way, they compensate for their economic "insignificance" by acting collectively and claiming to represent special interests. When they are ignored, trade associations publicly voice their opinions and demand to be heard by the state. The asymmetrical relationship with the state, whenever bourgeois fractions act separately, conditions a different game. As Schattschneider argues:

> Since the contestants in private conflicts are apt to be unequal in strength, it follows that the most powerful special interests want private settlements because they are able to dictate the outcome as long as the conflict remains private.... Therefore, it is the weak, not the strong, who appeal to public authority for relief (1956: 40).

This game, it must be pointed out, is typical of "normal" political circumstances. When general interests are perceived to be at stake, and private settlements cannot dictate the outcome, there is a need for class coordination for the weak as well as for the strong.

Business action is directed toward decision-making centers, but will change according to the nature of the political system. The way political action is directed is influenced by political culture and the institutional rules of the political game. In Latin America, the political system is characterized by two factors: (a) the centralization of power in the hands of the executive branch, (b) the predominance of clientelism in power relations. What matters for the national bourgeoisie is access to power and this power is concentrated in the executive, despite regime changes (authoritarian, democratic).[22] Accordingly, the national bourgeoisie uses the firm and/or trade associations to establish a direct contact with the executive to develop a clientelistic relationship. The fact that political parties are unimportant during authoritarian regimes, and that democracies are strongly presidentialist, reinforce the tendency of the national bourgeoisie to rely on the firm and trade associations as permanent forms of organization (Chalmers 1972: 401-421; Thompson 1987: 1-2). As James Malloy argues, in Latin America, "group strategy...is used mainly to penetrate the state through the executive apparatus to extract specific concessions. Parties and legislatures are not the preferred vehicle for interest representation." (Malloy and Seligson 1988: 252).

However, the predominance of firms and trade associations over political parties as organizational forms is relative and subject to change over time. Political parties are more significant in transitions from authoritarian rule and during democratic periods (when elections take place, or whenever legislatures play a critical role). Political instability, thus, also reinforces the role of the firm and trade associations as organizational forms. But it does not follow that political parties are irrelevant. It has been argued that, since democracies depend on votes and businessmen are a privileged minority, it is preferable for them not to become directly involved in the political process. In that sense, whenever democracy reigns, businessmen are more dependent on political parties. As Schattschneider argues "The business community is too small, it arouses too much antagonism, and its aims are too narrow to win the support of a popular majority" (1956: 42-43).

Political parties are not so much a vehicle for interest aggregation as a vehicle for establishing alliances or building compromises with other social groups. Parties help to avoid political isolation. In other words, if the national bourgeoisie restricts its political activity to firms and trade associations, it reduces its possibility of establishing alliances. This is one of the costs of a restricted political game.[23] Identification with political parties, however, is troublesome for businessmen because their interests are placed at greater risk as a result of political competition. This is more so in Latin America, where the predominance of political antagonism over compromise implies that the losers in the political game can be negatively affected or punished. Thus, firms and trade associations are more reliable and flexible vehicles to channel business political activity. This attitude does, however, reinforces the bourgeoisie's political isolation and poses a difficult dilemma because isolation makes business people more vulnerable to governmental political (revolutionary) attacks.

The Cuban case shows very clearly that bourgeois social and political isolation, combined with internal divisions, can be fatal whenever confronted with a revolutionary force. Latin American societies have tremendous income distribution gaps, combined with ethnic cleavages.

When these elements emerge in politics, they lead to all forms of mass mobilization, forms that are often violent. Business people in Latin America are a select and wealthy elite, usually of European origin, whose position of power and privilege does not enjoy legitimacy and often generates envy.[24] Social isolation, in these circumstances, becomes a problem, more so when the Latin American bourgeoisies have made little effort to link themselves to civil society by promoting cultural activities and/or becoming involved in philanthropic activities. Social and political isolation can be broken if philanthropic initiatives are taken and involvement with political parties becomes the norm. If these initiatives are not generalized it is because the national bourgeoisie finds it undesirable or risky to link themselves to the rest of society. However, if businessmen begin to "open up" socially and politically, it indicates a change of behavior which will modify their political strategy and transform them as political actors.

Leadership and Political Mobilization

Bourgeois political mobilization patterns are directly influenced by the type of issues being discussed on the political agenda; it is the very nature of these issues that triggers the need to react and defend its interests and that conditions its possibilities of acting collectively or individually in response. The effectiveness of business political mobilization depends not only on the existence of organizations but also on the quality of leadership.

The issues that force the national bourgeoisie to mobilize itself politically are: (a) labor and popular sector demands that represent a threat to its interests, whether channeled directly or mediated by leftist or populist parties; (b) expansion of non-private forms of property, usually by governments who take over and nationalize firms owned by the national and/or foreign bourgeoisie and; (c) competition by foreign capital in the domestic market, particularly in economic sectors where the national bourgeoisie is strong.

The first issue corresponds to the classic social conflict between labor and capital and to the more general conflict over income redistribution between the impoverished masses and the privileged minorities of the region. This issue, which affects all fractions (national and foreign, strong and weak), usually becomes more important under democratic governments because it grants political freedom to all players, including the labor unions and the left. The issue of income redistribution is less important under right wing dictatorships because they tend to suppress all forms of popular mobilization.

The second issue involves the defense of private property against the expansion of public firms and/or state-sponsored cooperatives and other forms of "social property." Whenever this issue becomes important on the political agenda, it prompts the unity between national and foreign capital in order to defend the realm of private property in society.[25]

The third issue corresponds to the conflict between foreign and national capital and between different sectoral fractions (sectoral clash). It affects the interests of some fractions of the national bourgeoisie (particularly the industrialists) as long as foreign capital invades its market or displaces national firms. This conflict generally centers around trade policies (protectionism or open trade) and foreign capital regulations. A nationalist-developmentalist policy gives priority to the internal market over the export sector, protecting the domestic market from foreign imports. This protectionist policy is usually complemented by norms that place limits on the development of foreign capital in local markets. A liberal-exporting policy emphasizes free market competition between local and foreign products, and among national and foreign capital. Additionally, exporters are favored as agents of capital accumulation since they can compete in the world market.

It is around these salient issues that the national bourgeoisie is most immediately mobilized. With the first two issues, there is more room for class cohesion since it is clear that the defense of general interests is likely to occur. With the third issue, disagreements within the national bourgeoisie (among those who either oppose or support a particular set of economic policies) are typical.

An effective and permanent defense of interests and demands of a greater power share are possible when the national bourgeoisie has been able to develop leaders. Leaders link members and fractions of the same class (internal role) and represent and bargain collective interests (external role). This double coordinating role is critical from a political perspective, as crucial as the individual and collective knowledge and determination necessary to make a firm solid and competitive in economic terms.

Collective leadership is nurtured in business organizations. This is the organizational setting where a special type of businessman, a community leader, develops a vision that goes beyond the firm and, eventually, fractional interests. Leaders identify and articulate global business problems through the development of a collective network. Sectoral trade associations and particularly peak (umbrella or comprehensive) associations that claim to represent the business sector as a whole, are crucial in leadership formation (Useem 1984: 143). These organizations offer a space to prove individual abilities and the opportunity to make contacts with all types of businessmen that belong to different sectors thus, facilitating class coordination whenever necessary.

Relations with the state and other social classes and groups and institutions are also mediated by business leaders who act as representatives of class interests. The bargaining process in which business leaders participate, either as representatives of firms or as heads of trade associations, is a school for political action that enhances their political awareness and sensitizes businessmen to political developments. This learning process is critical because it reveals the limits and possibilities of the political game.

Notes

1. Giddens, for example, considers that class analysis necessarily expresses "the connection between the economic order and other institutions of society." See Stanworth and Giddens (1975: ix).

2. On the importance of individual access to the state in the case of Third World bourgeoisies, see Paix (1990: 728).

3. On the Marxist theory of the state, see Jessop (1982).

4. Marx asserts that "the executive of the modern state is but a committee for managing the common affairs of the whole bourgeoisie" (1955: 12). The problem with instrumentalism is that it is an argument based on the assumption that state actions clearly represent the interests of the bourgeoisie. Thus, the analysis of the mediations between the bourgeoisie (and its distinct fractions) and the state is considered irrelevant. For a contemporary use of instrumentalism, see Asborno (1988: 4).

5. For a critique on elitism, see Meisel (1962). Antonio Gramsci made an early critical statement on elitism from a Marxist perspective. He asserted that "Mosca's so-called 'political class' is nothing but the intellectual category of the dominant social group." For Gramsci, the bourgeoisie and its "intellectual category" are not separated, but rather intimately related (1983: 6).

6. Giddens supports the idea that a restricted notion of elites may be complementary rather than opposed to class analysis. That is, elites can be found within social classes. See Stanworth and Giddens (1975: x-xi). The concept of elite is used here in a restricted sense to indicate a select minority which has leadership functions in firms, trade associations (business leaders) and the state apparatus (political class).

7. It must be noted that the degree of bourgeois influence on the state does not depend directly on the social origins of the state elite, as Miliband (1969) argues. The origins of the state elite can be diverse but, in spite of that, the state always needs and seeks the support of the bourgeoisie. The bourgeoisie, in turn, needs and seeks the support of the state.

8. In Western Europe, Germany has been analyzed as an "historical aberration" because of "the failure of a proper bourgeois revolution." German "peculiarities," as compared to England, have been extensively discussed by Blackbourn and Eley (1984: 12-13).

9. For a distinction between the heuristic and historical contents of the concept of social class, see Thompson (1979: 34-39).

10. For the Marxist debate on the national bourgeoisie that took place in the Third International or Komintern, see Claudín (1975: 265). In Latin America, both Mariátegui and Haya de la Torre have discussed the issue. See Mariátegui (1975) and Haya de la Torre (1985: 1). More recent remarks can be found in Prieto (1983) and Canak (1984: 7).

11. It is interesting to note that Weeks admits that "this is a controversial interpretation" (1985: 248).

12. On the discussion about the decomposition and recomposition of Latin American dominant classes (from landed oligarchies to industrial elites), the most interesting study is that of Graciarena (1967).

13. Cardoso has pointed out that considerations about the role of foreign capital changed after World War II, because from then on multinational corporations became interested in the Latin American industrialization process. Earlier discussions about the "nationalist" stance of the national bourgeoisie were based on the idea that foreign capital played an anti-industrialization role, allied with the landed interest of the exporting oligarchy (1977a: 7-40).

14. The cultural argument was first developed by Lipset (1967). Recent versions of modernization theory, highly critical of native industrialists, portrayed as "mercantilists," are found in Soto (1989). Soto, however, believes that cultural factors are not an obstacle for economic development. A new type of emerging business people, the informal entrepreneurs, seem to have the cultural requirements needed to develop capitalism. See Soto and Schmidheiny (1991: 9). For a critique on the "absent qualities" argument, see Wils (1979: 16-17 and 166) and Acuña (1985: 23).

15. The most significant contribution can be found in Cardoso and Faletto (1979). Revisions made to his approach are also interesting if one wishes to pursue the debate further (1979: 7-40).

16. Soto (1989) has studied in detail the informal entrepreneurs of Lima but he never made any effort to analyze in depth the entrepreneurial practice of "mercantilism." His analysis must be taken more as a political and ideological manifesto about the evils of "mercantilism" and the potential qualities of informal entrepreneurs than as a sound study of Peru's business class.

17. Portes does not take into account the *grupo* phenomenon in his attempt to "map" the class structure of Latin American societies (1985: 7-38).

18. There is a growing body of literature on the Latin American *grupos* from different theoretical perspectives, Marxist and non-Marxist. For a non-Marxist perspective on *grupos*, see Leff (1976: 97-122), Chueca and Alfaro (1974),

Strachan (1976), Sanfuentes (1984: 131-169), Soberón (1985: 61-75), Reaño and Vásquez (1988) and Camp (1989). For a Marxist perspective, see Lagos (1965), Dahse (1979), Acedo (1981), Cardero and Domínguez (1982), Nuncio (1982), Silva Colmenares (1983), Cordero and Santín (1986), Hughes and Quintero (1987), Asborno (1988), Green and Laurent (1988), Minella (1988), Azpiazu and Basualdo (1989), Rozas and Marín (1989), Stolovich, Rodríguez, and Bértola (1988), Schvarzer (1989), Malpica (1989), Anaya (1990) and Alcorta (1992).

19. O'Donnell (1978b: 9) and Acuña (1985: 34) critically consider the economic weakness assertion.

20. The concept of the "bourgeoisie" differs from that of the "petit bourgeoisie." This study considers as part of the national bourgeoisie both the *grupos* and the sectoral fractions. The petit bourgeoisie belongs to another strata. On a similar distinction for a European country see Marceau (1989: 47-48).

21. Secrecy and intimacy are typical elements of big business/state relations, as several authors have repeatedly pointed out. See Child in Leff (1976: 123), Useem (1984: 98), Stolovich, Rodríguez, and Bértola (1988: 11, 35) and Schvarzer (1989: 10). Secrecy, for obvious reasons, makes research on this topic particularly difficult.

22. Malloy (1988: 352) asserts that, "In the end, access to power and control over distributable goods is the name of the game, not form of regimes."

23. Its position in society, as well as its ethnic-cultural background makes the national bourgeoisie an isolated minority. The tremendous income distribution gap delineates an image of a privileged island surrounded by a sea of poverty. This image is reinforced by the fact that the Latin American business elites are mostly from European origin. It is not only a question of status. "Color" also reinforces this isolation. Bourgeois links with civil society can be built through political parties and also through firms and trade associations. Foundations and charity activities, however, are quite rare in Latin America, a region where corporate philanthropy is almost non-existent. The critique on business in not only based on envy but also on the fact that those who have wealth seem to be particularly selfish. The opposite is true in the U.S., where corporate sponsorship of cultural activities, education and health services, as Michael Useem argues, "also makes good business" (1984: 119).

24. On the question of business legitimacy in Latin America, see Leff (1976: 533), Sanfuentes (1984: 160) and CEDIS (1988: 26). The issue of "envy" is particularly important in this sense. It has been analyzed by Leff (1986: 11).

25. Domínguez (1982) argues that nationalism makes the study of coalitions in Latin America more complex. Nationalist coalitions form around attempts to reject foreign capital, but both national and foreign capital may join forces to halt threats to expropriate the private sector.

3

The Economic Power Structure in Contemporary Peru

The political analysis of the national bourgeoisie cannot be seriously undertaken without mapping the economic power structure as a whole and assessing its changing, evolving nature. This is particularly important because the paths or models toward economic development, as well as the economic weight and geographical location of different economic agents, have been subject to intense changes, influenced by both internal and external forces.

In Latin America, the economy has been traditionally centered around the primary-exporting area and developed by landowners, foreign enclaves and plantations. This old structure was first shaken during the Great Depression of the 1930s, a crisis that encouraged the adoption of an alternative model of economic development centered around the manufacturing industry. In the 1950s, the model of import substitution industrialization became generalized in the region. In this period, the process of change was led by the state and, in various cases, it came accompanied by radical anti-oligarchic and nationalistic reforms. In the 1980s, when the century's second Great Depression hit the region, a new trend was set in motion. In this third period, inward-oriented industrialization was declared "exhausted" as a model of economic development, private property was privileged and economic development now began to be centered around export diversification. Economic power, thus, has shifted hands and its most dynamic agents have been located along different economic axes.

The concept of economic power structure refers to the economic resources possessed by specific social agents according to the type of property they possess: private property (national and foreign), public property (owned by the state) and social property (rural cooperatives and *empresas de propiedad social*, owned by peasants or workers). These property agents are located in one of two following geographical areas:

urban-industrial and primary-exporting. The urban-industrial area is composed of such sectors as the manufacturing industry, construction, utilities and services. The primary-exporting area is composed of such economic sectors as agriculture, mining, oil and fishing. There are important differences between these two economic areas. First, the urban-industrial area, as its name indicates, is located in the cities while the primary-exporting area is located in the countryside. Second, the primary-exporting area produces raw materials that are mostly exported to the world market while economic sectors in the urban-industrial area operate mostly in the domestic market. Thus, the two areas have different geographical locations and different market orientations.

The approach used in this chapter is both dynamic and comprehensive. It is dynamic because it assesses changes taking place in the economic power structure in the long-run, covering more than four decades and looking at three distinct periods. It is comprehensive because it considers all economic agents and takes into account all the driving forces of change. Changes in the economic power structure have to be assessed by identifying the forces that promote it, whether internal (domestic) or external (international).[1] This book will emphasize both sets of factors.

The comprehensive and dynamic approach, together with the consideration of both internal and external factors as the driving forces of change, is particularly important to overcome past analytical problems. Several scholars have studied structural changes in Peru by focusing mostly on one particular period (the 1968-1975 period), by analyzing the leading area of the economy in a given period and by focusing on the analysis of specific agents: The oligarchy, the state, the industrialists and multinational corporations. In addition, the analysis of social and economic change in Peru and Latin America has often been marked by the importance attributed either to external or internal factors. Modernization theory, for example, strongly emphasized the role of internal factors (industrialists) as promoters of change, while dependency theory placed the emphasis on external factors.[2] Alain de Janvry has correctly pointed out that both internal and external factors have to be taken into account (1981: 22). The analysis of change, according to this perspective, focuses on the interconnection between the external and internal factors rather than giving priority to one set of factors over the other.[3]

In the case of Peru, the changes in the economic power structure were as follows. The first period began in the mid-nineteenth century and lasted until 1968. It was characterized by the preeminence of private capital (national and foreign) under the leadership of the landed oligarchy. In this oligarchical period, the economy was geared toward the development of primary-exporting activities such as minerals, oil, cotton, sugar and wool although urban-industrial development started to take place around Lima, the capital of Peru, in the 1960s. The second period started in 1968 and ended in 1975. It was a period of change led by the state against the oligarchy and foreign capital.[4] In this period, economic growth was centered around the urban-industrial area and supported in import substitution industrialization policies. The third period, the present one, started to unfold in 1975. It was characterized by a process of backlash politics: The weakening of the state as an economic agent and the strengthening of private agents (privatization). The economy was "liberalized," deregulated, opened to international competition, and oriented toward the export of raw materials and non-traditional exports.

Period I: The Oligarchy and the Agro-Exporting Economy

The traditional image of Peru's economic power structure at the beginning of the century was that of a country where national economic power was associated with the agro-exporting oligarchy. The ruling classes were unmistakenly identified with a handful of families who owned large estates (*haciendas*). The owners of *haciendas* were divided into two groups: The modern landowners (agro-exporting oligarchy located on the coast) and the traditional ones (known in Peru as *gamonales*, located in the highlands). A third partner also came into play: The foreign enclaves (mining and oil companies linked to the world market). Other minor economic agents were the commercial bourgeoisie linked to foreign capital (*compradore*)[5] and a small and feeble nucleus of emerging industrialists. Power, thus, was concentrated in the hands of the exporting oligarchy and located in rural areas.

This traditional power structure was already changing in the 1960s, when both external and internal forces were beginning to challenge the privileged position of the landed oligarchy and to promote the development of the manufacturing industry. These changes took place between private owners and were caused by the internal dynamics of Peruvian capitalism that developed the urban-industrial area and the new orientation of international forces (penetration of foreign capital in both the urban-industrial area and in new mining ventures and fishing).

Development of Private Capital

From the 1950s to the late 1960s, two changes were already visible. First, the presence of foreign capital in the Peruvian economy became stronger and much more diversified and a modern urban-industrial bourgeoisie began to develop (Malpica 1968: 21-23). The landed oligarchy concentrated its interests in agriculture and also had investments in other economic sectors. Its predominance in modern coastal agriculture was evident. Prior to 1968, 181 families with properties of more than 500 hectares possessed more than 50 percent of the coastal land. Among this group, 44 families owned properties of more than 2,000 hectares (25 percent of the coastal land) (Valderrama and Ludmann 1979: 19; Favre 1971: 110). In addition, the old oligarchy also had significant interests in urban development firms and in the export/importing business, but not in manufacturing industries, fisheries, banking or insurance enterprises (Valderrama and Ludmann 1979: 37-41).

In the 1960s, the industrialists were already an emerging nucleus of economic power, limited by the growing presence of multinational corporations (Malpica 1968: 11). According to data available, 242 subsidiaries of multinational corporations were created between 1940 and 1969. In some cases, there was an association with national capital: 46 of those companies (19 percent), were associated with national capital as minority shareholders; and 68 (28 percent), were controlled by national capital (Anaya 1974: 41). These facts then show that neither a massive takeover nor the formation of joint ventures led to the development of a "satellite" bourgeoisie. Rather, the association between national private capital and foreign private capital became possible because the first was already developing.

The new fraction of the national bourgeoisie, with strong roots in the manufacturing industry, was also present in other modern sectors (retail trade, construction, banking and insurance), making more diverse the economic power structure. Land development by medium-sized agricultural landowners on the outskirts of Lima was also significant (Malpica 1968: 2). The presence of these newcomers was a result of accelerated urbanization and the rapid expansion of the domestic market that occurred in the 1960s, particularly during the first Belaunde administration (1963-1968).

Changes were no less felt in rural areas, although the presence of the *gamonales* was still an important obstacle to economic modernization. As the domestic market developed (with the construction of roads and the growth of cities in Lima and the provinces), Peru's power structure also became more complex. The economic predominance of the landowners became less clear in the highlands. Merchants, owners of buses and trailers, and small-sized and medium-sized industrialists gradually became part of the regional social landscape.

In summary, changes in this first period in terms of property agents were important in two ways. First, foreign capital penetrated deeply into the Peruvian economy, being associated in some cases with national capital. Second, alongside the relative loss of importance of the agro-exporting oligarchy and the *gamonales*, a new bourgeois nucleus emerged in the urban-industrial area of the economy. Although the agro-exporting oligarchy was still the most powerful national class fraction, a more diversified power structure was being shaped and the oligarchy's economic preeminence was put into question.

The New Structure of Exports

In terms of economic areas, the situation was as follows. Although the coastal oligarchy dominated Peru's modern agricultural economy, agriculture gradually lost its economic importance as a key exporting activity because of the emergence of other exports such as fishmeal and minerals. Foreign capital was particularly active in developing new export products. According to Rosemary Thorp and Geoffrey Bertram, the percentage of export production by foreign firms rose from 45 percent in 1960 to 50 percent in 1967 (1978: 296). The diversification of the exporting base, caused by the development of new open cast mining investments by U.S. companies (copper in Toquepala by Southern Peru Copper Corporation, the Marcona iron by the Marcona Mining Company) and a boom in the fishing industry, modified the exporting base and strengthened the importance of foreign capital. Shane Hunt estimates that by 1965 American capital controlled almost 100 percent of oil and iron exports, 88 percent of copper, 67 percent of lead and silver, 30 percent of fisheries, 23 percent of sugar and seven percent of cotton (cited by Cotler 1978: 275-276). In 1955, agricultural products represented 42.3 percent of the value of exports, mining 40.9 percent and fish and fishmeal products 5.7 percent. By 1965, agricultural products had declined to 23.5 percent, while mineral products rose to 42.2 percent, and fishmeal products rose to 27.5 percent. This trend continued after 1965 (Fitzgerald 1981: 102). It must be pointed out that the oligarchy's interests in mining or fishing was not significant. In fishing, foreign capital also maintained substantial economic interests alongside oligarchical investments and some emerging entrepreneurs such as Luis Banchero, the tycoon of Peruvian fisheries.[6]

The Development of Manufacturing and the Domestic Market

Although fishing and mining gained greater importance in the primary-exporting area of the economy than did agricultural exports, the urban-industrial area gained the highest overall rate of growth.[7] In 1960, manufacturing industry displaced agriculture as the largest contributor to the GNP (20 percent versus 18.5 percent for agriculture). However, the combined contribution of agriculture, mining and fishing was still higher than that of manufacturing, construction, and utilities (30.3 percent versus 25.8 percent). Five years later, the manufacturing sector had become even more important, and the urban-industrial area as a whole predominated over the primary-exporting area (Fitzgerald 1981: 102). In addition to the expansion of the manufacturing industry, economic sectors such as banking, commerce and services also grew in importance. They represented 37.4 percent of the GNP in 1965, in comparison with 35.9 percent in 1960. This general trend has continued up to the late 1980s.[8]

By the mid 1960s, the stronger presence of foreign capital in manufacturing and banking was already evident. According to Thorp and Bertram:

>...by the late 1960s something like 40 percent of total fixed assets in the manufacturing sector were foreign controlled...parallel with foreign investment in manufacturing went a dramatic renationalization of banking, with the share of total banking assets under foreign control rising from 36 percent in 1960 to 62 percent by 1968 (1978: 295).

The development of the urban-industrial area was at the same time supported and stimulated by a higher integration of the Peruvian domestic market. There was massive migration from rural areas to the cities, primarily to the metropolitan area of Lima-Callao. The population of the capital city grew fast. It represented 9.9 percent of the country's population in 1940, 18.4 percent in 1961 and 22.9 percent in 1972 (Fitzgerald 1981: 127). Lima, traditionally the center of political-administrative power, also became the center of economic power when, by 1968, 80 percent of Peru's manufacturing industry became concentrated there (Cotler 1978: 289). These changes reflected the modernization process that Peruvian society was undergoing, economically as well as demographically.

Period II: The State and the Urban-Industrial Economy

The most drastic modification in the economic power structure of independent Peru took place in the 1968-1975 period. The driving force of change was the Armed Forces led by general Juan Velasco Alvarado, an army officer characterized by his fervent nationalism and the enmity he professed to the landed oligarchy. During Velasco's administration, particular private economic agents suffered from governmental actions while others were benefited. The national bourgeoisie was modernized and strengthened. This period is mostly characterized by the emergence of a strong state and new non-private forms of property and the will to accelerate the industrial transformation of the economy. External factors, however, are also present, particularly in terms of providing credit to a financially thirsty government.

Evaluation of the changes that took place in this period is important because most of the political and academic literature on Velasco tended to emphasize its intended objectives, and disregarded the global impact produced in Peru's economic power structure.[9] Even the literature published after his downfall has this bias.[10] What concerns us here is not the analysis of Velasco's goals but the deep transformation in the economic power structure it generated.

Entrepreneurial Pluralism

Velasco's administration fostered "entrepreneurial pluralism," that is, the emergence and development of new forms of property (public and social), that existed alongside private property. These new firms were generated mostly through the expropriation of land and foreign firms. Other less significant modifications occurred when new firms were created or sponsored by the state. Expropriation primarily affected foreign capital and landowners, and to a less degree, national capital.

Social Property. The liquidation of both the agro-exporting oligarchy and the *gamonales* as power factors in Peruvian society was the most far reaching modification of power in the republican period of Peruvian history (Bamat 1978: 137 and 139).

It was during the implementation of the agrarian reform (May 1969 to July 1976), that the state expropriated a total of 11,664 *haciendas* holding 8,066,929 hectares (Valderrama 1976: 22). The reform affected the "sugar and cotton barons" as well as the less powerful *gamonales*. The expropriated land was transferred primarily to agrarian cooperatives (Cooperativas Agrarias de Producción, CAPS, and Sociedades Agrícolas de Interés Social, SAIS). The members of CAPS and SAIS represented 57.7 percent of the beneficiaries and about 70 percent of the adjudicated land was concentrated in their hands. Other non-private agents, such as the Peasant Groups and the Peasant Communities, controlled 26.1 percent of the adjudicated land, while the remainder was held by individual proprietors (3.9 percent). The agrarian reform, despite its radicalism, was not imposed on the small and medium agricultural proprietors with parcels of less than 30 hectares of land. But they were a minority group. In fact, power in the rural areas was no longer concentrated in the private sector.

It must be pointed out that although social forms of property were not restricted to agriculture, they had very little economic significance. Beginning in 1974, the state promoted the formation of *empresas de propiedad social* (worker management and ownership). At the end of the Velasco period, there were only eight firms owned and directed by 2,840 workers. Another 63 were "in formation," and 452 remained "under study" (Tueros 1983: 180-181). As a result of its delayed implementation, social property of this type was placed in a very precarious condition.

The State. The development of the state economy by Velasco's government was unquestionably spectacular. In 1968, only a small nucleus of state-owned firms and regional corporations existed: a total of 47, employing 20,000 workers. The major public firms were the development banks (industrial, agrarian, mining, mortgage and housing banks), the steel industry (SOGESA), a small oil refinery (Empresa Petrolera Fiscal), a cement plant (Yura), a fertilizer plant (Cachimayo) and some regional electric power corporations (Santa, Mantaro). By Latin American standards, the state's presence in the economy was considered relatively small (Thorp and Bertram 1978: 290).

As of December 1975, the state exerted control over a total of 174 firms, employing approximately 90,000 workers. One hundred-nine of these firms (62 percent) were acquired as a result of expropriations (mainly of foreign capital and to a less extent, of national private capital located in anchovy fishing, cement, paper and some media firms). The remaining firms were either newly created or those inherited from the previous government.

By implementing the "structural reforms," the state became a leading economic agent even more important than foreign capital. The state assumed a monopolistic position in electricity, telecommunications, cement, iron, steel, paper, anchovy fisheries (extraction and transformation), railroads, water and sewerage utilities, the commercialization of exports and the acquisition of publicly needed imported goods. In other cases, particularly in extractive mining and banking, it maintained a very important but not a dominant position.

The state also came to play an important role in the financial system. The expropriation of three banks (Popular, Continental, Internacional), coupled with the strengthening of development banks and the creation of the Development Finance Corporation, made the state a strong financial agent. A similar process occurred with the creation of PetroPeru and CentrominPeru, because it transformed the state into an important oil and non-ferrous metal producer. Both the expropriation of newspapers and the strong participation of the state in radio and television firms, coupled with the creation of the National Information System, represented a quasi-monopoly in the information business. In shipbuilding, by strengthening the Naval Industrial Service, the state became the only large shipbuilder.[11]

It is interesting to compare 1968 (the year of Velasco's coup) with 1975 (the year of Velasco's fall). State participation in the economy rose from 13 percent to 23 percent of GNP (Instituto Nacional de Planificación 1980: 101). In a short period, the state became the most powerful agent within the economic structure.

Public firms, however, had several weaknesses. In terms of management, the central problem derived from the lack of independence of its managers from the state. This forced public firms to become directly involved in the political dynamics of their respective ministries.

The instability of the Peruvian political process altered the chain of command whenever there were cabinet changes. Political clientelism influenced the appointment of personnel and directors and aggravated the management problems. In addition, the state commitment to meet political-social goals (through subsidies) also negatively influenced the ability of management to produce sound economic results. Corruption finally exacerbated the economic problems of public firms, a problem that became particularly serious in the 1980s. One paradox of the transformation of the state as a key economic agent was that the foreign financing of public firms increased from 11,336 million *soles* in 1974 to 18,174 in 1975 (Bamat 1978: 165). Financial dependence, however, soon became a problem. When the budget deficit of public firms had climbed from 19,452 million *soles* in 1974 to 35,224 million in 1975, loans stopped and financing became more difficult, weakening the role of the state as a tool for economic development (Banco Mundial 1981: 182).

The Entrepreneurial Reform: Comunidades Laborales. The relative loss of importance of private capital in the 1968-1975 period was partially a result of the creation of labor communities (*comunidades laborales*), or co-partnership schemes.[12] The *comunidades laborales* were supported by the gradual purchase of shares (no more than 50 percent) transferred from private owners to the new collective owner (the labor community), through the annual distribution of a percentage of the profits (20 to 25 percent depending on the sector). This scheme involved economic sectors such as manufacturing, mining, fishing and telecommunications. One outstanding characteristic of this reform was that it affected firms of all sizes. However, the reform was not applied to all economic sectors (commerce, finance and construction were exempted) and its progress was slow and beleaguered with obstacles. Most entrepreneurs sought mechanisms to delay the gradual acquisition of their property by labor communities (Durand 1977). In 1974, there were 89 mining labor communities that held 48,253 workers and 2,882 industrial labor communities had another 165,194 workers. In a five year period, these labor communities could only accomplished the transfer of 3.9 percent of the capital in mining, and 26 percent in manufacturing industries (SINAMOS 1975: 8). Foreign and national capital were able to successfully slow down the transference of private property to the hands of the labor communities.

Foreign Capital and "Financial Dependence." Velasco's revolutionary government also produced a drastic alteration of the power structure in terms of the presence of foreign capital in the economy via expropriations, renegotiation with existing firms and the promotion of new forms of foreign investment (Hunt 1975: 302; Portocarrero 1976: 20; Goodsell 1974: 141-165). Although the presence of foreign capital within the economy was reduced and redefined, the role of foreign capital as the provider of external credit greatly increased.

The expropriation of foreign firms was quite significant, particularly in the oil industry (International Petroleum Company, Refinería Conchan-Chevron), mining (Cerro de Pasco Corporation, Marcona Mining Company), fishing, agriculture (W.R. Grace Company mainly, via the agrarian reform), communications (ITT), transportation (Peruvian Corporation) and banking (Banco Continental controlled by the Chase Manhattan Bank and Banco Internacional controlled by the Chemical International Bank). In manufacturing, with the exemption of chemical and paper firms owned by W.R. Grace, there were no expropriations (Guasti 1983: 197). The old multinational firms that symbolized foreign power in the country at the beginning of the century (the International Petroleum Company, the Cerro Corporation, W.R. Grace and the Peruvian Corporation), vanished from the scene (Hunt 1975: 332). Velasco also conducted direct negotiations to attract investments under new agreements, the most significant being those signed with Southern Peru Copper Corporation and Occidental Petroleum. In manufacturing, a number of firms were created under a new modality of joint ventures. The most important case, in terms of the size of the investment, was signed with Bayer, the powerful German chemical and drug corporation, for the production of acrylic and synthetic fibers for the textile industry. Other less significant cases were the agreements signed with multinational corporations such as Volvo and Perkins to produce diesel engines (Motores Diesel Andinos) and with Massey-Ferguson to produce tractors (Tractores Andinos).

In manufacturing and banking, new laws were issued to reduce the presence of foreign capital and enhance that of national private capital. In banking, the laws stipulated that every new banking firm should be fully owned by national investors. At the same time, foreign participation in existing banks and insurance companies was to be reduced to the maximum of 20 percent of capital (Sánchez Alvabera 1984: 54-55; Sifuentes 1988). In manufacturing, the government issued a new law that forced 230 multinational corporations to be transformed gradually into mixed firms, until national capital reached 51 percent (Guasti 1983: 194; Cavanagh 1980: 58). In the case of automotive assembly, the procedure was also intended to "rationalize" the industry; from a total of 11 automotive assembling plants, only five remained (Volvo, Volkswagen, Toyota, Nissan and Chrysler) (Hunt 1975: 320-326).

The outcome of Velasco's nationalistic policy was a decline in the importance of direct foreign investment in the economy and especially in the primary-exporting area.[13] According to Laura Guasti, "manufacturing corporations maintained generally low levels of new investment in Peru and limited their reinvestment to existing plants and stock" (1983: 197). From 1969 to 1975, the percentage of GNP controlled by foreign capital had declined from 22 percent to 11 percent.[14] However, the importance of external factors was still significant because the government found alternative sources of credit in international private banks and the Peruvian economy continued to be highly dependent on the world market.

A significant portion of the expropriated firms was owned by American corporations. The Velasco government's first act was the military intervention and takeover of the International Petroleum Company, a decision that had serious consequences. The U.S. retaliated by imposing a credit blockade.[15] This confrontation was ended with the signing of the Greene-Mercado agreement in 1974, which provided adequate compensation to the expropriated U.S. firms (Cavanagh 1980: 166). Nevertheless, credits from agencies such as the Agency for International Development, Eximbank, InterAmerican Development Bank and the World Bank, did not substantially increase after the signing of the agreement. The desperate need for credits forced the government to find alternative sources. Simultaneously, the increasing liquidity of international private banks made the Euromarket the primary provider of external credit. According to Barbara Stallings, what resulted was: "A dramatic change in the size and structure of Peru's public sector foreign debt. The debt leapt from $1.1 billion in 1968 to $2.5 billion in 1973; and by 1976, it had soared to $5.5 billion (1983: 166). The effect of Velasco's changes was a decline in the "dependence" on direct foreign investment and an increase in the "dependence" on international credit.

In addition to the increasing importance of "financial dependence," Peru was still solidly linked to the world market. Peru not only sold its products to external markets but continued to import inputs for the manufacturing sector, foodstuffs and weapons at faster rates. This fact showed the limits of Velasco's self-sufficient policies and the constraints posed by external forces. The multilateralization of Peruvian trade and investment increased the state's room to maneuver but did not eliminate the dependent condition that the government was attempting to overcome.

National Private Capital: Weakened? Since the inauguration of his government, Velasco made a differentiation between the "oligarchy" and the "industrialists." The former was the political target of his regime and the latter an ally. However, once the law of *comunidades laborales* was enacted in 1970, the government established a distinct criterion. It started to emphasize the difference between "dialoguing and modern industrialists" (allies of Velasco) and "traditional entrepreneurs" (who opposed its reforms).[16] This distinction was related to the reform's diverse impact on the national private sector. It was negative in some cases but positive in others.

The agrarian reform, the nationalization of fisheries,[17] the enterprise reform (*comunidades laborales*) and the policy of assigning basic manufacturing industries to the state (where national capital existed), as already explained, had a negative but differentiated impact on the private sector. The last two reforms had a limited negative effect on industrialists. The nationalization of the cement plants only affected isolated firms and the *comunidades laborales* reform had a more general impact, but was constrained by the slow acquisition of property by the labor communities. However, the private sector benefited directly and indirectly from other types of measures.

Those landowners who already had combined investments in the agriculture and manufacturing sector were transformed into "modern entrepreneurs" thanks to the agrarian reform, a significant fact, particularly in the case of the *grupos*, the emerging modern economic conglomerates. Romero, Picasso and Olaechea Alvarez Calderón, all of them former landowners, increased their links to the banking system and promoted the formation of manufacturing industries.[18]

Both the nationalist policy and the strategy of promoting import substitution industrialization had a positive influence on the development of a modernized Peruvian bourgeoisie who, under the guidance of the state, became a vital economic agent. In some cases, Velasco's policy gave way to the voluntary withdrawal of foreign capital and the subsequent purchase of foreign firms by national entrepreneurs. Anderson

Clayton, a U.S. company that owned an industrial-commercial cotton-oil complex, sold its interests at a low price to the Romero *grupo*, who then became more powerful in this economic sector. It should be noted that this same *grupo* was the first to convert agrarian bonds (obtained as compensation for the expropriation of its cotton and cattle *haciendas*), into capital for the installation of a modern export cotton spinning mill (Reaño and Vásquez 1986: 140-157). Other important firms were also purchased by powerful national investors. CUVISA, a large textile firm, and the Alianza and Minsur mines were purchased by the Brescia *grupo* (Becker 1983: 180). In the case of banks and insurance companies, the government restricted foreign participation to 20 percent and the effect was highly beneficial to private national capital. The progressive nationalization of foreign manufacturing firms did not produce the same results because the sale of 51 percent of the shares to nationals was done gradually and could not be fully accomplished before the law changed in 1978.

Industrial policy benefited national capital and strengthened considerably the national bourgeoisie. The "absolute protection" of the domestic market (a list of more than a thousand goods that could not be imported), coupled with easier access to credit and the Peruvianization of the banking sector was positive to the national bourgeoisie. In the case of the automotive industry, the policies of "rationalization" and progressive integration of national parts permitted the creation of a myriad of small-sized and medium-sized spare parts manufacturing industries.

It is important to understand that the state did not negatively affect all economic sectors. The *comunidades laborales'* reform, as previously noted, was not applied to construction, commerce or banking. Large commercial exporting/importing firms such as Berckemeyer, Ferreyros and A.F. Wiese were not touched, and their influence grew considerably as a result of the displacement of oligarchical interests and foreign export/importing firms. Banks such as Crédito, Lima and Wiese were favored by Velasco's nationalist banking policies.

Insofar as the state became the central agent of the economy, the reforms did not encourage the rapid strengthening of the emerging sectors of the national bourgeoisie. The central nucleus of national capital was no longer the agro-exporting oligarchy. Only scattered medium-sized and small-sized proprietors remained as representatives of the private sector in rural areas. The set of Velasco's reforms, together with the dynamism of industrialization, brought about a complicated process of internal recomposition of the remaining bourgeois fractions. However, as a result of the government's policies, the Peruvian bourgeoisie was modernized and fortified.[19]

Due to the effect of the agrarian reform (and also the nationalization of the fishmeal, cement and electricity firms) the weight of national private capital as a percentage of GNP dropped from 34 percent in 1968 to 27 percent in 1975. But in the case of construction, commerce and banking, as shown in Table 3.1, the net balance was highly favorable.

TABLE 3.1 Participation of National Capital in the GNP, 1968-1975
(in Thousands of *Soles*)

Economic Sectors	1968	1975
Agriculture	56	--
Fishing	15	01
Mining	14	12
Manufacturing industry	109	104
Construction	13	22
Utilities	04	--
Banking	07	11
Commerce	70	80

Source: Based on data drawn from FitzGerald, *Economía política del Perú, 1956-1978*. Lima: Instituto de Estudios Peruanos, 1981. p. 410.

Changes in Economic Sectors. In the 1968-1975 period, the economic structure moved toward the development of the urban-industrial area at a faster, intense rate. Governmental priorities forced the pace toward industrialization and were quite effective in de-emphasizing growth in the primary-exporting area. Sectors such as manufacturing and construction developed rapidly thanks to the demand-stimulation generated by import substitution industrialization policies. In 1968, when Velasco came to power, manufacturing and construction already represented 29.7 percent of the GNP. At the end of the period, their weight in the economy increased to 31.8 percent. Economic sectors such as agriculture, fishing and mining, sectors that represented 24.7 percent of the GNP in 1968, dropped their participation to 18.2 percent in 1975 (FitzGerald 1981: 314).

It seemed a dramatic modification of historical patterns that Peru's economy was now centered in the cities and modern industrial plants, not in the rural areas, mines and oil fields as in the past. The dynamism of this process, however, was weak as the analysis of the next period will prove. In addition, some degree of economic development occurred in the primary-exporting area. Two U.S. multinationals invested in newly discovered oil fields (Occidental Petroleum and Belco Petroleum), sharing with Petroperu, a public firm, its presence in this now critical exporting sector. A non-traditional group of exports (known as *exportaciones no tradicionales*), also developed since 1970. It constituted a heterogeneous conglomerate of commercial, manufacturing and mining firms, that grew moderately without becoming an important element in the export economy. These diverse economic activities represented only 3.3 percent of the overall exports in 1970 and 10.8 percent in 1973, but dropped to 7.3 percent in 1975 (Gutierrez 1981: 268). In the years that followed, non-traditional exports did not experience a major economic dynamism.

Period III: Privatization and the Export Economy

The third period is inaugurated in 1975, when General Francisco Morales Bermúdez displaces Velasco from power with civilian and military support and initiates a number of changes. Morales Bermúdez will open a transitional period, both economically and politically. Economically, the government will gradually abandon import substitution industrialization policies and de-emphasize the role of state as a key economic agent. It is a process of backlash politics where the national private sector and international financial organizations back conservative political leaders in order to liberalize the economy. Politically, the military will agree to return to the barracks after a Constitutional Assembly is formed and, later on, general elections called. Of the first three democratic governments (Fernando Belaunde, 1980-1985; Alan García, 1985-1990; Alberto Fujimori, 1990-1995), only two (Belaunde and Fujimori) will agree to carry on the process of economic liberalization. García will attempt to stop the process but generating the conditions to make state-led growth possible will be very difficult.[20]

In the third period, privatization reigns. The abandonment of the reforms will be manifested in the weakening of "social property" firms and, to a lesser extent, public firms. Power, thus, gradually returns to the hands of private owners. But re-privatizing the economy will prove to be easier to accomplish than to develop a new export-oriented economy. The debt crisis and the continuing economic recession will slow down the process of economic change, together with the political opposition to it that emerges in this period. This opposition, it must be noted, was strong enough to try to reverse the process during García's administration.

External forces will play a critical role in this process of policy and economic change.[21] However, their power will be manifested more as the increasing influence of international financial organizations on policy-making and regulating access to international credit rather than as increasing direct foreign investment. The recomposition of the economic power structure, thus, is more centered around national private capital, that is to say, the national bourgeoisie.

Strengthening Private Capital

Social Property and the Comunidades Laborales. General Morales Bermúdez and President Belaunde severely weakened social property and the *comunidades laborales*. In the case of social property, the state could no longer maintain its promotional and financial support and gradually the firms were left on their own (Cárdenas 1983: 321; Tueros 1983: 861-862). Many of these firms quickly encountered financial difficulties and a private sector unwilling to cooperate with them.

There were similar problems in agriculture. In this sector, Morales Bermúdez ended the agrarian reform in 1976 and the state ceased to promote and subsidize rural cooperatives. Belaunde intensified the backlash with new agrarian legislation that favored the small-sized and medium-sized private farmers and provided incentives for the parcelling out of rural cooperatives (Méndez 1983; ENDA 1986). The parcelling process was strongly developed in the non-sugar producing coastal cooperatives where, by 1985, according to estimates by Flavio Figallo, two-thirds of the rural cooperatives had been parcelled out (1987: 21-22).

In the case of the *comunidades laborales*, the trend toward reprivatization followed quite a similar path. With Morales Bermúdez, decisive changes took place when a set of norms was approved and, as Javier Iguiñiz puts it, sought to maintain the name of the institutions but "emptying them of any co-partnership and co-participatory content" (1988: 31-32). In manufacturing, as in mining, the *comunidades laborales* ceased to be coproprietors of shares and instead became holders of bonds and "labor shares," which did not represent the equity capital of the firm. In addition, an individualistic logic was encouraged by a provision stipulating that individual workers (rather than the *comunidades laborales*) should be the proprietors of such bonds or "labor shares" with the potential of being for sale on the stock market.[22] Belaunde followed a similar path introducing legislation that, on the one hand, provided that small firms were excluded from the reform sector and, on the other hand, allowed the dissolution of existing *comunidades* in exchange for a more generous system of profit distribution.

García and Fujimori also continued this trend. Fujimori, in particular, took a decisive step forward in terms of privatization in the rural sector thanks to a legislative decree issued in March 31, 1991. For the first time since 1969, the year the agrarian reform was initiated, the government authorized the sale and mortgage of land and authorized private firms to own and manage up to 150 hectares of land.[23]

The Strong State is Weakened. The tendency toward privatization was not as strong a force in the case of public firms. Their number declined slowly despite the rhetoric of several governments about it. Only in the 1990s, under Fujimori's government, the privatization process was accelerated and several public firms (such as AeroPeru, HierroPeru, Compañía Peruana de Vapores, Tintaya, etc.) were sold out.

With Morales Bermúdez there were isolated cases of reprivatization. The anchovy and tuna fishing fleet of PescaPeru was transferred to private hands, but fishmeal processing remained in the hands of the state. With Belaunde, fishmeal processing and sales of fishmeal by private firms was also tolerated, despite the existing legislation. In the case of cement firms, a state monopoly was converted into a group of mixed capital firms (49 percent in the hands of the state and the rest private); the negotiation for this formula was started under Morales's government and the formula was finally adopted under Belaunde.[24] Mass media firms were totally reprivatized during Belaunde's administration.

Belaunde also put an end to the state's monopoly in a number of fields: Commercialization of export commodities such as minerals, fishmeal, cotton and coffee; and also in the domestic commercialization of human-consumption fishing, fertilizers and agricultural food products. In the production of basic inputs, the state no longer had a monopolistic position. Added to the aforementioned case of cement, private firms were allowed in the paper, fertilizer, tobacco and palm oil industries. Only in sectors such as electricity and services, the ones least attractive to private interests, did the state maintain a monopoly. If a certain number of firms were taken over by the state, this was because the firms were indebted to development banks and once bankrupt they passed to the hands of the state. Despite Belaunde's plans, generalized reprivatization of state-owned firms remained incomplete due to both the opposition by APRA and United Left's in Congress, and the resistance of unions allied to blue-collar and white-collar workers employed by public firms. Lack of interested buyers, national and foreign, also proved to be a problem.

In other cases, the state, through the Development Finance Corporation, acquired a minority participation as shareholder in firms fully managed by private capital. It contributed to the creation of these firms and provided subsidized credits. Several of these firms, such as Textil Piura, Sogewiese Leasing, Sociedad Cervecera de Trujillo, Cervecería del Norte, the Recuperada and Condesa mines, were firms controlled by the *grupos* (Romero, Wiese, Bentín, Lanata Piaggio and Benavides de la Quintana). In general, the state held a subservient position with regard to private capital. In isolated cases, such as the mining project of Tintaya, where the private sector displayed a lack of interest, the state played a developer's role. There were also cases where important mining deposits were owned by the state and private capital was allowed to operate them.

By July 1985, the state was the majority owner of 234 firms (134 nonfinancial and 100 financial), completely owned 173 firms, and had less than 50 percent of the shares in 61 firms (Alva Castro 1985: 13). At this time, the state firms constituted a disarticulate body with serious administrative and financial problems. The progressive decay of the state sector of the economy, despite isolated cases of successful management and adequate profitability, reached dramatic levels in 1983 due to both the high losses accumulated since 1981 and severe financial indebtedness. According to a Treasury report from 1982 to 1984, net losses increased 32 times (Contraloría General de la República 1985: 21).

Foreign Capital: Big Benefits, Not Much Investment. Foreign capital enjoyed major benefits since 1975 and improved its relative position in some sectors (oil industry) but the general trend was different than that of the 1960s and 1970s. Instead of increased investment in Peru and Latin America, direct foreign investment tended to decrease until the 1990s.[25]

Between 1980 and 1984, US$1,736.6 million were invested in oil: Contracting corporations, (Oxy, Belco), received 1,183.4 (68 percent) and the rest went to Petroperu (Campodónico 1986: 99 and 105). In other activities such as mining, commerce, manufacturing industry and banking, there were no significant reinvestments or new investments. Despite the changes in mining, oil, industrial and banking legislation and the modifications introduced in the *comunidades laborales*, there were practically no significant cases of direct foreign investment in the Peruvian economy.[26] In banking, the Belaunde administration authorized the entrance of foreign banks, but none entered. According to the Inter-American Development Bank, direct foreign investment in Peru has declined dramatically since 1981. In that year, foreign investment was US$128 million, declining to 46.4 million in 1982, 37.4 million in 1982, -87.1 million in 1983 and -1.0 million in 1985 (Inter-American Development Bank 1987: 458 and 1990: 297). This trend showed slight increases in the second half of the 1980s and declined again in the early 1990s. The 1985-1990 annual average foreign direct investment rate of only US$25.5 million shrank down to 2 million in 1990 (Wise 1992: 14). In addition, the remittances of multinational corporations substantially increased, as well as foreign debt payments, which resulted in a continuous decline of international reserves (Campodónico 1986: 107).

Thus, the weight and importance of direct foreign investment in the economy was not substantially modified for a number of years despite the changes in governmental priorities which granted concessions allowing foreign capital to operate with greater freedom and under better conditions.

In the first half of the 1980s, foreign capital was still largely concentrated in oil and mining (69 percent of its investments were in these industries) and, secondarily, in the manufacturing industry (18 percent) (Sánchez Alvabera 1984: 3). By 1983, the oil multinationals produced 72 percent of crude oil (Campodónico 1986: 137). In mining, in the same year, foreign capital on average produced 45 percent of overall output, with the strongest output being in copper where it produced 73 percent of total output (Aste y Obando 1987: 61). By 1981, the offices of foreign banks located in Lima represented a mere seven percent of the net worth of the deposits (Sánchez Alvabera 1984: 51 and 140).

In the 1975-1985 period, international banks and international financial organizations became highly influential in the decision-making process due to Peru's increasing external indebtedness and continuing lack of foreign reserves. The magnitude of foreign debt rose dramatically, resulting from new loans and the sharp rise in international interest rates (from an average of seven percent in the first half of the 1970s to 11 percent in the second half, and 14 percent in the early 1980s).[27] The growing external debt and the difficult financial and economic position of the country, made the International Monetary Fund the primary influential institution in the design of orthodox economic policies in the 1975-1985 period. Although its influence stopped during the García administration (1980-1985), it continued as soon as Fujimori came to power. In 1990, Peru, a country considered the "world's worst debtor," turned again to international financial organizations for advice and credit.[28]

The National Private Interests. Since 1975, national private capital gained prominence vis-à-vis the state and foreign capital. However, even if privatization policies strengthened its position in the economic power structure, other policies tended to negatively affect its interests. Liberalization policies also implied fewer subsidies and trade protection. In addition, the serious and prolonged deterioration of the Peruvian economy also weakened the national private sector in many ways: Increased financial burdens, no major new investments, no technological renovation, dramatic cost increases (including "security costs" because of terrorist attacks).

The redefinition of the state's economic functions strengthened the role of national private capital in such industrial activities as paper, cement, fertilizers, agriculture, fishing, international trade and banking. In the case of the labor communities, private capital again became the only owner of shares both in mining and the manufacturing sector. The paralysis of the agrarian reform and the progressive parcelling out and privatization of the agrarian cooperatives gave the small-sized and medium-sized farmers greater dynamism as economic agents and it opened up the opportunity for other agents to invest in agriculture.

However, the strengthening of national private capital in this period, as compared to that of the former period, was also due to foreign investor's lack of interest in the Peruvian economy.

If it is true that Morales Bermúdez authorized the formation of "multinational banks" (such as Arlabank and Extebandes), these banks did not have a strong position within the banking system. The most important change in this same period was the *grupos'* consolidation of control over the private banking system. Banco de Crédito del Perú, the most important Peruvian bank, was managed by foreign interests until 1979, when Dionisio Romero, leader of the Romero *grupo*, organized an alliance of shareholders with other *grupos* (Raffo, Brescia, Nicolini) and took over direction of the bank.[29]

During Belaunde's administration, the formation of new private banks (foreign and national) was authorized. In banking and insurance firms, the level of shareholder participation permitted to foreign capital increased from 20 to 33 percent (Sánchez Alvabera 1984: 59-60). However, banks such as the Chase Manhattan Bank, the Morgan Guaranty Trust, City Bank, the Bank of Tokyo, the Bank of America, SUDAMERIS and Wells Fargo Bank, (all banks that had initially shown interest in the Peruvian banking market), finally decided not to invest. National capital strengthened its position in the banking system with the creation of new banks such as Banco Latino (controlled by the Lanata Piaggio and Majluf *grupos*) and Banco Mercantil (controlled by Picasso and Navarro Grau *grupos*). In 1991, Banco Interandino opened its doors, formed by Carlos Rodríguez Pastor, a Peruvian international investor, with the support of the Benavides de la Quintana *grupo*. As Table 3.2 shows, the *grupos* were in complete control of the banking system.

The End of Domestic Industrialization. In the third period, the changes of the relative importance of the primary-exporting area versus the urban-industrial were another key element. Changes, however, were significant in terms of the decreasing dynamism suffered by the urban-industrial area, a process that was not accompanied by a surge of export activities.

The idea to strengthen the primary-exporting area (as well as non-traditional exports) encountered many problems despite the importance

TABLE 3.2 Commercial Banks: Percentage of Shares Controlled by *Grupos*, 1986
(in Millions of *Intis*)

Banco de Credito del Peru: (Capital: 573.6 million *intis*)	%
National Capital	
Romero *grupo*	11.87%
Brescia *grupo*	08.09%
Nicolini *grupo*	05.7%
Raffo *grupo*	03.18%
Foreign Capital	
Ubeerseebank	13.61%
Banque Sudameris	04.86%
Banco Wiese: (Capital: 262 million *intis*)	
Fundación Wiese	10.44%
Wiese de Osma family	18.82%
Wiese de la Puente family	08.94%
Wiese Moreyra family	05.70%
Arias Schreiber Wiese family	04.24%
Picasso *grupo*	11.74%
Banco Mercantil: (Capital: 75.3 million *intis*)	
Lanata-Piaggio *grupo*	21.86%
Majluf *grupo*	12.01%
Francisco Pardo Mesones	15.41%
Jorge Gildemeister Kraft	15.37%
Banco Latino: (Capital: 46 million *intis*)	
Picasso *grupo*	50.09%
Benjamín Perelman Zetter	35.00%
Banco de Lima: (Capital: 80.9 million *intis*)	
Olaechea Alvarez Calderón *grupo*	73.32%
Benavides de la Quintana *grupo*	03.62%
Picasso *grupo*	00.40%

Source: The data in this table are drawn from *The Peru Report* "The Peruvian
Financial System at the Time of the Expropriation." Peru Reporting, E.I.R.L.,
1987; and data obtained from the Superintendencia de Banca y Seguros.

of oil between 1978 and 1982. Mining and fisheries had very marked good and bad years, but they did not enjoy steady development or experience a great leap forward. Mining and oil, two key exporting activities, represented 51 percent of overall exports in 1975, and rose to 84.2 percent in 1985.

The exports of fisheries and agricultural products tended to decline in importance (with the exception of coca), while at the same time non-traditional exports increased moderately, representing only 20 percent of the overall exports in the first half of the 1980s. In the second half of the 1980s and early 1990s, non-traditional exports declined because of lower profit rates caused by changes in the exchange rate (Pfaller 1989: 35). The real boom occurred, as noted, in the coca industry, an illegal activity that dynamized and corrupted the economy at the same time.[30] In terms of the debt issue, the growing foreign debt service absorbed a considerable amount of resources and remained unsolved (Ugarteche 1986).

Manufacturing and construction lost dynamism with the recession of the domestic market (1976-1978, 1983-1985, 1989-1990), and increased competition with foreign goods (1978-1985, 1990-1991). For the first time in a period of 35 years (1950 to 1985), the urban-industrial area stopped to be an engine of economic growth. The paralysis of the urban-industrial area, combined with the absence of a dynamic primary-exporting economy, indicated the seriousness of the Peruvian economic crisis.

Conclusion

The analysis of the economic power structure in contemporary Peru, both in terms of the relative weight of property agents and the primacy of a given economic area, can be summarized as follows. In the first period, the economic power was in the hands of private capital, national and foreign, and the economy geared toward the primary-exporting area. The landed oligarchy was the hegemonic national class fraction, sharing power with the gamonales (traditional landlords) and foreign capital (mainly located in agriculture, mining, oil and fishing). However, significant changes were already visible in the 1960s in terms of the growing power of industrialists and the entrance of multinational corporations in the urban-industrial area. The new economic agents were industrializing the economy at a faster pace in the late 1960s. In the 1968-1975 period, the reforms induced by a radical military government provoked a dramatic modification of the economic power structure. With the agrarian reform, the agro-exporting oligarchy and the gamonales disappeared as power factors and, in addition, several foreign companies were nationalized. The state became a leading economic agent, with public firms in every major economic activity. The state also became the promoter of non-private forms of property (agrarian cooperatives, labor communities and social property firms). In this period, the economy was oriented toward the development of the urban-industrial area, an area where national capital expanded and diversified its interests. In the period inaugurated in 1975, a process of backlash politics took place. The state (together with all the "social" forms of property) was considerably weakened as an economic agent. The idea of using the state as a tool for economic development was also abandoned. Private property became again predominant in the national economy. A process of de-industrialization was initiated and development oriented toward traditional and non-traditional exports. But the persistence of numerous problems (a continuing economic recession combined with a debt crisis, chronic social unrest, increasing political violence and constant policy instability) slowed down the re-orientation of the economy around exports. In the third period, foreign capital did not invest in new ventures even if it had the opportunity to penetrate the banking sector and mining and oil industries. National capital became, by default, a more important investor, but still concentrated its interests in the urban-industrial area of the economy.

Notes

1. Brown (1988: 256) provides a useful list of "exogenous forces": world commodity markets, multinational corporations, international trade, financial institutions, international loan practices, technology transfer and the like.

2. See Lipset (1967) and Frank (1969 and 1972). A good synthesis of these two theories is found in Klarén and Bossert (1986). Contemporary authors such as Soto (1989), go back to the dilemma posed by the modernization paradigm, that is, neglecting the importance of external factors and overemphasizing internal factors.

3. It is worth mentioning that the analysis of changes in the Peruvian economic power structure will help to make clear this interconnection, because it shows how it varies over time. External factors, always intertwined with internal ones, for example, tend to be more influential in the first and third period, but not in the second.

4. Several authors consider Velasco's government as a historical turning point. See Quijano (1971: 49), Thorp and Bertram (1978: 327) and Fitzgerald (1981: 163).

5. The concept of the *compradore* bourgeoisie was coined in the Far East, in the eighteenth century, when Portuguese merchants traded with native agents in

order to buy and sell products in China. The *compradore* was a national agent strongly identified with foreign interests.

6. On the fishing boom of the 1960s, see Caravedo (1979: 47-50).

7. For an analysis of the limitations of the "import-substitution industrialization" model of the 1960s, see Beaulne (1975). See also Anaya (1974: 43).

8. For that reason, several authors stress the importance of the "urban-industrial pole" of the economy. See Quijano (1971: 49), Cotler (1978: 289) and Fitzgerald (1981: 101).

9. The description of the Velasco government as the "Peruvian experiment," a concept used by Lowenthal (1975: 20), clearly expresses this bias.

10. See Lowenthal and McClintock (1983) and Franco (1983).

11. It should be pointed out that some basic industries were created as joint ventures between foreign capital and state capital. The most remarkable case was that of Bayer Industrial.

12. On industrial labor communities, see Durand (1977 and 1982a). On the mining labor communities, see Iguíñiz, Sulmont and Quintanilla (1985).

13. Sánchez Alvabera evaluates the overall importance of foreign investment for that period (1984: 54-55). According to more recent sources, such as Anaya (1988b: 25), direct foreign investment in Peru dropped from US$836 million in 1971 to 755 in 1976.

14. FitzGerald (1981: 167). Estimates of the National Planning Institute reveal the same trend although percentages vary. See Instituto Nacional de Planificación (1980: 83).

15. The financial blockade lasted until 1971 according to Stallings (1983: 162).

16. The government's position on this issue can be seen in Velasco (1972: 291-301) and Franco (1983: 348-349). The negative reaction of industrialists to the reforms are fully documented in a book published by the National Industrial Society. See Sociedad de Industrias (1977). The importance assigned to the state in the economy and the *comunidades laborales* casts doubt on the arguments of Dore (1980) and Weeks (1985), who have considered the national industrialists as the driving force of change and the power behind the throne.

17. It must be noted that Velasco's government provided more generous compensation to private owners in the case of the fishing sector. See Malpica (1976) and Caravedo (1979: 84-85).

18. The Romero *grupo*, initially very strong on cotton agriculture and cattle ranches in Piura, on the Northern Coast, was the most important case. See Reaño and Vásquez for Romero (1988: 43-96) and Malpica (1987) for other cases.

19. On this, both Bamat (1978) and Becker (1983) agree, but they identify different bourgeois fractions as the heirs to the old oligarchy.

20. For the Morales Bermúdez and Belaunde administrations, see Franco (1983), Palmer (1984) and Scurrah (1987). For the García administration, see Wise (1990). Paredes and Sachs (1991) provide information for the García administra-

tion and discuss the new policy orientation of the Fujimori administration. For the discussion of the pendular movement of Peruvian policies, see Schydlowsky (1986), Ortiz de Zeballos (1989) and Gonzales de Olarte and Samamé (1991).

21. Lowenthal and McClintock (1983: xiii).

22. For changes of *comunidades laborales'* legislation, see Durand (1982a) and Iguiñiz, Sulmont, and Quintanilla (1985: 29-33).

23. *The Andean Report*, (March, 1991), p. 67.

24. On Morales Bermúdez's attempt to reprivatize the cement plants, see Durand (1982b: 104).

25. According to the Inter-American Development Bank (1987: 458), private direct foreign investment in Latin America was US$7,492 million in 1982, 5,680 in 1983 and 3,429 in 1984. In 1980, a Council for the Americas (1980) risk analysis report found little optimism of U.S. corporations toward the Peruvian economy.

26. On mining, see Aste (1984); on manufacturing, see Ogata (1981: 86); on banking, see Sánchez Alvabera (1984: 59-61) and Sifuentes (1988).

27. On the Peruvian debt, see Ugarteche (1986: 76).

28. According to an article written by Nicholas Asheshov in the *Institutional Investor* (September 24, 1990: 4), the IMF-WB weekly, the harsh stabilization plan adopted was "written word for word by the fund team."

29. Journalistic reports called the takeover "Operation Entebbe," in reference to the similarly impressive raid of Israeli commandos in Africa, see *Oiga* (April 9-16, 1979) and (April 16-23, 1979). A detailed study of the takeover can be found in Reaño and Vásquez (1986: 168-171).

30. On the coca business, see Gorriti (1988), Lee III (1988) and McClintock (1988). The difference between Peru and Colombia is that Colombia manufactures cocaine with coca provided by Peru and Bolivia. In Colombia, the economic power structure has been altered by the emergence of drug traffickers as a new fraction of the bourgeoisie. In Peru, drug traffickers are economically important only at the local level.

4

The Internal Structure of the National Bourgeoisie

The internal composition of the national bourgeoisie was also modified from the 1960s on, while major changes in terms of the relative weight of property agents and the orientation of the economy were taking place. The transformation of the national bourgeoisie, however, was more difficult to detect and analyze. The process was slow and remained obscure, especially at the beginning. This, in turn, fueled an intellectual controversy about the new profile of power within national private capital. In particular, about the identity of the new hegemonic fraction in post-oligarchic Peru.

In 1975, when the Velasco period was over, the power of the old landed oligarchy vanished. This radical alteration of the power structure was provoked by political, not economic factors. Once the oligarchy was removed from its leading position, national economic power was basically left in the hands of industrialists, bankers, merchants, miners. But at the same time, a gradual process of investment diversification was taking place, an economic process that remained undetected for many years. Only when the state was under attack and the privatization of public firms well developed, did the profile of the power pyramid begin to be debated. The basic question was to identify the heir to the oligarchy, that is, the class fraction which occupied the apex of national capital. But the influence of old paradigms to interpret the internal diversification of the national bourgeoisie and the difficulties of identifying changes at the beginning of a transitional period, forced analysts to offer different and contradictory interpretations. Some identified the new hegemonic class fraction with the industrialists (a fraction linked to the development of the urban-industrial area), others with the miners (a typical fraction of the primary-exporting area), while a third interpretation saw the economic conglomerates, the *grupos*, as the heirs to the oligarchy.

The Urban-Industrial Bourgeoisie

In the late 1970s, Thomas Bamat started to support the thesis of the economic preeminence of the "urban-industrial bourgeoisie." Bamat argued that the heirs to the oligarchy had to be essentially found in the manufacturing sector, stating that "...the heart of the bourgeoisie is industrial and not something else" (1978: 248). However, since this class fraction was also immersed in activities such as construction, commerce and insurance, Bamat preferred to conceptualize it as an "urban-industrial bourgeoisie." Several problems are found in sustaining this argument.

To begin with, Bamat's analysis is limited to a given time frame (1968-1978) and focused only on one area of the economy (urban-industrial). Bamat wrote at a time when industrialists were still seen as powerful and influential economic agents. Quiet internal changes, the diversification mentioned by Bamat, were already underway but they were not yet sufficiently developed to allow the analyst to grasp the importance of the *grupo* phenomenon. The *grupos* did not limit investments to the urban-industrial area of the economy and this process became visible only in the 1980s. Bamat was not in a position to foresee the tendencies toward deindustrialization that developed in the 1980s, a process which weakened the fractions linked to the domestic market, but not the *grupos*. The *grupos*, because of their links with banking and their diversified investment portfolio, had enough flexibility to adapt themselves to the new economic trends of the third period. It should be added that the definition of the bourgeoisie as "urban-industrial" is somehow ambiguous. Bamat's "urban-industrial" bourgeoisie seems to constitute a unified class fraction but, in fact, it does not. Within the urban-industrial area several sectoral fractions can be identified: industrialists, constructors and merchants.

The Miners

A second interpretation emerged in the early 1980s and located the most powerful class fraction of the national bourgeoisie in a different economic axis: the primary-exporting area. David Becker supported a thesis opposed to Bamat's. According to him, the "urban-industrial bourgeoisie" was not the leading economic fraction but the miners were. Becker argued that Velasco destroyed the power of the oligarchy, creating at the same time the conditions necessary for the fortification and modernization of a new bourgeoisie. This new bourgeoisie was to be found on a different economic axis, the Peruvian medium-sized mining industry (*mediana minería*). For Becker, the miner's hegemony was due to "...the preponderant position of the mining industry in the nation's economy" (1983: 239). In the early 1980s, this sector enjoyed an economic boom, a situation that allowed miners to be independent from finance capital. Becker's argument also has a number of shortcomings similar to those found in Bamat's.

Becker studied the mining sector without achieving an overall view of the economic power structure as a whole. The temporal scope of his analysis was also limited as he focused on a particular time frame (1977-1981). At this time, the mining-exporting entrepreneurs developed rapidly because they were enjoying a boom period (bonanza development according to Becker's definition). The key factor behind the boom was the sudden improvement of international prices for minerals (particularly for non-ferrous metals). Consequently, the importance assigned by governmental policies to these exporting activities shifted in their favor. Profits at this time were extraordinarily high in medium-sized mining, so it was possible to agree with Becker's opinion that this economic sector was independent of finance capital (1983: 239). In the following years, however, medium-sized mining profits declined sharply as a result of a collapse in international prices and then became heavily indebted to finance capital (Aste and Obando 1987). The problem with Bamat's approach is that the connection between mining and other capital has not been studied and the growing tendency of the *grupos* to participate in medium-sized mining was not discovered. *Grupos* such as Romero, Brescia, Lanata Piaggio, Wiese and Picasso, for example, were either already in the mining sector or had strengthened their presence in that sector in the first half of the 1980s. It would be correct to assert that medium-sized mining was (and still is) the power center of private national exporters, but to state that the miners gained "...ascension to the seat of societal power" is certainly a clear overestimation of the miners importance in the economy as a whole.

The *Grupos*

Although Bamat and Becker make opposing arguments, both authors have as a starting point the assumption of a definite link between specific economic sectors and fractions of the bourgeoisie. This assumption is valid if the task is to identify only sectoral fractions of the bourgeoisie, which exist as medium-sized capitals but it is not sufficient to identify the apex of national economic power. The apex of this economic structure, as has been implied before, is occupied by the *grupos*.[1] Those fractions located below them, in the intermediate part of the pyramid, are the sectoral fractions. Therefore, both the miners and the industrialists are located in the intermediate part of the pyramid.

The *grupos* are characterized by a diversified investment portfolio. The *grupos'* firms are thus located in several economic sectors and a relatively high level of economic power is concentrated in their hands. Seven of the biggest *grupos* (Romero, Raffo, Bentín, Nicolini, Lanata Piaggio, Ferreyros and Brescia) conduct business in at least five different economic sectors (Durand 1988b: 42). With regard to their economic power, Ludovico Alcorta has estimated that 14 *grupos* accounted for 12 percent of the GNP in 1983 (Alcorta 1987: 67). Specialized reports on the top companies show that, side by side with state firms and multinational corporations, the *grupos* appear in the third rank of Peru's leading companies (led by *grupos* like Nicolini, Romero, Brescia, Bentín, Lanata Piaggio).

A reference to the number of firms listed in Peru's top 1500 firms that are directly controlled by the *grupos*, together with other indicators presented in Table 4.1, provides a clear idea of its economic might. Twelve of the major *grupos* own 240 firms of the top 1500 firms, including most of the private banks and insurance companies (*The Peru Report* 1988). Romero had a total of 35 firms, Brescia 49, Raffo 13, Nicolini 27, Ferreyros 29, and Bentín nine. All these *grupos* were major shareholders

TABLE 4.1 The *Grupos*: Indicators of the Economic Preeminence of the Five Major Peruvian Conglomerates

Grupo	Number of Firms	Economic Diversification		Firms on Top 1500
		(a)	(b)	
Brescia	46	31	25	39
Nicolini	36	05	31	27
Lanata Piaggio	47	03	44	27
Romero	64	09	55	35
Wiese	32	02	30	18

a Primary-exporting area: mining, agriculture, fishing.
b Urban-industrial area: manufacturing industry, service, banking, finance, insurance.

Source: The data in this table are drawn from Carlos Malpica, "Los verdaderos dueños del Perú." Fascículo de *La Voz*, Lima September-November 1987. *The Peru Report* "The Top One Thousand Five Hundred Companies in Peru." Lima: Peru Reporting, E.I.R.L, 1987.

of Banco de Crédito. The Benavides de la Quintana *grupo* has 15 firms in the list and Olaechea Alvarez-Calderón has six, both linked to Banco de Lima. Lanata Piaggio has 27 firms and Majluf eight, and both *grupos* are linked to Banco Mercantil. Picasso has four firms and this *grupo* is linked to Banco Latino. Wiese has 18 firms and this *grupo* totally controls Banco Wiese. The number of firms controlled by the *grupos* is certainly much higher among the firms not on the top 1500 list and on which there is little information available. These too must be taken into account.

Although more recent studies of Peru's economic power structure do not hesitate to assign the *grupos* top ranking (Anaya 1990; Malpica 1990; Alcorta 1992), the problem inadequately answered in some works is the specific characteristics of the *grupos*. Eduardo Anaya, for example, argues that:

> The key element in every *grupo* is the existence of a commercial bank linked to a number of agricultural, mining, fishing, manufacturing, construction and real estate, commercial, storage, insurance and banking, mass media, etc., firms. The commercial banks become its core element, the "brain trusts" around which, in turn, dictate to the pyramid of the *grupo* the action program to follow (1987a: 4-5).

Anaya is right in pointing out the investment diversification of the *grupos* and in highlighting the importance of their control over commercial banking. Nevertheless, commercial banks have not become, in several cases, the core element of the *grupos*.

The process of capital diversification has been more varied and complex than that described by Anaya. The only case in which the bank is properly the *grupos'* brain trust is that of Wiese.[2] But if the cases of Banco de Crédito and three of the recently formed banks (Latino, Mercantil, Interandino) are closely examined, it may be observed that several already-formed *grupos* take control of an already-existing bank, or form a new commercial bank. The *grupos'* link with the banks is a basic and essential strategy for assuring their expansion, but it does not follow that the bank is the brain trust of the *grupos*.

What is important about the *grupos'* involvement in banking and insurance companies is rather the broadening of economic interests, a trait already developed thanks to their diversified investment portfolio. The *grupos'* interests and vision of the economy is not limited to one or two economic sectors. They cross structural boundaries, both within each economic area and between areas.

The more powerful *grupos* exist as highly articulated units administered through entrepreneurial holdings and family ties rather than through banks. Commercial banks, in most cases, are one of the *grupos*' important firms, however, the direction of the *grupo* is not necessarily located in the bank.

Banco de Crédito, for instance, is controlled by several *grupos* and does not function as the brain trust. The bank fell under the control of several *grupos*, under the leadership of Romero and Raffo, and including the participation of other *grupos* such as Brescia and Nicolini. Banco de Crédito, then, is not the brain trust of a *grupo*, since it did not direct all the firms of those *grupos* who control it. In the case of Banco Mercantil, the *grupo* alliance includes Lanata Piaggio and Majluf, and in Banco Latino's case, the Picasso and Navarro Grau *grupos*. Each *grupo* has an independent direction, but they share control of the banks. The direction of the *grupo* is located in productive firms rather than in the banks: Industria Textil Piura for Romero, Tejidos La Unión for Brescia, Backus and Johnston for Bentín, Compañía Nacional de Cerveza for Lanata Piaggio, Tejidos San Cristóbal for Raffo, Minas Buenaventura for Benavides de la Quintana, Nicolini Hnos. for Nicolini, Negociación Vitivinícola Tacama for Olaechea Alvarez Calderón and Bodegas Vista Alegre for Picasso.[3]

Another element requiring clarification is the nature of the *grupos*' link with foreign capital, insofar as the *grupos* have been characterized as an "intermediary bourgeoisie," that is, they are controlled by and subordinated to foreign capital.[4] The *grupos* have diverse types of links with foreign capital (financial, technological, commercial) and, in some cases, some form of property association. Activities such as banking and insurance[5] are where the *grupos* have an overall interest and where there is a strong association with foreign capital. The central point here, however, is that, in terms of property and management, the *grupos* keep control over the firms themselves. Hence, the *grupos* are not an intermediary bourgeoisie, but rather a fraction associated to foreign capital which retains independent decision-making capabilities.

Lastly, the *grupos*' link to the world market is another topic of discussion that deserves attention. Several studies on *grupos* indicate that this is not a valid argument since their firms operate in both markets, domestic and external (Malpica 1987 and 1990; Anaya 1990; Alcorta 1992). The link to the world market is indicated by the fact that the *grupos* own big export/import firms[6] and operate in the world market through the sale of primary and manufactured products.[7] Therefore, the *grupos*' firms combine operations in both markets and do not necessarily concentrate in one of them. Nevertheless, it is important to point out that the *grupos* are in the process of expanding their investments in the primary-exporting area.[8]

Conclusion

The internal structure of the national bourgeoisie has suffered a subtle but important transformation since 1968, when the landed oligarchy was displaced by the military as the most powerful national dominant class fraction. Its process of economic consolidation became visible in the 1980s when the *grupo* phenomenon fully emerged. The apex of the pyramid was thus replaced by the diversified *grupos* and not by the sectoral fractions (the urban-industrial bourgeoisie, according to Bamat; the miners, according to Becker). The sectoral fractions, with their concentration of economic interests in one economic sector, occupy a lower, subordinate position in the power pyramid and can be considered the heirs of the old power elite. These changes can be summarized as follows. In the mid 1960s the most powerful class fraction was the landed oligarchy, the predominant sectoral fractions were the exporters and the emerging sectoral fraction the industrialists. Twenty years later, in the mid 1980s, the most powerful class fraction were the *grupos*, the predominant sectoral fraction the industrialists and, finally, the re-emerging sectoral fractions the exporters.

The differences between the *grupos* and the sectoral fractions are based on size and type of economic interests. The power of the *grupos* derives from their firms' strategic location among the nation's top firms and from the fact that several firms are owned by one conglomerate. Both factors reveal an extreme concentration of economic power that is unparalleled by any other national class fraction. The *grupos*'s distinctiveness is their diversification of economic interests, a phenomenon facilitated and accelerated by their control of the banking system. Their vision of the economy is not limited to one specific economic sector, as is the case of the sectoral fractions, but is the economy as a whole. The *grupos*' firms operate in both areas of the economy (urban-industrial and primary-exporting) and also have different market orientations (domestic and world market). These elements draw a new map of the national bourgeoisie's internal structure in contemporary Peru and help to identify the different business players of the political game.

Notes

1. The *grupos* can be considered a "new bourgeoisie" because they have only recently attained a prominent economic position. Their origins go back to the period between the last decades of the nineteenth century and the first decades of the twentieth century. The *grupos* were formed on the basis of firms developed by descendants of European immigrants such as Romero (Spain);

Brescia, Raffo, Lanata Piaggio, Picasso, Nicolini (Italy); and Wiese (Germany). They started their businesses in different economic sectors (agriculture, manufacturing industry, banking, mining) and, later on, in the 1970s, initiated a rapid process of economic diversification. See Durand (1988b).

2. Most of the *grupo*'s firms are controlled by Banco Wiese, but the A&F Wiese commercial firm should also be considered as a second holding company. This *grupo*, then, is controlled through two centers.

3. Information about most *grupos* is found in Malpica (1987) and (1990), Anaya (1990) and Alcorta (1992). For the Romero *grupo*, see Reaño and Vásquez (1988). For the Lanata Piaggio *grupo*, see Chueca and Alfaro (1974). For the Bentín *grupo*, see Sánchez (1978).

4. The Communist Party of Peru (known as Sendero Luminoso) and other Marxist-Maoist organizations state that the *grupos* are a *compradore* bourgeoisie, that is, intimately linked to foreign capital.

5. Foreign capital was a shareholder in seven out of 15 insurance companies in 1986. Assicurazioni Generali SPA (Italy) has 19 percent of the shares of the Atlas insurance company, and it is under the direction of the Isola *grupo*, the major shareholder. La Fondiaria SPA (Italy) has 16.2 percent of the shares of La Colmena, and is controlled by the Nicolini *grupo*. Ralli Brothers Ltd. (USA) has 14.4 percent of the shares of Internacional, controlled by the Brescia *grupo*. The Uberseebank AG (Switzerland) has 11.7 percent of the shares of El Pacífico, and is controlled by the Romero *grupo*. The Insurance Company of North America (USA) owns 12.8 percent of the shares of La Positiva, controlled by the Ferreyros *grupo*. Three foreign companies own 14 percent of the shares of Rimac, controlled by the Brescia *grupo* (The Standard Marine Insurance Co., The British Fire Insurance Co., The London and Lancashire Insurance Co.). Riunioni Adriatica di Sicursa (Italy) owns 19.2 percent of the shares of El Sol, controlled by the Lanata Piaggio *grupo* (*The Peru Report* 1987: 149-158).

6. The following *grupos* also operate most of Peru's major import/export firms: Wiese (A&F Wiese), Brescia (Importadora Ferretera and Mercantil Lima), Nicolini (La Comercial Importadora), Romero (Consorcio Distribuidor), Ferreyros (Casa Ferreyros), Lanata Piaggio (Comercial Saenz Peña). See Malpica (1987) and *The Peru Report* (1987).

7. The Romero *grupo* owns three firms directly involved in traditional exports (Calixto Mostert, Oleaginosas Pisco and Cia. Industrial Peru Pacífico) and two in non-traditional exports (Industria Textil Piura and Universal Textil). The Brescia *grupo* exports minerals (Atacocha, Castrovirreyna Cia. Minera and Minsur) and also non-traditional textile exports (Tejidos La Unión and Hilos Cadena Llave). The Wiese and Bentín *grupos* export fishmeal and canned and frozen fish through their joint venture, Del Mar, a leading company in the fishing industry. The Picasso *grupo* and other *grupos* (Benavides de la Quintana and, to a lesser degree, Lanata Piaggio, who owns a small-sized mine), are all involved in the export of minerals. The Nicolini and Raffo *grupos* export textiles (Tejidos de

Ica and San Cristóbal, respectively). See Ministerio de Economía y Finanzas (1987).

8. Information on investment projects presented by the major *grupos* to the government in 1987, shows that the *grupos* have started to emphasize investment in the primary-exporting area and non-traditional export sector. Some grupos (Brescia, Raffo and Romero) own companies located outside Peru as part of this process of outward expansion. See Malpica (1987 and 1990).

5

Forms of Organization and Mediation with the State

The national bourgeoisie participates in the political process through organizations such as political parties, trade associations and the firm. The importance of these organizational forms as channels of political participation varies according to the nature of the political system, the economic significance of the different class fractions and the collective ability of the national bourgeoisie to redefine its relations with the state.

This chapter analyzes the forms in which the different fractions of the national bourgeoisie (the *grupos* and the sectoral fractions) have organized themselves as political actors. It also studies a pattern of mediation between the national bourgeoisie and the state that was established in the late 1960s and lasted until the first half of the 1980s. In this period, lack of cohesion among the different fractions was common and state elites were able to take advantage of it. Failed attempts by the national bourgeoisie to overcome this situation occurred two times, in 1974 and 1977. These attempts to unite class fractions, and mobilize them collectively for political purposes, revealed that a new trend was gradually being set in motion. The failed unitary experiments served as a central learning experience because business leaders became aware of their political weaknesses and discovered which circumstances were more favorable to class unity.

Political Parties and the National Bourgeoisie

The national bourgeoisie's internal economic structure, as well as its forms of organization, were profoundly re-defined during the Velasco revolutionary period (1968-1975). The key dominant class fractions developed forms of political organization and types of relationship to the state in a period where political power continued in the hands of military

66

leaders for 12 years and access to policy-makers did not depend on political parties and Congress. The national bourgeoisie had to rely on the firm and the trade associations to have access to the state. But the limited role political parties play in terms of business interest aggregators is also due to two other factors besides the incessant recurrence of military governments. First, the concentration of decision-making capabilities in the hands of the executive during democratic periods is a factor that diminishes the importance of Congress and, therefore, political parties. Second, business people have developed a political culture that emphasizes accommodation to changing political circumstances (different regimes and different ruling parties). Business people show little concern for party politics. If they do so, it is to defend specific interests and, on that basis, they have developed clientelistic links with a number of political parties since Peru returned to democracy in 1980.

The most important political parties linked to the national bourgeoisie were the Popular Action party (formed in 1956), the Christian Popular Party (formed in 1966) and the American Popular Revolutionary Alliance (APRA, formed in 1924). All of them were excluded from the political system during the Velasco period and, only later on with the transition to democracy, they began gradually to re-enter the political arena.

Business Political Pragmatism

Generally speaking, the Peruvian business people have not been inclined to participate actively in political parties or to get engaged in ideological debates. Not surprisingly, business leaders have often repeated that businessmen are self-confined, centered mainly on business issues, willing to accommodate themselves to the shifting political situation rather than to attempt to influence political outcomes.[1] Wils, in his study of Peruvian entrepreneurs, states that industrialists have traditionally "felt alienated from parliamentary politics in Peru. Seventy-two percent of them considered all parties worthless." He depicted the industrialist as a man "who is concerned with immediate and concrete problems...a busy individual who quite probably has not much time for politics" (Wils 1979: 163 and 167). Francisco Martinotti, a representative of small manufacturing industries and director of the National Industrial Society, makes a similar point, stating that "...in Peru the entrepreneur has concerned himself more with the firm than with the country."[2] References to the "splendid isolation" of the entrepreneurs and the "divorce that has existed between politicians and entrepreneurs" are constantly stated by representatives of the national bourgeoisie. Gabriel

Lanata Piaggio, head of one of the leading family *grupos*, evaluated the performance of the national bourgeoisie as a socio-political actor in similar terms:

> We have devoted ourselves to defend our firms and to entertain ourselves as much as we can, we have not been able to keep in touch with the rest of the population, with what was happening in government. We have never been interested in driving around the country in our luxury cars, on beautiful and bumpy roads, stopping in small villages and finding out what was going on with the rest of Peruvians (*El Comercio*, April 17, 1988: 1).

Lack of participation in political parties has business leaders out of the public eye and out of touch with society as a whole, since political parties aggregate a variety of interests. Political action has been more secret than public, more based on interest groups than on civil political organizations. Business leaders, then, have played politics protected by factory walls and isolated from the majorities.

The traditional entrepreneurial approach to politics has been that it is more important to have a direct, often clientelistic relationship with the state, than to develop an organic link with political parties and, therefore, society as a whole. The pragmatic approach was based on the idea that the state is the center of the decision-making process and nothing else counts. Lanata Piaggio frankly admits it: "We have concerned ourselves with having the right connections and looking for our friends in government so that we can obtain price increases, foreign currency and credit facilities" (*El Comercio*, April 17, 1987: 1). They know that despite regime changes, the state apparatus is the institution that most influences their firms' performances and has a direct impact on all economic issues.

Rather than a definite affiliation to a political party, what existed was a pragmatic tendency among business people to link themselves to the government in office (whether military or civilian, headed by Popular Action or APRA), as long as this government did not attempt to affect the interests of the national private sector. The average businessman in Peru was thus accustomed to the "politics of conformity" (Wils 1979: 165).

The same attitude prevailed when there was political competition and political parties became relatively more important. If this was the case, the national bourgeoisie tended to establish personal links with party leaders and support the fund raising campaigns, instead of openly participating in party politics and establishing a more substantive connection based on shared ideas and beliefs. In some cases, according to a Vice Minister of Industry, political leaders were on large firms' payrolls on a permanent basis to make sure that whenever the time came, the firm already had a contact in Congress, the cabinet or the state bureaucracy.[3]

Entrepreneurial pragmatism can be observed in attitudes toward political parties especially in the 1980 and 1985 general elections, the first to be held since 1963. Immediately before the 1980 elections, results were uncertain because of a tough competition between the main political contenders, APRA and Popular Action. Only in the last week did the undecided voters back Popular Action, the party which in the end, won the election. During the campaign, Alfredo Ferrand, head of the National Industrial Society, while answering questions about his attitude toward the presidential candidates stated: "My campaign slogan is 'Forward, Bedoya is the path'"[4]. Ferrand merged the party slogans of Popular Action ("Forward"), the Christian Popular Party ("Bedoya is the bet"), and APRA ("APRA is the path"). Another statement, made by *grupo* leader Dionisio Romero, corroborates the argument. Romero affirmed that his *grupo* always contributed to presidential campaigns: "Campaigns are very expensive and party resources scarce. Thus, they [the political parties] look for good willing people to finance their campaigns," adding that:

> I talked personally with the three main political parties and to the three we [the entrepreneurs] told how much money we were going to give. We are collaborating with democracy. We talked with leaders of APRA, Popular Action and the Christian Popular Party and collaborated with all three (*La República*, August 14, 1987: 18).

The entrepreneurial attitude has been to side with the winner and, therefore, to prefer political parties that have stronger mass support, rather than to openly identify themselves with parties that, although having well-defined entrepreneurial ideologies, have poor chances to win an election.

The Christian Popular Party is a typical example of a pro-business party without much business support. Although throughout the 1970s and early 1980s it proclaimed itself the defender of business class interests, the Christian Popular Party was not recognized as such by the national bourgeoisie. The reason for the entrepreneurial lack of interest in this party was its inability to obtain mass support and, therefore, of getting elected (Conaghan 1988a: 61). An entrepreneur criticized Luis Bedoya, head of the Christian Popular Party, for "campaigning using silk gloves instead of getting in touch with the poor, with people in the provinces."[5] Popular Action, a party with a less-defined pro-business sector stance that generally appealed more to populist tactics, had more backing from the national bourgeoisie. As Fernando Belaunde, Popular Action's founder, and twice President of the Republic (1963-1968, 1980-1985), openly admits, "the entrepreneurs know that we have the votes, and that is why they are interested in us."[6]

Executive Power

The centralized nature of the political system is the other explanatory factor of the limitations of political parties as vehicles of interest representation for the national bourgeoisie. Political parties are not important because Congress has always played a limited role in lawmaking since rules and laws are enacted mostly by the executive. This uneven balance of powers between the executive and the legislative branches has been recently reinforced by the Peruvian Constitution of 1979 because it confers on the President more than one way of using extraordinary legislative powers (Bernales and Rubio 1981: 372-375). According to Hernando de Soto, one of the central characteristics of the Peruvian political system is the importance of the executive as primary issuer of laws and regulations:

> The executive branch enacts, without consultation, over 98 percent of all decisions adopted by the two branches. Parliament, whose pluralism and openness to press and public scrutiny may lessen the possibility of arbitrary legislation, issues a little over one of every hundred laws promulgated in Peru. As a result, most decisions are made without democratic consultation and, what is worse, the vast majority of them are specific resolutions which are almost never published (1989: 196).[7]

Agreeing with this assertion, a leader of the Confederation of Private Entrepreneurial Institutions said in an interview that "the relation with powers is defined according to our priorities, first the executive, then the legislative and finally political parties."[8]

The "irrelevant" role of political parties as interest aggregators then is not so much based on the alternation of military and civilian regimes so typical of Latin American politics but on another trait that has been less explored: on the concentration of powers in the hands of the executive and a business political culture that has traditionally emphasized pragmatism, that is, accommodation to shifting political circumstances. But lack of an organic link between political parties limits the national bourgeoisie's chances of developing relations with the masses, the poor. The pragmatic game is effective in terms of defending particular interests but it reinforces its social isolation.

The Firm and Trade Associations

The most important and permanent types of organization used by the Peruvian bourgeoisie to play politics are the firm and the trade association. What remains unclear is whether the firm is more important than the trade association and to what extent all fractions operate politically in the same way.

Scholars such as Thomas Bamat, David Becker and Manuel Castillo argue that trade associations are the primary type of organization of the Peruvian bourgeoisie. According to them, the different bourgeois fractions clearly express their diversity of interests mainly through trade associations (Bamat 1978: 255-256; Becker 1983: 258; Castillo 1981). The trade associations-as-a-key-organization approach is based on the idea that the difference among fractions depends basically on their diverse sectoral economic interests. Based on this diversity, each fraction forms a trade association that will represent specific (sectoral) business interests: banking, commerce, mining, fishing, manufacturing industries, etc.

Other authors, particularly Anthony Ferner, offer a different view. Ferner argues that the "modern" fractions of the industrial bourgeoisie use a variety of vehicles (the firm, the trade association and other entrepreneurial institutions), while more "traditional" and weaker fractions rely mainly on trade associations (1982: 159-160, 167-168). His argument (that the powerful "modern" fractions use a variety of means, while medium-sized capitalists are constrained to trade associations), is a useful distinction. However, a more precise definition of the internal differentiation of the national bourgeoisie should be drawn instead of the somewhat vague references to "modern" and "traditional" fractions.

In fact, there is not one single or main type of organization common to all fractions of the national bourgeoisie. The emphasis on one particular type of organization varies according to the economic resources available to these fractions: the powerful *grupos*, on the one hand, and the weaker sectoral fractions on the other hand. This argument will be explained in detail.

The Grupos: Firm and Trade Associations

The *grupos* make up the most powerful fraction of the national bourgeoisie. Their power derives not only from concentrating wealth but also because their economic presence is felt in several economic sectors at the same time. Thanks to investment diversification, the *grupos* possess a varied number of firms located in different economic activities, firms located in the urban-industrial area as well as the primary-exporting area. Therefore, they have the advantage of membership in as many sectoral trade associations as they have firms in different economic activities.

Germán Reaño and Enrique Vásquez, drawing on a specific case, the Romero *grupo*, claim that this *grupo* seeks both a direct link to the state via the firm and an indirect one via trade associations (1986: 201). The *grupos'* presence in trade associations will reinforce their power. This assertion is based on the fact that one of the managers of the Romero *grupo*, Miguel Vega Alvear, was the head of the National Industrial Society and the Confederation of Private Entrepreneurial Institutions in 1985, and the Romero *grupo* took advantage of it to have special access to the state

Indeed, the *grupos* generally combine a number of strategies, direct and indirect, to link themselves to the state, but the role of trade associations is not necessarily as important as that of the firm. The *grupos'* participation in trade associations is, in general, not regarded as essential. The reason for the *grupos'* participation in collective associations is because this organizational form is important to establish a link with other fractions of the bourgeoisie, but is not a channel of access to the state. The *grupos* participate in trade associations to mediate in the struggle of interests among different fractions and individual firms. That is, they moderate or influence the type of demands raised by the sectoral fractions, and the way in which these demands are channeled to the state by trade associations.[9]

Information revealed in several interviews helps to reinforce the argument. A leader of the National Industrial Society, when questioned on the interest that the *grupos* may have in trade associations, answered that "they want the trade association not to do certain things." That is, the *grupos* participate in trade associations (either through direct or indirect representation) to veto certain demands raised by the sectoral fractions. The association, rather than serving as a channel for gaining access to the state, actually serves the *grupos* to relate themselves with the minor fractions of the national bourgeoisie. This prevents trade associations from endangering the defense of their own particular, individual interests. With regard to that, a manager of CONFIEP, Peru's business confederation, made the following revealing statement:

> The *grupo* leaders do not actively participate in the associations, but their firms are certainly there. They follow very closely what goes on in the associations and let their opinion be known. They do not attend the meetings personally but send their people, their "front men." They are neither indifferent nor absent.[10]

Traditionally, the heads of the *grupos*, with very few exceptions, have tended to keep undercover, out of sight. As part of this low-profile strategy, they usually avoid holding key posts in trade associations. The entrepreneurs interviewed have always argued that terrorist actions against firms and kidnapping of business people, common phenomena in Peru since 1980, forced them not to play any public role.[11] However, this is a long standing attitude, which existed prior to the emergence of the threat factor.

Terrorism and kidnapping actually reinforced an attitude that originated in the late 1960s and the early 1970s. The low-profile strategy of the *grupos* goes back to the Velasco period when the emerging bourgeoisie witnessed the liquidation of the oligarchy. At that time, businessmen associated the visibility of oligarchic power, and their public image as an extremely powerful group of wealthy families, with their demise. Public exposure, according to them, made the arrogant oligarchy politically vulnerable. Velasco then generated what can be called an expropriatory trauma. Fear of governmental decisions against the private sector reinforced business isolationism. Juan Antonio Aguirre Roca, former President of the National Industrial Society in 1977-1978 and head of the business confederation in 1992, states that Velasco "was resentful of the rich and powerful. He believed that economic success was a sin." This situation forced the new bourgeoisie to adopt a different attitude than that held by the oligarchy.[12] Instead of showing off, they opted for concealment, avoiding public scrutiny. Their low-profile strategy was publicly acknowledged by Dionisio Romero:

> We have been very careful to limit our power to productive activities only, without participating either in television, radio or newspapers, since we consider that the presence of economic power there would have been considered unhealthy (*La República*, August 14, 1987: 19).

Although Romero had enormous economic resources available, he decided, as other *grupos* did, not to openly invest in the media, and publicly appear as an economic power.

The case put forth by Reaño and Vásquez, that the Romero *grupo* increases its power by having one of its managers head a trade association, actually demonstrates how *grupos* like Romero choose to use its managers as the *grupo* representative, so that the head of the *grupo* may keep undercover.[13] In an interview with a manager of the Ferreyros *grupo*, he frankly stated that "the rule is to avoid public posts."[14] The *grupos* play the political game in the shadows, close to the power centers and as far as possible from the public eye. Martinotti acknowledged the curious political behavior of the *grupos* in the following way:

I feel that the heads of the *grupos* should have played an active role in the business class, acting as leaders, showing why they became successful entrepreneurs.... They have not been interested in participating in public life. On the contrary, they have lived at the margin of trade associations, they have not participated actively.[15]

In sum, an important characteristic of the *grupos'* behavior is that their leaders have traditionally preferred to keep a low-profile and so have avoided public scrutiny.[16]

The study of trade associations' Executive Boards in a given period (1985-1986), demonstrates that the heads of the *grupos*, with very few exceptions, kept a low profile inside trade associations.[17] This is also the case of the Association of Banks, the organizational *locus* of the *grupos*. The Association was headed in 1986 by Francisco Pardo of Banco Mercantil (Pardo's only property is 15 percent of Banco Mercantil's shares). Commenting on this situation, one manager of the Banco Mercantil said in an interview:

The Association of Banks should be presided over by Romero, Raffo or Wiese. This is not the case. The *grupos* do not want to get personally involved. The man who has resources in Peru does not want to take any risks.[18]

The same phenomenon is seen in the Association of Insurance Enterprises, where the majority of firms are owned by *grupos*. The Association was presided over by Jorge Harten, general manager of Popular and Porvenir, the latter being a state-owned firm. In five other major trade associations (Association of Exporters, National Confederation of Merchants, National Mining and Petroleum Society and the National Industrial Society), the heads of the *grupos* are present although not in key posts.[19] Hence, it can be assumed that, as a general rule, the *grupos* opt for a second-line executive post, one that does not make them into public figures. In some cases, they send their managers as representatives of the *grupo* to the trade association's Board of Directors. Cases like Vega Alvear, from the Romero *grupo*, who acted as President of the National Industrial Society and the Confederation of Private Entrepreneurial Institutions, also occur in six other trade associations and one entrepreneurial institution, where other *grupo* managers are members of the Board of Directors.[20] As may be expected, because of the *grupos'* extended control over insurance companies, most managers of firms owned by the *grupos* appear in the directory of the Peruvian Association of Insurance Companies.[21]

Therefore, it becomes clear that the *grupos* were not indifferent to

participation in trade associations' activities. They directly have participated in these associations by placing themselves in second-line posts, or
by positioning their managers in important posts. However, they did
not show a major concern on trade associations as channel of access to
the state because they strive for political power through the firm.

It is via the firm that the *grupos* link themselves to political power
centers, (mostly to the executive), by mobilizing a varied scope of organizational, human, and material resources available to them.[22] For the
most part, they act independently of each other: Each *grupo* defends its
particular, selfish interest. However, there are occasions when the *grupos*
also act as a class fraction by collectively mobilizing the resources of a
number of *grupos* for the purpose of pursuing common goals. A simple
coincidence of interests is not the only factor involved. The *grupos* are
independent entities and often compete among themselves, but they
have common interests too.[23] This commonality of interests is based in
part on the fact that the *grupos* are, in a significant number of cases,
minority shareholders of other *grupos'* firms, since most leading firms
sell part of their shares through the Lima Stock Exchange. The directories of the major *grupos*, at the same time, are interlocked: the same
director participates in a number of firms. Shared ownership and interlocked directories have created a network among the *grupos*, a space for
coordination whenever necessary.[24] The fact that the *grupos* are small in
number and that the propertied families and *grupo* leaders travel in the
same social circles are additional factors that facilitate intra-*grupo* coordination.

One particularly important space for coordination are the banks. As
was already mentioned, the banks in Peru were created or are controlled
by more than one *grupo*. The case of Banco de Crédito, Peru's most
powerful private bank, is a good example of a coalition of the major economic conglomerates, because the wealthiest *grupos* (Romero, Raffo,
Nicolini, Brescia and Ferreyros) were all members of the Board od Directors.[25] These links among the *grupos* (property and interlocking direc-
torates), tie together the major banks and the top nonfinancial firms and
redefine the perception of economic interests. As Maurice Zeitlin argues
for the Chilean case, the banks:

> ...[T]ake on a crucial political-economic role in integrating the simultaneous
> and potentially contradictory financial, industrial and commercial interests
> of the wealthiest families, whose various investments span these ostensibly
> separate sectors (1988: 114).

The *grupos' modus operandi* to have access to the state depends basically on informal strategies for contacting and influencing both state offi-

cials and cabinet members (and occasionally, members of Congress). Through this silent mechanism, the *grupos* obtain the protection of state officials. Norms and regulations needed to operate their empires, and valuable information from direct sources (an important asset for business life), are obtained through the *grupos's* direct penetration of the state. Information becomes extremely valuable in a society where the state intervenes in so many ways to fix prices (interest rates, wages, taxes, exchange rates) and where political and policy instability is fairly normal.[26] Information allows the *grupos* to anticipate events and legal provisions that are crucial to the growth and profitability of their firms.[27] The ability to keep in contact with state officials and cabinet members varies, of course, according to shifting political circumstances (cabinet and government changes). Part of the *grupos' modus operandi* is their adaptability to changing circumstances. They have developed a capacity to "manage uncertainty" by silently restructuring contacts and personal relations within the state whenever a major cabinet or governmental change occurs.[28] Not only the members of the clan (each one with its own contacts) are involved in this strategy. The law offices and consulting firms and the personal connections of the *grupos'* managers also play a role in the networking process. All this networking permits them to easily adapt the *grupos'* overall strategy to shifting circumstances. If the contacts of the clan, and its network, do not work, the possibility of coopting politicians, ministers and officials is always available, more so when public posts are used as a mechanism of upward social mobility (or an opportunity for corruption).[29] The possibility of a constantly renewed clientele is always there and the links with the state apparatus are so deep that, even when cabinet or government changes occur, the *grupos* generally manage to be well-informed and to assure themselves a privileged relationship with the state.

This game is played in secrecy, a necessary condition for success.[30] Since both the *grupos* and state profit individually from this connection, a connection that conspires against the national interest which the state in principle defends, it is imperative to avoid public exposure. Both the *grupos* and state officials run the risk of being denounced by their numerous political opponents, who suspect the dealings but rarely have concrete evidence to condemn them.[31]

A working relationship between the *grupos* and the state is exemplified in several interviews to both managers and high state officials. A retired manager of the Wiese *grupo* stated that Guillermo Wiese, the *grupo* leader was "very respected, and the economic activities of the *grupo* well appreciated by all governments."[32] A former President of the Peruvian Chamber of Construction and well recognized business leader claimed that "the super entrepreneurs believe that everything is settled with a mountain of money."[33] A director of the Association of Exporters interviewed, emphatically and crudely stated that in the bureaucracy almost everything depends on "grafts and political favors."[34]

The testimonies of several public officials coincide with that of the entrepreneurs. An high state official of the Development Finance Corporation (COFIDE) claimed that when credits are denied to a *grupo's* firm: "The *grupos* call the President of the Republic, and the President calls the President of COFIDE."[35] A Director of the Ministry of Industry claimed that "it is not correct to say that the state is neutral. Each minister arrives with his own group." According to this testimony, state officials are "ordered from above" to facilitate licenses or grant exceptions. He added that influence of the *grupos* has to be taken into account whenever decisions are taken: "One [the state official] has to be careful with the *grupos*. If a firm is sanctioned and you do not know it is part of a *grupo*, you are fired. That has happened here."[36] An official of the National Planning Institute said that "the *grupos* know better than smaller firms how to move themselves inside the state apparatus and have several other forms of influence." He continued, "some officials feel important because they meet the big shots, they greet him and that counts."[37] Another official of the Ministry of Economy and Finances claimed that "the important matters are settled in closed meetings or dinners between the *grupos*, the Vice Minister and the advisers."[38]

Several scholars who have examined the nature of economic power in Peru (Ludovico Alcorta, Folke Kafka, Soto and Malpica), claim that the *grupos'* secret and clientelistic *modus operandi* is the norm rather than the exception. The problem, however, lies in the fact that none of them provide sufficient data to demonstrate how it works. According to Alcorta, "a great concentration of economic power necessarily implies a political influence comparable to their economic influence." The *grupos'* political influence, continues Alcorta, is manifested in the granting of "specific favors, most likely, tax exemptions, favorable credits or governmental pressure on labor unions" (1987: 87). However, he does not provide data which confirms this. Soto supports a similar argument in his studies of "rent-seeking" entrepreneurs. "Rentism," according to him, is a resource useful in the competition to obtain favors from the state, favors that ensure earnings not derived from direct productive effort. Soto in particular claims that:

> The legal system changes as the relative position of those who manage to influence the government changes. This is why we often hear that our system lacks uniformity and stability, our laws are negotiable, there is legal anarchy, and what matters is not what you do or want, but what politician or bureaucrat you know. Nor should it be surprising that bribery and cor-

ruption are characteristic results of a legal system in which competing for unearned income has become the predominant form of lawmaking (Soto 1989: 191).

The problem with Soto, as with Kafka (1983), one of his disciples, is twofold. First, he lacks systematic research on this issue. Soto's study focuses research mainly on the informal sector, despite the fact that his theory claims to understand the logic underlying both the formal and the informal sector. Second, he includes very broad and diverse participants in what he calls the "redistributive coalitions" (unionists, consumers, entrepreneurs), without any distinction among the power differential of these diverse interest groups. Soto's main interest in comparing the formal sector (involved in rent-seeking practices and, therefore, privileged), with the informal sector (small-sized informal entrepreneurs, operating outside the legal system), is to prove that the informal sector does not participate in redistributive coalitions and that the "formal sector" as a whole is involved in rent-seeking practices. The question of who among the formal sector benefits most from this competition of unearned income remains unanswered. There are key distinctions to be made within the formal sector (that is, between the *grupos* and the sectoral fractions) and not only between the formal and informal sectors to shed more light on this question.

Malpica, who has published several studies from a class perspective on the ruling elites, asserts that a select, concealed, and permanent link between the *grupos* and political power has always existed (Malpica 1987, 1990). The problem with Malpica's study is lack of analysis of the phenomenon as a whole. He basically depicts the *modus operandi* of each *grupo* in a descriptive way. Because of that, it is helpful to synthesize his conclusions.[39] According to Malpica, the major *grupos* (Romero, Raffo, Brescia, Bentín, Lanata Piaggio, Nicolini, Ferreyros, Benavides de la Quintana, Picasso, Wiese, Baertl and Alvarez Calderón) knew how to adapt themselves to the Velasco reforms and, in some significant cases, benefited from them. After Velasco, the *grupos* kept up their links with both military and civilian governments, thus, regime changes did not alter this pattern of a privileged relationship between the *grupos* and the state. The links between economic and political power were largely of an informal nature. Family contacts and friends, the so called "F" connection, helped to get the *grupos* to stay in touch with state officials on a permanent basis. Favors to senior officials (two Presidents included), or their families, opened the doors of the government's higher circles. In some cases, the *grupos* have used positions in the public administration to penetrate the higher circles. Based on these different mechanisms the *grupos* usually managed to prevent the adoption of rules that affected them, to modify rules that negatively affected them, and, in addition, to obtain specific favors from government officials that favored their firms. The problem with Malpica is that he does not quote any sources or publish data that supports his argument, but at least he shows an inside knowledge about the logic of power relations in Peru that is recognized even by his critics.[40]

What is interesting about these arguments, despite the theoretical and methodological limitations, is that all scholars point to a pattern of political influence that grants specific favors to individual firms rather than to a more general and open influence on the policy-making process.

It must be noted that the primary goal of the *grupos* has not been, as might be expected, to influence the orientation of economic policies or specific sectoral laws. They followed a more pragmatic approach, preferring to exercise their influence to change specific articles in a legislation rather than publicly opposing or backing macroeconomic policy changes. The *grupos*, thanks to a diversified investment portfolio, have easily adapted themselves to policy changes. In addition, since it has been possible to obtain specific favors for their firms, policy changes did not always necessarily have a negative impact on the *grupos* interests. What mainly concerned them was what state officials define as the "small rule," that is tailored legislation, legislation custom-made to serve the interests of the *grupos*.

In this context, the political know-whom, as long as the state remains colonized by the *grupos*, is more important than the technological know-how. Since the late 1970s, economic policies that favored this privileged pattern of *grupos*/government relations have greatly dismantled state protectionism and interventionist policies. The *grupos*, however, have shown an ability to obtain tailored legislation, a practice that has often conspired to give coherence to major policy changes that emphasize international competitiveness as well as deregulation. In this sense, the political ability of the *grupos* is unparalleled.

It is important to point out that if the *grupos* profit from this relationship, the state elites also obtain specific political results. In some cases, that goes beyond the personal interests of state officials. State elites enjoy greater room to maneuver in terms of the policy-making process because there is a pact with the *grupos*, the most powerful class fraction. They know that business response to policy changes will not be strongly opposed because of this pact. Business demands, particularly those of sectoral fractions, have been generally diffused and, therefore, less politically effective. The power game between the *grupos* and the high state official is usually a game of mutual cooptation, highly functional to both partners, because the global direction of macroeconomic policy is mostly left to the political class in exchange for tailored legislation benefiting the *grupos*. The state can expand its room to maneuver in the policy-making arena because the national bourgeoisie is fragmented, divided into several fractions, unable to coordinate among themselves and often competing against each other.

The Sectoral Fractions and Trade Associations

The sectoral fractions of the national bourgeoisie, compared to the *grupos*, have a weaker but well defined position in the economic power structure. They are not as powerful as the *grupos* and their interests are limited to specific economic sectors. Since the firm does not have the economic significance of the *grupos*, it cannot mobilize material and human resources as effectively as can an economic conglomerate.

Occasionally, some firms might succeed because of personal contacts with high state officials, but rarely do they have a chance to establish a permanent relationship with the political power apparatus as a whole. The sectoral fractions do not have the clout necessary to obtain tailored legislation and their concerns are mostly restricted to the defense of the general economic, legal and labor issues of each particular economic sector. The norms and regulations of these issues apply to all sectoral firms and constitute the main concern of trade associations. Therefore, the primary organizational form of the sectoral fractions is the trade association, an organization that claims to be representative of an economic sector and, as such, is entitled to dialogue and participate in negotiations with the state.

In order to clarify the question of representation and the presence of medium-sized firms in trade associations, a more detailed analysis is necessary here.[41] The question of sectoral representation is defined in the following way. First, the trade association's degree of sectoral representation is estimated according to the importance of trade association members as compared to the total number of firms of every economic sector (organizational density). Second, leaders of each trade association are identified by the economic importance of their firms within each economic sector. It is important to remember that *grupo* representatives (with few exceptions) do not generally lead trade associations, and that, in each trade association, members may range from representatives of multinational corporations to *grupos*, big sectoral firms and even small firms.

A detailed study of the membership and leadership of seven of the most important, oldest and best established trade associations of key economic sectors (manufacturing industry, pharmaceutical industry, fishing, mining, agriculture, construction and commerce), provides an answer to the question of what kind of firms are predominant in Peru's business trade associations.

The National Industrial Society (formed in 1896) had 1,654 members in 1985 versus a total of approximately 14,000 firms in the manufacturing industry. The Society represents only 11.8 percent of the total number of manufacturing industrial firms, but its members are the major ones in terms of the total value of the sector's production. According to one of its leaders, the Society's firms produce approximately 80 percent of the gross output value of the manufacturing industry.[42] In the case of the textile committee (one of the oldest and better organized), total membership includes only 80 firms (representing 26 percent of the total number of firms), but these firms manufacture 75 percent of the gross output value for 1984.

The classification of members by size follows the criteria defined by the Society in 1986, that it is measured in terms of their assets. Big industries (4 to more than 7 million *Intis*) represent 16.1 percent of the associates, medium-sized industries (250,000 to 3,99 million *Intis*) represent 20 percent and small-sized industries (up to 249,999 *Intis*) represent more than half of the associates.[43]

The Executive Committee of the National Industrial Society is composed of thirteen members: seven of the directors are included in the categories 1A and 2A ("big firms"), two are included in the categories 3A, 4A and 5A ("medium-sized firms") and four are included in the categories 6A, 7A, and 8A ("small-sized firms"). The majority of Directors (seven out of thirteen, 54 percent), represent big firms while the firms in this category are only 16 percent of the total members. In some committees, such as the committee for textiles, with an Executive Committee of eight members, big firms clearly prevail: seven of the members are in category 1A, and one is in 2A.

In the case of pharmaceutical laboratories, a branch of the manufacturing industry that has a separate trade association, the primary organization is the Association of Pharmaceutical Laboratories of Peru (ALAFARPE, formed in 1965). The total number of firms associated with ALAFARPE is 67, about half of the total number of firms in that particular industry (130 firms). ALAFARPE has 22 of the 24 major producers, representing 72 percent of the firms located in that industry, producing 75 percent of the gross output value. ALAFARPE represents mostly firms of greater economic power and it is led by big firms.[44]

In the case of fisheries, the National Fishing Society (SNP, formed in 1952), includes 108 firms (producers of canned and frozen fish products) out of a total of 152 (71 percent of the total number of fishing firms). Such firms represent 96 percent of the total production of canned fish. In the case of frozen fish producers, the firms associated in SNP produce 71 percent of the total output of frozen fish. The Society's Board of Directors includes 19 members, 12 of whom are canned-fish producing firms. Of those 12 firms, nine (75 percent) are among the 20 major producers, responsible for 47 percent of the total output of canned fish for 1986. With regard to frozen fish, the members of the Board (seven in total), represent firms that produced 57 percent of the total output of frozen fish for 1986.

The National Mining and Petroleum Society (SONAMINPET, formed in 1896), has 120 members and there are approximately 200 firms in the mining sector. Thus, the Society represents about 60 percent of the mining sector firms.[45] Its Board of Directors has seats for 18 members, most of whom are representatives of "medium-sized" mining. According to the Ministry of Energy's regulations, "medium-sized" mining includes those mines producing from 350 to 5,000 metric tons of minerals daily. The major mining firms are represented on the Board: eight of the ten top silver-zinc-and-lead-producing firms of the "medium-sized" mining strata. If the total number of mining firms with representatives on the Board are taken into consideration,[46] the economic representation of the Society becomes clearer. For 1986, the firms controlled by the members of the Board produced 63 percent of the nation's total zinc output, 47.7 percent of the nation's total lead output, and 63 percent of the nation's silver output.

In the agricultural sector, the National Agrarian Organization (ONA, formed in 1980), is the key trade association representing the private sector. ONA has 245 committees and a total membership of approximately 250,000.[47] The Board is composed of eight members, most of them affluent medium-sized farmers (seven out of a total of eight). Within ONA, the National Committee of Rice Producers (the most powerful committee), has 66,000 members, practically all of the nation's rice producers. The President of the Committee, Gustavo García Mundaca (also the head of ONA in 1987), is a successful rice producer in Ferreñafe (a valley on the North Coast) and owner of a medium-sized farm of 60 hectares. The other four members of the Board own properties ranging from 15 to 47 hectares.

In construction, the entrepreneurs have successfully organized themselves in the Peruvian Chamber of Construction (CAPECO, formed in 1958). CAPECO includes 1,048 (60 percent) of the nation's 1,755 construction firms and basically represents the big and medium-sized construction firms. The Board is composed of seven members and, the big, medium-sized and small-sized firms are also represented on the Board. Big firms, according to Chamber's regulations, always have two seats on the Board. Twenty-two of the 25 largest firms are members of CAPECO.

In commerce, there are two big confederations, the Confederation of

Chambers of Commerce (CONFECAMARAS, formed in 1970), and the National Confederation of Merchants (CONACO, formed in 1945). The first confederation includes Peru's biggest import/export firms (from Lima and the provinces) with a total of 66 regional Chambers of Commerce and Industry. The Lima and Arequipa regional chambers (both founded in 1887), are the most powerful ones, particularly the first one. The Lima Chamber of Commerce, the most important economically, includes approximately 4,000 firms (28 percent) of the nation's 14,500 firms. This membership includes most of the big and-medium-sized commercial firms. Nevertheless, CONFECAMARAS has 25 members on its Executive Committee and, in contrast to other trade associations, only four of the biggest firms are represented (16 percent).

The National Confederation of Merchants is the organization which competes with CONFECAMARAS. It basically includes medium-sized and small-sized firms, but does not limit itself to commerce or industry. It also has more local committees: a total of 187 committees versus CONFECAMARAS' 66. CONACO claims to have a numerous membership (approximately 100,000) and to represent mostly small-sized firms. However, a close look at its Executive Board shows that big firms control five out of 16 seats (31 percent).

In sum, sectoral trade associations are more representative in terms of economic power (associates represent a significant percentage of sectoral output), than in terms of their representation of a majority of firms located in every economic sector. Only the National Agrarian Organization has an almost total representation of producing firms. In all cases of the seven trade associations studied above, they represent more than 70 percent of the output of their respective economic sector. Organizational density, however, measured in terms of representation of the number of firms of each economic activity, varies from 11.8 percent to 28 percent in the case of the National Industrial Society and the Lima Chamber of Commerce, to more than 90 percent in the case of some of the National Agrarian Organization's most active committees. In terms of the associations' leadership, the characteristics are quite clear. First, only national firms are members of the Board of Directors or Executive Committees. Second, very few Directors or Presidents are leaders or managers of the *grupos*: three are found in the National Industrial Society, one in the National Fishing Society, two in the National Mining and Petroleum Society, one in the Lima Chamber of Commerce and none in the rest. Third, small-sized firms are underrepresented in all cases.[48] Typically, leadership positions are held by representatives of "big" sectoral capitals not related to the *grupos*.

For the sectoral fractions, trade associations are the most important type of organization. Individually, their firms are not powerful enough to establish permanent links in effective ways with the state apparatus and cabinet members. But what they cannot do individually they can accomplish collectively. According to several interviews given by trade association directors, the firms need coverage by trade associations in order to "be heard" by state officials.[49]   Access to the state depends heavily on being a member of a trade association that claims to be representative and, therefore, has a right to be heard.

In order to understand the political role of the association it is important to take a look at the way each organization defines its goals.[50] According to trade associations' statuses, these organizations agree to perform mainly two types of functions, internal and external. The internal function is to provide services, (information and legal advice), to all members, and to arbitrate conflicts between members. The external function, based on the formal representation of a particular economic sector, is to bargain with "others" (labor unions, the state). A trade association is said to be representative as long as it is able to include a significantly large number of members (organizational density) and/or group members that are important in terms of their economic weight. A trade association that is "representative" enjoys public recognition, that is a formal recognition by the state and the recognition of society as a whole.[51] In Peru, trade associations do not usually deal directly with labor unions because labor conflicts are mostly mediated by the state. In addition, as mentioned above, business social isolationism prevents trade associations from playing a role in the rest of society.[52] Therefore, the trade association's most important external activity is the representation and defense of sectoral interests in relation to the state.

Not having direct permanent access to the state, as is the case of the *grupos*, sectoral fractions count mostly on their organizational resources. Each individual trade association maintains and fosters relations with the ministry of each sector, on the basis of being "representatives" of an economic sector. However, the level of importance these relations have depends on the participation of sectoral fractions in governmental coalitions and the macroeconomic policy orientation the state adopts.[53] If a specific sectoral fraction does participate in a governing coalition and this participation is based on a specific policy orientation, the doors of the state are usually open to the minor fractions of the national bourgeoisie.

Pattern of Mediation

In order to understand how, in a given period, firms and trade associations are engaged in a complex relationship with political power, it is necessary to look at the larger picture to explain the existing mediation patterns between the state and the national bourgeoisie.

A specific pattern of mediation was established after Velasco's revolution, once profound modifications in the economic power structure, politics and society began to take place. Prior to 1968, trade associations, particularly the National Agrarian Society (controlled by the agro-exporting oligarchy), had institutionalized access to a number of state agencies but such access was cut off by Velasco. Instead, Advisory Committees were formed and the governmental practice of appointing individual entrepreneurs (linked to *grupos* in many cases) was initiated (Bamat 1978: 201; Durand 1982b: 66-67; Ferner 1982: 167-169). A new power game between the state and the national bourgeoisie was being developed in the late 1960s and 1970s. The link between the state and "modern entrepreneurs" (the *grupos*), was almost immediately established by appointing hand-picked entrepreneurs to the Advisory Committees and by Velasco's initiative to sponsor "little dinner groups" at the presidential palace on Sundays.[54] At the same time, Velasco favored the tactic of isolating trade associations who opposed reforms and gave preferential treatment to those trade associations willing to support his government. Instead of pursuing unity, individual trade associations swung from open confrontation to collaboration. In this period (from 1968 to 1980), the national bourgeoisie was internally divided since each fraction decided separately (frequently in conflict with each other), how to confront the state. The state elites, in turn, reinforced this pattern to further their own position. It was easier for state elites to put into practice reforms with a fragmented national bourgeoisie, a class whose fractions were unable to coordinate and agree on a similar course of action. Business people used to refer to this pattern of mediation with the state as Velasco's "sausage policy," that is, to take the business sector "by slices" (Conaghan 1988b: 19).

During this period, some attempts were made by the state to control or constrain trade associations, by intervening directly in the associations' affairs. This approach was applied in only two cases and succeeded in only one. In one instance, Velasco tried to and succeeded in eliminating the old agrarian trade association (the oligarchical National Agrarian Society) (Bamat 1978: 209; Monge 1988: 31). In a second instance, the state tried to intervene in the internal affairs of the National Industrial Society by imposing regulations on elections of members of the Board (including workers, as representatives of *comunidades laborales*), but failed to do so because of an active, well organized opposition by the Society.[55] The National Industrial Society succeeded in remaining autonomous but paid the price of being essentially cut off from the state (Bamat 1978: 211; Castillo 1982: 59-60).

What happened in these two cases does not mean that, in general, relations between the state and trade associations were normally based on confrontation. The National Agrarian Society's trade association was eliminated by the state because it was the organization of the landed oligarchy. A confrontation was inevitable in this case. In the case of the National Industrial Society, a direct political confrontation with Velasco's government occurred because of the Society's resistance to the *comunidades laborales* and to the government's attempts to place representatives of the *comunidades* (known as *comuneros*), on the Society's Executive Board. This line of action was not attempted with other trade associations. Cases of direct confrontation were limited to the National Agrarian Society and the National Industrial Society. In all other cases, despite the reforms, trade associations tried to link themselves to the state apparatus and to collaborate, whether they agreed or not with the Velasco reforms. Given the circumstances, a strong state shaped a pattern of relations with business where individual trade associations had to choose between making war and facing the consequences or collaborating. The national bourgeoisie was not only economically weak but, also, most of all, politically weak.

What must be kept in mind is not the different tactics adopted by trade associations (direct confrontation or tactical containment) (Bamat 1978: 212-219), but the fact that the state was able to determine a general pattern of relations established with almost every dominant class fraction. This pattern was consolidated with other actions. Cooptation of individual entrepreneurs occurred when the government offered membership in the Advisory Committees, or was invited to belong to the President's inner circle. This cooptation reinforced the lack of unity among the emerging *grupos* and sectoral fractions of the national bourgeoisie and among sectoral fractions.

The state established a pattern of association with the sectoral fractions organized into trade associations that varied according to specific cases. In the case of the industrialists, a sectoral fraction that decided to challenge state-led reforms, the state's response was to isolate it. At the same time, state elites established close relations with other trade associations, those willing to collaborate for pragmatic reasons or out of fear.

This pattern of mediation was continued by the next two administrations (Morales Bermúdez, 1975-1980; and Belaunde, 1980-1985), although relations between the state and the national bourgeoisie were more positive because of the pro-business orientation of governmental policies (rights of private property and labor laws). The state, in cooperation with the private sector, began dismantling the reforms and changing labor legislation. These policies were initiated by a military government and continued by a civilian one. However, despite changes in economic policies, and of political regime, the pattern of mediation between the state and the national bourgeoisie continued into the 1980s because the issues being discussed changed but each class fraction continued to act separately and the government succeeded in "slicing" apart business fractions.

Because of the novel economic policy orientation (liberalization, privatization, deregulation), both miners and import-export merchants defended free-trade and favorable exchange rate policies, while others, mainly industrialists, claimed a "cheap dollar" policy and the protection of the domestic market. This typical economic clash of interests was particularly evident during the Morales Bermúdez and Belaunde administrations.[56] Both governments gave priority to the primary-exporting area and made decisions without consulting trade associations negatively affected by those policies. At the same time, the state enjoyed the support of those trade associations which benefited from macroeconomic policies, in addition to the *grupos'* support (or silent acquiescence).

The pattern of relations between the state and the national bourgeoisie was based on a balance of forces between the two that favored the state because the national bourgeoisie lacked internal unity and was politically isolated. This pattern was clearly revealed also at the Annual Conference of Executives, an event which congregated entrepreneurs from all economic sectors and the state elite to discuss current political issues. The Peruvian Institute of Business Administration (IPAE, formed in 1959), the organizer of the Annual Conference of Executives, played a different role than did trade associations. IPAE was important because it reinforced the pattern of mediation between a strong state and a weak national bourgeoisie in a particular way. The Institute was conceived of as an educational organization, but it also played a political role because it organized an annual conference that provided a link between the state and the bourgeoisie. During the 1970s, the Velasco and Morales Bermúdez's military governments used the Conference as a channel to dialogue with the private sector, helping to institutionalize the Conference as the most important annual meeting between the state elites and business leaders. At this conference, entrepreneurs had an opportunity to speak, and state officials, (usually Ministers and other important state officials such as the heads of the Central Reserve Bank and the Development Finance Corporation), also had a chance to make their viewpoints explicit. The forum served as a fruitful exchange of opinions in a period where political parties were banned, Congress closed and the mass media under tight government control. The conference was organized by individual entrepreneurs who represented big business. Their leaders were all linked to multinational corporations, the *grupos*[57] and a handful of big firms. They chose the speakers and agreed with the government on the topic to be discussed every year. The rest of the private sector was invited to attend. The Conference, therefore, was basically an opportunity for dialogue, useful to both the state and the national bourgeoisie.

Two key factors revealed the limited importance of the Conference for the national bourgeoisie as a collective player. First, at the Conference business leaders always spoke on an individual basis, representing individual not class or fractional opinions. Second, the event was just a conference, not a space where decisions could be adopted and negotiations could take place.[58] Trade associations, it must be remembered, were the only organizations to claim the "representation" of the private sector and, therefore, allowed to negotiate with state officials. The Institute did not attempt to interfere with the associations' right to bargain with the state, however, since trade associations lacked a business confederation, the Conference was seen as the "mouthpiece of the private sector." The Conference organizers always avoided or prevented confrontations with trade associations. They claimed that the Conference did not interfere with the associations' rights because it was neither formally representative of the private sector, nor was it a space for negotiations. However, the Conference's leaders enjoyed a privileged relationship with high state officials and used the occasion to exchange ideas and arrange private dealings. In addition, the state elites saw in the Conference an opportunity both to know the opinion of the private sector and to defend the government's viewpoint on a number of issues. The existence of the Annual Conference of Executives did not improve the bargaining capabilities of the national bourgeoisie. Class fractions were still divided and did not have a collective representative organism because the existence of the Conference did not change the fact that relations with the state were still based on a divided, politically disorganized national bourgeoisie. The Conference, since other channels of dialogue were nonexistent, was better than nothing, and therefore tolerated by most business people.

Attempts to Form a Business Confederation

The pattern of mediation established in this period posed a serious problem for class cohesion because it challenged the ability of the national bourgeoisie to overcome internal divisions, and limited its influence on the policy-making process. Reactions to this situation came mainly from the industrialists, that is, the class fraction that did not enjoy a positive or privileged relationship with the state during the Velasco administration.

Two factors, internal and external to the national bourgeoisie, contributed to generate the conditions for class unity among trade associations: (a) the formation of a leadership willing and able to carry on the project of internal unity and, (b) the appearance of a critical juncture that generated conditions for class solidarity, as to develop a learning process.[59] These factors appeared together simultaneously at several different moments in the 1970s. Unity was to be built gradually around issues concerning the whole class, in conditions under which trade associations' leaders could handle the negative impact of the objective difference of interests among class fractions. Unity through a business confederation was seen by trade associations' leaders as the way to become politically active on a permanent basis.

The national bourgeoisie's initial experience started with Velasco who carried on the "structural reforms" without consulting those affected by them. His government systematically ignored trade associations' demands to stop the reforms and to be informed of policy changes. Only the Annual Conference of Executives served as a forum to dialogue about the structural reforms. But the state had no obligation to take into account the demands of trade associations, or hear the opinions of disaffected entrepreneurs who dared to criticize its actions at the Conference. The links established through the participation of individual entrepreneurs in Advisory Committees continued despite the reforms because those entrepreneurs accepted the rules of the game imposed by the state.

In the Velasco period, industrialists in particular (and the sectoral fractions of the national bourgeoisie in general), repeatedly felt that the state had the power to impose reforms, partially because the bourgeoisie's internal divisions weakened its bargaining position. The National Industrial Society openly criticized the Annual Conference of Executives because a dialogue between entrepreneurs and the state took place at that event in a moment when relations with industrialists were cut off. The Society was also openly opposed to the governmental tactic of appointing individual entrepreneurs to Advisory Committees. The Society's opinion on this particular issue was very clear: Only entrepreneurs nominated by trade associations were true representatives of the private sector. Demands for state recognition of trade associations as representative organizations and for entrepreneurial formal participation in state organisms, started to emerge in the heat of events. The isolation of industrialists from political power was initially denounced by the National Industrial Society in 1974, when industrialists accused Velasco's government of "Discrimination in the dialogue with omission and disregard for representative organizations.... Dialogue and collaboration requests are only for handpicked persons."[60] A leader depicted the situation in the Velasco period in the following way: "The structural reforms of the military government were approved when the manufacturing firms were at an early stage of development and the Peruvian entrepreneurs fragmented, accustomed to act in isolation."[61] State officials, used to playing with the national bourgeoisie's internal divisions, knew that the weak trade associations lacked a business confederation capable of uniting and politically empowering them.

In this period, a generation of business leaders, particularly although not solely, in the National Industrial Society, learned in tough negotiations with state officials to be on guard and to develop defensive mechanisms. Leaders like Raymundo Duharte, Juan Antonio Aguirre Roca (National Industrial Society), Julio Piccini (Peruvian Chamber of Construction), and Edgardo Palza (Peruvian Institute of Business Administration), searched for an opportunity to create links among trade associations and foster class cohesion. They defined themselves as "*gremialistas*," business leaders strongly identified with the interests of the *gremio*, the trade association. This self-definition implied that they were capable of distinguishing whenever necessary between the individual, selfish interests common to all business people and the collective interests of the business class as a whole.

The failure to form a business confederation on two occasions (1974 and 1977), strengthened the conviction of the "*gremialista*" leaders that lack of unity limited the national bourgeoisie's role in national politics, and that state elites were consciously blocking any unitary attempt.[62] In their view, Velasco's nationalizations and the economic empowerment of the state, the attack on private property rights (*comunidades laborales*), the attempts to reduce the power of the private sector by developing non-private forms of property (rural cooperative, social property), the elimination of the National Agrarian Society and the governmental interference with the internal affairs of National Industrial Society all debilitated the business class as a whole. And they occurred because the national bourgeoisie could not oppose or prevent the government from doing it. Their clear inability to stop governmental actions was due to internal divisions in combination with a conscious state policy to divide the business sector in order to conquer it.

The opportunity to create the Front presented itself when Velasco nationalized the fish meal industry in 1974. The National Industrial Society, stressing the need for class unity, attempted to create an organism called the "Front for the Defense of Private Property." The potential for unity was present because of common fears of several bourgeois fractions toward continued expropriation of national capital. The threat of nationalizations, however, was not enough to overcome fears of governmental punishment. Some trade associations (the National Mining and Petroleum Society, the Association of Exporters and the National Confederation of Merchants), preferred to avoid direct confrontation with Velasco's strong government on this occasion. These trade associations were not willing to risk the good relations established with the state. Despite the opposition of the National Industrial Society, which fought openly against the Velasco government, the three trade associations mentioned above, as well as the emerging *grupos* and the entrepreneurs who organized the Annual Conference of Executives, managed to maintain a positive relationship with the state and avoided the risks of confrontation. The fact that the Conference continued to be held at a moment when the Front was being organized helped Velasco to manage the industrialists' pressure. He knew very well that the national bourgeoisie was internally divided, and unable to agree on how to oppose the government's reforms that were rejected in private by all entrepreneurs. Velasco was fully aware of the national bourgeoisie's political weakness and acted accordingly.

The other unitary attempt was made in 1977 in a different political context. That year, a deep political and economic crisis unfolded as the Morales Bermúdez government faced increased pressures from the labor movement and demands for elections in a year when the economy was suffering a recession. The mass movements radically opposed both the austerity measures (the first of a series to be adopted to cope with economic crisis) and changes in labor legislation that favored the private sector. The government was heavily indebted, in need of foreign exchange, but not willing to adopt the "shock treatment" favored by international banks and the International Monetary Fund. At this critical juncture, the government was forced to turn to the private sector in order to both seek support to stop labor protest and to bargain with the international financial organization to obtain foreign exchange without adopting a tough stabilization program. The National Industrial Society and six other trade associations saw the danger of political chaos and the potential for unity. At this moment, they decided to create the Union of Private Entrepreneurs and claim participation in the cabinet.[63] The Union, once created, helped the government solve the crisis, and the situation soon stabilized: An electoral deadline was agreed upon (to ease social tensions) and international credit was restored on the condition of adopting a stabilization program. However, once the political crisis dissipated, internal disagreements among sectoral fractions on economic policies immediately developed. The new cabinet formed after the crisis included one representative from the Union (Gabriel Lanata Piaggio, a *grupo* leader who at that time represented the industrialists' position), however, within the cabinet and within the business sector there was no agreement on the economic policies to be adopted.

Free trade policies prevailed at the end. A sharp reduction of trade barriers and raising of interest rates affected the industrialists and other fractions linked to the domestic market. Both policies, issued without consulting the industrialists, had the backing of the miners and import/export merchants. The *grupos* remained silent, as usual, but they also privately backed the government's policies because such policies benefited the banking sector. In order to isolate the industrialists, the state elites lent support to the Association of Exporters, subsidizing non-traditional exports. All these factors weakened class cohesion. Not only did Union members disagree on economic issues but Lanata Piaggio had to resign because his positions in the cabinet did not prevail.[64] A few weeks later, the Union ceased to exist.

In 1977, the unitary attempt failed both because of internal disagreements and government maneuvers to weaken the Union. Another factor that contributed to this dissolution was the inability of different trade associations to adopt democratic procedures for selecting Union leaders. Internal rivalries broke out in a moment when unity was being eroded because of diverse economic interests and when the government was attempting to divide the business class.

In the first half of the 1980s, the situation in terms of the relations between the national bourgeoisie and the state, remained more or less the same. The drastic lowering of trade barriers by Belaunde's democratic government was opposed by the industrialists and supported by exporters and import-export merchants. Lack of unity even among industrialists continued. Some Committees of the National Industrial Society (Textile, Shoes, Garment, Metalics) fiercely opposed open-trade policies but most of the Society's leadership did not enthusiastically back them, because Ernesto Lanata Piaggio (Gabriel's brother), a *grupo* leader elected President in 1982, decided not to openly oppose Belaunde's policies. However, the Society's leadership could not prevent individual Committees from defending their interests and confronting government policies. This time, the committees in favor of protectionist policies, found an ally in the Association of Exporters. The elimination of subsidies for non-traditional exporters made possible a united front of those committees opposed to economic liberalism and the Association of Exporters, who now joined forces in its efforts to stop the new economic policy orientation. Internal class divisions among the national bourgeoisie, however, prevailed in the end. The open-trade policy was backed by both the National Mining and Petroleum Society and the Lima Chamber of Commerce. The Annual Conference of Executives avoided any confrontation with the state and continued to emphasize "dialogue." The *grupos*, as usual, backed the government. Demands of some of the Society's Committees and the Association of Exporters were isolated and lacked strength. Not even Congress could play a positive role in defending protectionist interests, because the legislation was adopted by the state in agreement with the World Bank, and also because congressmen favorable to these demands did not dare at this moment to oppose current economic policies.

But despite the divisions, a learning process developed. Experience accumulated throughout this period was concentrated in a number of trade associations' leaders, the "*gremialistas.*" They continued to pursue the creation of a business confederation as a way to strengthen the national bourgeoisie's bargaining capabilities. The numerous setbacks helped them to assess the "hard way," as Gian Flavio Gerbolini (head of the Textile Committee at this time) declared, as to why unity was lost.[65] In 1984, this goal was finally attained when the Confederation of Private Entrepreneurial Institutions (CONFIEP), backed by eight trade associations, was created. This time, the exogenous and endogenous conditions necessary for success were present. The severe economic recession of 1983-1984 negatively affected all economic sectors, (mining and agriculture, as well as sectors related to the domestic market) and forced all fractions to seek policy alternatives. Even the *grupos* decided to abandon their support to open-trade policies and backed the industrialists' demands. The goal of forming a business confederation was considered urgent and necessary for business leaders because the proximity of general elections, to be held in May 1985, was an opportunity to convince the new government to change economic policies. In addition to that, the threat factor helped to galvanize the national bourgeoisie. In 1984, it was clear that the Shining Path, an aggressive guerrilla movement, could not be defeated by the army and that even a new guerrilla organization, the Tupac Amaru Revolutionary movement, was being formed. The 1984 Annual Conference of Executives, expressing the entrepreneurial mood, now assumed an unusual role: It provided the "*gremialistas*" with an opportunity to develop a "National Plan," that is, to collectively propose policy alternatives. In November, the same month the Conference was held, the Confederation was formed. Referring to the political importance of class unity, Julio Piccini, head of the Peruvian Chamber of Construction and first President of the Confederation of Private Entrepreneurial Institutions declared in his inauguration speech that:

> CONFIEP is the unity within diversity. In the past natural discrepancies were translated in sterile confrontations or inmobilism. CONFIEP, today, pretends to act...as a space for dealing with sectoral differences, differences that are subordinated to the national interest (*Industria Peruana*, November 1986: 35).

The unity achieved through CONFIEP was the most important attempt to overcome the pattern of mediation between the national bourgeoisie and the state established since 1968. For the first time, there was a critical juncture that helped to provide unity among different fractions of the national bourgeoisie, and a strong internal entrepreneurial movement, lead by the "*gremialistas*," to create a business confederation. In the 1970s, these two factors could not be adequately combined: A collective leadership was still in the making and internal divisions prevailed; the critical junctures often stressed the diversity of fractional interests over bourgeois class interests; and the state elites succeeded in opposing business unitary attempts. In the meantime, the leadership was learning its first political lessons. The continuity of the learning process inaugurated during the Velasco administration is explained by a former President of the Association of Exporters:

> Things like the Union [of Private Entrepreneurs, UEPP] and CONFIEP are definitely a response to a fear of a repetition of something like Velasco...there was no union in the private sector and Velasco was very clever in a way. He took the private sector by slices.... And now we have learned our lesson that we have to be together in the big issues. So the private sector is more aware of these dangers (Conaghan 1988b: 19).

Although in 1984 unity was clearly expressed through the Confederation, it was still unclear whether CONFIEP could consolidate itself and become a permanent expression of business organizational unity. It must be remembered that only eight trade associations supported it. In addition to that, the *grupos'* support was mostly due to the circumstances rather than conviction. The formation of a business confederation did not mean that the pattern of relations was finally modified. It was just the beginning of a new period where a chance for class unity and the political empowerment of the business sector vis-à-vis the state was opened. The transition from one pattern of mediation between the state and the national bourgeoisie to another will be explained in the following two chapters, when the political activation of the national bourgeoisie is studied in detail.

Conclusion

In the post-oligarchic period, from 1968 onwards, the different fractions of the national bourgeoisie organized themselves for political purposes in varied ways. The firm and the trade association, rather than political parties, served as the primary, most important institutional mechanisms for mediating with the state. Political parties played a minor role even though Peru returned to democracy in 1980 because the concentration of power in the hands of the executive made parties less important, and business political culture, remained unconcerned with party politics.

The firm and trade associations, the more important organizational forms of the national bourgeoisie, were used in accordance with the political needs and economic resources of the various fractions. The *grupos*, economically more powerful than the sectoral fractions, relied mostly on the firm. The *grupos* did participate in trade associations but in secondary positions or through their managers. Their leaders preferred to occupy second-line posts in order to exert influence over sectoral fractions, not to gain access to the decision-making process. The economically weaker sectoral fractions relied more on trade associations as the most effective means of gaining access to the state because the scarce resources mobilized by their firms could not guarantee permanent access to the state.

The pattern of mediation between the national bourgeoisie and the state was shaped in a context characterized by the internal divisions between the *grupos* and the sectoral fractions, and among sectoral fractions. The state usually enjoyed the support of the *grupos*. Even in the face of regime and policy changes, the *grupos* almost always opted to back state elites, because their diversified investment portfolio and their ability to obtain specific advantages from state officials made accommodation a rational choice. The state elites were able to isolate those sectoral fractions not favored by current state economic policies. In doing so, they were able to keep under control political pressures that would have otherwise affected the decision-making process.

The national bourgeoisie lacked a business confederation that represented its general interests. At the Annual Conference of Executives, state officials were able to dialogue with entrepreneurs from all economic sectors but on an individual basis. The Conference did not represent the private sector and could not serve to foster negotiations between the state and the national bourgeoisie. State elites favored the Conference because it provided an opportunity to dialogue with individual, isolated entrepreneurs who, nevertheless, opted to attend the Conference to obtain information and establish contact with high state officials.

The leaders of key trade associations known as the "*gremialistas*," attempted several times to overcome internal divisions. The "*gremialistas*" tried first to create a united front of trade associations in 1984 and, later on in 1977, a business confederation. These attempts at unity finally succeeded in the 1984 critical juncture, when the leaders of seven trade associations finally found an opportunity that was favorable to class solidarity and the formation of a business confederation. The pattern of mediation between the state and the national bourgeoisie was now being changed but still needed to be consolidated.

Notes

1. See the speeches of Alberto Sacio León, manager of an oil company, and Juan Antonio Aguirre Roca, a cement manufacturer, in the 1984 Annual Conference of Executives. See IPAE (1984: 35-38, 301-303).

2. Interview conducted by the author, published in *Quehacer* (November-December 1987: 33).

3. Interview with business leader in Lima (July 21, 1992).

4. Bedoya was the presidential candidate of the Christian Popular Party in the 1980 general elections.

5. Interview with Edgardo Palza, Lima, November 20, 1986. See also the declarations of textile industrialist Jorge Mufarech, in Durand (1984: 19-20).

6. Interview conducted by Maxwell Cameron in Lima, March 16, 1986.

7. The estimate is based on a 40-year period (1945-1985), including both military and civilian governments.

8. Interview with Edgardo Palza, Lima, November 20, 1986.

9. The same is true with regard to multinational corporations, another powerful and solitary player. As Becker points out, Southern Peru Copper Corporation, a member of the National Mining and Petroleum Society and the most powerful private mining firm in the country, "...relies on one-to-one negotiations with the state to protect its interests; [and] it treats its society membership as a public relations gambit" (1983: 261).

10. Interview in Lima, November 20, 1986.

11. Interview with Edgardo Palza. Lima, November 20, 1986.

12. The new bourgeoisie thought that the oligarchy was overexposed in a period when Peruvian society became politicized. In a different society, one which welcomes economic success, Aristotle Onassis, who enjoyed and used publicity in the U.S. for business purposes, used to say that "The more people read about the myth, the less they will know about the man" (Evans 1986: 99). The Peruvian new bourgeoisie, in contrast, was totally unwilling to promote any myth about its economic might.

13. The same tactic has been applied by the Ferreyros *grupo*.

14. Interview in Lima, June 12, 1986.

15. Interview published in *Quehacer* (November-December, 1987: 36).

16. The nationalization of the banking system in July 1987 made it possible for Peruvian public opinion, for the first time, to be informed about the *grupos* and their leaders. Prior to the nationalization, the majority of *grupo* leaders rarely made declarations or allowed their pictures to be taken by photographers.

The nationalization brought the heads of the *grupos*, such as Dionisio Romero and Juan Francisco Raffo (both of Banco de Crédito) and Guillermo Wiese (Banco Wiese), to public attention. Other equally powerful *grupos* (Brescia, Nicolini, Ferreyros and Bentín), never made public appearances, not even in such critical circumstances as the nationalization of the banks.

17. The membership list of each trade association and the directory of the executive committee was given by trade associations. Additionally, sources such as Malpica (1987) and *The Peru Report* (1987, 1988), provided useful information about the *grupos*. The economic significance of the trade associations' firms was based on disaggregate statistics obtained from the different sectoral ministries for the same period.

18. Interview in Lima, August 3, 1986.

19. In the Association of Exporters, Pedro Olaechea Alvarez Calderón, head of the *grupo*, is Second Vice President and Luis Ducassi Wiese, a member of the Wiese *grupo*, is a director of one of the Association's committees. In the National Confederation of Merchants, Jorge Picasso Salinas, one of the heads of the *grupo*, is Second Vice President. In the National Mining and Petroleum Society, Mario Brescia and Luis Picasso, heads of their respective *grupos*, are directors. In the National Industrial Society, Gabriel Lanata Piaggio, head of the *grupo*, is Second Vice President. Also Luis Queirolo Nicolini and Jorge Picasso, members of their respective *grupos*, are Directors.

20. Edward Holme, manager of Tejidos La Unión of the Brescia *grupo*, was Secretary of the Board of Directors and President of the Textile Committee; George Schofield, manager of Universal Textil (Romero *grupo*) was also a member of the same Board of Directors. Luis Razzeto, manager of Del Mar (a firm controlled by *grupos* Wiese and Bentín), was Secretary-Director of the National Fishing Society. In the National Confederation of Merchants, Jaime Cáceres, manager of El Cóndor insurance company (Wiese *grupo*), appeared as Director. A manager of the Brescia *grupo*, Phillip Munn of Importadora Ferretera, appeared also as Director of the Lima Chamber of Commerce. In the case of the Peruvian Institute of Entrepreneurial Administration, the *grupos*' managers also hold key positions. Miguel Vega (Romero *grupo*) was Second Vice President. Oscar Espinoza (Ferreyros *grupo*) and Jose Mariátegui (Lanata Piaggio *grupo*) appeared as Directors.

21. The following managers are members of the Association's Board of Directors: Two managers of the Romero *grupo* (Miguel Pérez of Seguros Peruano-Suiza and Arturo Rodrigo of Seguros El Pacífico); one manager of the Wiese *grupo* (Jaime Cáceres of Seguros El Cóndor); one manager of the Bentín *grupo* (Carlos Ortega of Seguros La Fenix Peruana), three of Brescia *grupo* (Adolfo Bedoya of Seguros La Internacional, Antonio Rodríguez of Rímac and Luis Salcedo of América Terrestre y Marítima); and finally, one of the Nicolini *grupo* (Giancarlo Landotti of La Colmena).

22. They also have a support network, useful to obtain information and

gain access to the state apparatus and the Executive. Two important elements in this support network are the law offices and consulting enterprises.

23. Takeover attempts are probably the toughest type of competition among *grupos*. In 1986, the Romero, Raffo and Brescia *grupos* attempted to takeover Backus & Johnston, the holding company of the Bentín *grupo*. Bentín was forced to make an alliance with the Wiese *grupo* to block the attempt. This had been the most important case of inter-*grupo* conflict of the 1980s.

To avoid the risk of a takeover, the *grupos* usually control more than 50 percent of the shares. There are some cases, like the Nicolini *grupo*, where the family controls 100 percent of the shares. Family quarrels may endanger this control too (as has been the case with the Berckemeyer *grupo*), but at the same time family members know that their economic support depends on the success of the *grupo* as a whole, a factor that favors family unity. Since family matters are also business matters, the head of the *grupo* is also the head of the family clan. Interview with member of the Picasso *grupo*. Lima, November 20, 1987.

24. Malpica (1987) has abundant data on this issue. Soberón (1986) offers additional information in his study of the firms that operate in the Lima Stock Exchange.

25. For information on Banco de Crédito, see Reaño and Vásquez (1988).

26. Emphasis on this idea was suggested by Javier Iguíñiz.

27. The La Fabril *grupo*, controlled by the Argentinian holding company Bunge & Born used to offer its powerful computer system to the Ministry of Economy and Finance. Technocrats used this computer to evaluate different policy scenarios, so La Fabril knew in advance what the government was planning to do. See Green and Laurent (1988: 164-165).

28. On the concept of management of uncertainty see *Nexos* (July 1986: 29-30).

29. This *modus operandi* is adapted to the national political culture, which favor personal contacts and reciprocity of "favors." The importance of favors and bribery is reinforced in periods of economic recession because state officials are more sensitive to the *grupos'* demands in a situation characterized by decreasing real salaries.

30. Scholars who study business/government relations have often pointed out the importance of this secret dimension of power. See Stolovich, Rodríguez, and Bértora (1988: 11,35), Schvarzer (1989: 10) and Leff (1976: 123).

31. In some cases, a discrete participation of *grupo* leaders in consultative organisms is sometimes necessary to indicate big business support of governmental policies. The best example is that of Dionisio Romero, a *grupo* leader and Peru's best known businessman, who became a member of Advisory Committees during the Velasco (1968-1975) and Morales Bermúdez (1975-1980) administrations. In addition, one of his managers, Vega Alvear, participated in a similar organism during the García administration (1985-1987).

32. Interview conducted by Patricia Zamalloa. Lima, December 10, 1987.

33. Interview in Lima, January 12, 1987.

34. Interview in Lima, January 15, 1987.

35. Interview in Lima, December 3, 1987.

36. Interview in Lima, September 14, 1987.

37. Interview in Lima, February 16, 1987.

38. Interview in Lima, August 18, 1987.

39. These conclusions are scattered through out his publication "Los nuevos dueños del Perú" (1987).

40. Carlos Malpica has been a leftist senator since 1980 and is well known for his denunciations of multinational corporations and governmental corruption.

41. "Medium-sized" firms are producers that occupy an intermediate position in the market, below public firms, multinationals and the *grupos'* firms, and above the petit bourgeoisie. They are "medium-sized" more in terms of their position in the economy as a whole, but can be considered "big" in the context of their own economic sector.

42. Interview with Francisco Martinotti, Second Vice President. Lima, February 19, 1987.

43. The exchange rate in 1986 was, on average, approximately 14 *Intis* to the dollar.

44. In contrast, smaller firms in the pharmaceutical industry prefer to be members of the Association of National Pharmaceutical Laboratories (ADIFAN, formed in 1982). ADIFAN has only 30 members which together accounted for 25 percent of the total output value of the pharmaceutical industry in 1984.

45. As one of its prominent members, the Society also has Southern Peru Copper Corporation, the only private firm that belongs to the "big-sized mining" strata and Peru's major producer of copper (61 percent of the nation's total of output value for 1986).

46. The number of firms represented in the Board of Directors is larger than the number of directors because some of them own more than one mine.

47. According to Monge (1988: 36), the most important committees in terms of membership are the Cotton (30,000), Rice (66,000), Potatoes (80,000) and Corn (80,000) Committees. It must be noted that trade associations usually exaggerate their total membership. This is particularly true in the case of ONA and CONACO.

48. The fact that the numerically predominant petit bourgeoisie do not enjoy a similar weight on the trade associations' Boards of Directors, has been the cause of several divisions. This is the case of the National Federation of Small Industry, formed in 1974 after splitting off from the National Industrial Society; the National Association of Pharmaceutical Laboratories, formed in 1980 after splitting off from ALAFARPE; and the Association of Small Mining Producers, formed in 1980 after splitting off from SONAMINPET. In terms of the subject matter of this book, it can be said that small-sized firms are still in the

process of becoming political actors. The first time an organization of small-sized industrial firms, the Association of Small and Medium-sized Industrialists (APEMIPE, formed in 1972), participated in politics was in 1990. APEMIPE's President, Máximo San Román, was in the presidential ticket of a new political organization, Cambio 90, formed by Alberto Fujimori, who won the elections in May 1990. The first political lesson learned by APEMIPE is that an open involvement in politics is dangerous for a trade association. Once President Fujimori and San Román became political opponents in 1992, APEMIPE lost contact with the state and was totally isolated from it. Interview with Rosa Gálvez, President of APEMIPE. Lima, May 29, 1992.

49. All the directors of trade associations interviewed agreed on this.

50. This study is based on the analysis of the statuses of seven trade associations.

51. It must be noted that in the case of Peru, without exception, trade associations have been created by entrepreneurs themselves and not through the influence of external agents such as the state, as in Mexico. There is no state corporatist tradition in Peru. Trade associations usually enjoy internal autonomy and easily obtain formal recognition by the state. Only the Velasco administration attempted to interfere with the National Industrial Society internal affairs but it was an isolated case.

52. The textile industry is an exception to the rule. Because of a tripartite agreement signed in the 1940s, the Textile Committee of the National Industrial Society, the Textile Labor Confederation and the state get together to agree on wages and working conditions.

53. The next two chapters deal with this issue.

54. According to Malpica (1987), Velasco formed an intimate group of business people and generals who got together every Sunday. The group was known as ALTECO, an acronym formed by the first two letters of the Spanish words for lunch, tea and dinner (almuerzo, té, comida). On the role of little dinner groups for business/government relations in the United Kingdom and the U.S., see Useem (1984: 98).

55. The National Industrial Society was able to challenge Velasco successfully on that issue. However, the government punished it by annulling the Society's formal recognition as the industrialists' trade association. See García de Romaña (1975: 79-80) and Durand (1982b: 59-64).

56. On the liberalization of the domestic market, see Banco Central de Reserva (1983). On the reactions of the industrialists toward this policy, see Germaná (1981), Durand (1984) and Castillo (1986).

57. The *grupos* were interested in the organization of the conference and had their managers on the organizing committee and, sometimes, as speakers. This was the case of Vega Alvear (Romero *grupo*) and Oscar Espinoza Bedoya (Ferreyros *grupo*) in 1985 and 1987. However, the heads of the *grupos* usually did not attend the conference as part of their policy to stay in the shadows and avoid

public exposure. One exception occurred in 1986, during the García administration, to be analyzed in chapter six.

58. According to Edgardo Palza, manager of the Institute for 15 years, the conference became important during Velasco's military government because it provided an opportunity to dialogue with entrepreneurs. The Conference functioned for state officials to obtain information about the entrepreneurs and sense their opinions. Their participation, along with the presence of Ministers and the President, enhanced its status as the entrepreneurial event of the year. See interview conducted by the author with Palza in *Quehacer* (December 1988-January 1989: 27-28). The author has attended this conference eight times since 1976.

59. Collier and Collier conceive critical junctures as "a period of basic change...which is hypothesized to produce distinct legacies." See Collier and Collier (1991: 29). In this book, a critical juncture is conceived as a political moment (*coyuntura*), where tensions between social classes and the state lead to attempts to modify the existing pattern of mediation between them. A key critical juncture is the moment where, in fact, this pattern is transformed, a new period is open and a number of distinct legacies can be identified.

60. Statement made by Raymundo Duharte, when he was head of the National Industrial Society. See Durand (1982b: 45). In several interviews (held in Lima in 1983, 1986-1988), Duharte always mentioned the bitterness industrialists felt not only toward the government but also toward entrepreneurs who played the government's game.

61. Statement made by Alfonso Bustamante, an industrialist from Arequipa. *La Prensa* (January 15, 1980: 3).

62. A study of these attempts at unification can be found in Durand (1987a).

63. In addition to the National Industrial Society, seven other trade associations joined the Union: The Association of Exporters, the Lima Chamber of Commerce, the Chamber of Commerce and Industry of Arequipa, the Association of Pharmaceutical Laboratories, the Peruvian Chamber of Construction, the Association of Car Manufacturers, and the Federation of Regional Chambers of Commerce.

64. It is important to note that at this time the Lanata Piaggio *grupo* was beginning a process of investment diversification and its interests were still concentrated in the manufacturing industry. The Lanata Piaggio *grupo* will invest in banking and the mining sector in the first half of the 1980s. Their changing position became clear when Ernesto Lanata Piaggio, Gabriel's brother, became head of the National Industrial Society in 1980 and did not openly criticize open trade policies.

65. Interview with industrialist Gerbolini. Lima, June 18, 1983.

6

Business Politicization and
Governing Coalitions

The first important sign of change in the pattern of mediation between the state and the national bourgeoisie was expressed in the formation and consolidation of a business confederation in 1984. This key event was part of a more complex process of business politicization that can be better understood by looking at the modes of bourgeois participation in the political process, in particular, by analyzing how the different fractions of the national bourgeoisie participated in governing coalitions.

This chapter will study in detail two governing coalitions. The first was formed by Belaunde's government in 1980, and oriented toward a liberal-exporting model of economic development. The second one was led by García, Belaunde's political opponent, who came to power in 1985. García, inspired by nationalist ideas, changed the governing coalition and oriented it toward a national-developmentalist model of economic development. The national bourgeoisie, was partially responsible for this new macroeconomic policy orientation and its participation in García's coalition forced them to become more actively involved in national politics. This process takes place in a context where democracy reigns again but operates in a highly unstable social, economic and political environment.

Belaunde's government was the first to be democratically elected after 12 years of military rule (Velasco and Morales Bermúdez). When he inaugurated his government in July 28, 1980, the governing coalition was already shaped. It included foreign capital, that enjoyed a close relationship with the state, the *grupos*, and the sectoral fractions linked to the world market (mainly import/export merchants and the miners). The coalition was based on an orthodox, liberal-exporting economic policy, that gave priority to both private property and exporting capital. By the end of Belaunde's term, the coalition was falling apart because the economic depression eroded the political foundations that sustained it. A general sense of dissatisfaction with Belaunde's government among the national bourgeoisie helped to undermine the coalition. The opposition was led by APRA and García who came to power in 1985.

Unlike Belaunde, García decided to adopt a heterodox, national-developmentalist economic policy, giving preferential treatment to national capital and protecting the domestic market. His coalition articulated the *grupos* (whose loyalties changed in accordance with the pendulum swings of Peruvian politics), and those sectoral fractions linked to the domestic market (mainly the industrialists).

In this period, the two governments tried to reproduce the pattern of mediation between the national bourgeoisie and the state studied in Chapter 4, but changes within the national bourgeoisie began to take place. In the mid-1980s there was an evident trend toward business unity that enabled entrepreneurs to begin to distinguish between general class interests, common to all fractions, and particular interests. The role played by a recently formed business confederation would be crucial to initiate a process of articulation of different interests. It is then a period that will lead to a transition: The signs of change are beginning to emerge but the old pattern of mediation is still at work.

Rise and Fall of Belaunde's Liberal-Exporting Coalition

Peru was one of the first Latin American countries governed by authoritarian regimes to return to democracy. Electoral promises and arm chair politics came with it. Popular Action, Belaunde's party, came to power in the 1980 elections with a high degree of electoral support (45.37 percent of the votes) (Tuesta 1987: 233). Although Belaunde never mentioned the adoption of liberal-exporting policies during the campaign, once in office his government favored that policy orientation, a policy inaugurated by his military predecessor in 1977 and widely held as unpopular.

The elites, the national bourgeoisie included, supported Popular Action because Belaunde had promised to defend private property and to reprivatize some of the firms nationalized by Velasco. However, the continuation of popular and elite support depended heavily on a real economic up-swing, particularly since Popular Action's ties with popular organizations were weaker compared to those of its opponents, APRA and the United Left.

At the beginning of his administration, Belaunde was also able to isolate the demands of those fractions of the national bourgeoisie affected by liberal-exporting economic policies, thanks to the support of exporters and the *grupos*. Initially, liberal-exporting policies were easily adopted in Congress because Popular Action made an alliance with the Christian Popular Party and thereby obtained a congressional majority (both parties had 32 out of a total of 60 senators, and 108 out of a total of 180 deputies) (Tuesta 1986: 49). In addition, because of Belaunde's "good payer" policy on the external debt, the 1980s started with a positive economic situation thanks to a continuous foreign credit flow and better terms of trade for Peruvian mineral and oil exports (Thorp 1984: 91).

Three years later, the economic situation changed and the opposition to the government started to developed and get organized. In 1983, the economy entered a period of deep and generalized recession and Belaunde's support rapidly eroded. Consequently, voters moved to the center (APRA) and the left (United Left) looking for an alternative solution. This shift in voters' attitudes surfaced in the municipal elections of November 1983, where the opposition parties had an impressive electoral victory. But the political pressure against Belaunde and his economic policy orientation came also from those fractions of the national bourgeoisie adversely affected by it. Popular and business dissatisfaction helped to erode the consensus between the two governing parties and within Popular Action. Thus, party support to orthodox policies also began to diminish. The most clear indication that Belaunde was being isolated and the governing coalition was collapsing, was when the *grupos* began to withdraw their support. This turned out to be a key factor that accelerated the coalition's demise and prepared the ground for García's victory.

The Liberal-Exporting Experiment

Shortly after his inaugural speech, and to the surprise of the industrialists, Belaunde opted for liberal-exporting policies. The way this policy was adopted was at the center of the political storm that would soon start. This crucial policy decision was taken mostly because Belaunde came under pressure from international financial organizations. Very few Peruvians were in favor of orthodox policies and only some conservatives and the class fractions linked to the external market openly advocated it. This political "surprise" was initially accepted because it was expected that foreign capital was going to invest in the Peruvian economy and the restoration of international credit would help the government start a much needed public works program. These high expectations convinced Congress to grant the executive extraordinary powers to allow the administration to establish a new legal basis to support the liberal experiment. In the first three months, a package of 240 legislative decrees was adopted and the specifics about economic policy became known to the national bourgeoisie (Wise 1988: 11).

It must be taken into account that the presidential decision to liberalize the Peruvian economy was adopted without consulting trade associations. In September 1980, the government reduced the level of protection from an average of 120 percent to a maximum of 60 percent. Soonafter, in February 1981, reductions and restrictions on the use of a generous subsidy, the Export Tax Reimbursement Certificate given to non-traditional exporters (CERTEX), was also approved by the executive (Durand 1984: 29). In addition, the negotiation of the external debt was left in the hands of the state, and the fact that debt policy permitted foreign creditors to benefit at the expense of local producers led to increasing tensions between industrialists and Belaunde's government. The rules of the game were being changed from above, without public consultation, in a way quite similar to that of the military government. If in the Velasco period the national bourgeoisie was forced to accept the socialist reforms, during the Belaunde administration it was forced to accept a policy destined to make them competitive by international standards. The difference was that, in this case, the political system offered the opportunity to organize the resistance to the new economic policy orientation dictated from above. However, the pattern of state/national bourgeoisie mediation still shows signs of continuity.

As soon as economic policies were adopted, they became the main target of certain fractions of the national bourgeoisie who felt betrayed by Belaunde's administration. Orthodox policies were openly rejected by trade associations such as the Association of Exporters and some committees of the National Industrial Society (Textiles, Shoes, Metal). Government backers, however, included the *grupos*, and trade associations such as the National Mining Society and the Lima Chamber of Commerce. Not surprisingly, in 1982 the National Industrial Society, led by Ernesto Lanata Piaggio, head of the family *grupo*, avoided a confrontation with Belaunde's government and helped to isolate the demands of the Society's most anti-orthodox policy committees. Internal divisions within the national bourgeoisie expanded the Belaunde government's room to maneuver (Iguiñiz 1986: 315-317). It should be noted that the industrialists' contacts with certain political leaders within Popular Action and the Christian Popular Party, were considered worthless to change the economic policy orientation. At the beginning, their isolation conspired against any possibility to broaden the opposition.

This situation began to change in 1983 when a critical juncture favorable to business politicization unfolded. By September of that year, the Lima Chamber of Commerce still gave its support to liberalization policies and openly defended Carlos Rodríguez Pastor, Minister of Economy and Finance and a former official of Wells Fargo Bank. However, this type of support became less frequent as the economic crisis deepened. Gradually, the national bourgeoisie became less internally divided, more unified, and more willing to intervene in the political process. Most fractions came to believe that, in order to search for an alternative political solution and policy orientation, and to halt the economic recession, unity was necessary. A deep and generalized recession made disagreements over economic policies less important. Consensus arose around goals such as "economic reactivation" and *concertación* (concerted action). From June 1983 onwards, class unity within the National Industrial Society became stronger. Carlos Verme, a shoe manufacturer, was elected President in June 1983. Shoe manufacturing was a branch of the economy strongly affected by open trade policies and the recession of the domestic market. In his inaugural speech, Verme called for unity among industrialists, implicitly criticizing his predecessor, Ernesto Lanata Piaggio.

The 1983 Annual Conference of Executives, (which took place shortly after municipal elections in which Popular Action suffered a setback), showed the trends set in motion. The industrialists on this occasion were strongly nationalistic and openly critical of government economic policies. Their leaders insisted on a solution to the crisis based on economic reactivation of the domestic market. This plan should have been sought through *concertación* between the state and trade associations, with the direct participation of the national bourgeoisie in the policy-making process. Juan Antonio Aguirre Roca, a cement manufacturer and well-known "gremialista" leader, remarked that "the most severe crisis of the country in the last century...obliges us to identify alternatives of immediate application to keep us from succumbing" (IPAE 1983: 10). Guillermo Arteaga, a milling manufacturer, claimed that "the productive system is shattered [because] the manufacturing sector was left at the mercy of legislation inspired on rigid economic schemes." He argued that such a dramatic situation had developed because the fate of the manufacturing sector had been "negotiated" with foreign interests. For industrialists like Arteaga, only a "realistic plan," elaborated through dialogue and *concertación*, could provide the basis for a solution (IPAE 1983: 79-70 and 82).

While industrialists openly criticized the government's orthodox economic policies and demanded immediate policy changes, the *grupos* adopted a more moderate approach. Nevertheless, a shift in their attitudes was a clear indication of their accommodation to changing circumstances. Gonzalo de la Puente y Lavalle, manager of the Wiese *grupo* and Belaunde's former Minister of Industry, argued that open trade policies were a factor in the crisis, but not its underlying cause.[1] He favored short-term emergency measures that would both benefit the private sector as a whole and "alleviate the situation of some sectors of the national manufacturing industry that are threatened by collapse" (IPAE 1983: 87-88). Juan Francisco Raffo, Vice President of Banco de Crédito and head of the Raffo *grupo*, surprisingly argued that "the high level of foreign indebtedness...is frustrating the country's chances for development," and that an economic policy "aimed to safeguard the external front," was "impairing the national productive apparatus." Raffo expressed his concern for the rising financial costs of national firms and proposed urgent measures "to achieve a reorganization of the assets of the private sector and a restructuring of its debts" (IPAE 1983: 204). At the 1984 Annual Conference of Executives, it was clear that the *grupos* were shifting to the winner's side.

On the government's side, President Belaunde avoided at the business Conference any reference to "dark issues" (the recession), preferring to talk about "brighter" subjects such as public works. Belaunde's stance indicated disillusionment with economic policies advocated by his Minister, Rodríguez Pastor, and the International Monetary Fund, because they threatened the continuation of public works, his favorite presidential initiative.[2] At this time, the Minister of Economy and Finance became almost the sole defender of orthodox policies. Rodríguez Pastor recognized that the results of the 1983 municipal elections indicated that the people's patience "was getting shorter" but attributed this to the people's rejection of the national bourgeoisie. According to Rodríguez Pastor, the electorate was critical not only of his policies, but also of "an entrepreneurial conduct unwilling to meet the demands of competitiveness and efficiency, and tempted by the comfort of monopoly and protectionism." He warned of the danger of politicians being tempted to respond to electoral results by taking "actions that appealed to the multitudes or provided immediate partisan advantages," that would sacrifice orthodox policies. He stubbornly insisted on the positive side of maintaining total support from international financial organizations such as the International Monetary Fund and the World Bank (IPAE 1983: 158-159 and 165).

The liberal-exporting coalition had clearly began to fall apart. The *grupos* changed positions and now decided to openly support the industrialists' demands at a time when the opposition parties (APRA and the United Left) were getting stronger and the balance of power within the government was shifting to a position in favor of pro-economic reactivation policies. The main factor behind this new political trend was the opportunities opened by the effect of the severe economic recession of 1983-1984.

The Economic Recession

Several factors (both external and internal) dramatically narrowed the government's economic room to maneuver and in the second half of 1983 a deep and generalized economic recession took place. The economic indicators were negative for all economic sectors. The GNP averaged a growth rate of -12 percent.[3]

There were a number of critical external factors that got combined to accelerate and deepen the recession: deterioration of the terms of trade, increasing interest rates and lack of international credit and foreign investment. The terms of trade, which had improved from 110 to 120 (1977=100) between 1979 and 1980, declined to 108 in 1981 and to 86 in 1982. Interest rates in the international market rose sharply from 1.5 percent in 1980 to 7.7 percent in 1981 and then 8.3 percent in 1982 (Thorp 1984: 84-87). This decrease in terms of trade and increase in interest rates aggravated the country's trade balance. That year, the Latin American debt hit crisis levels in 1982 and private international banks became unwilling to keep providing credit to Latin America, including Peru, a country that was not being adequately rewarded for its "good payer" policy. The lack of interest in the Peruvian economy shown by foreign investors, and the deterioration in terms of trade, meant that the exporting sector was unable to serve as an engine for economic growth. So evident was their situation that the mining sector was also calling (together with manufacturing industrialists of several branches) for "emergency plans." The mining industry was heavily indebted and also suffered a dramatic decline in earnings.

Internal factors, such as a natural disaster and a recession in the domestic market, helped to aggravate the situation. In 1983, the *El Niño* sea current changed its pattern and negatively affected fishing and agriculture by provoking heavy rains and an equally destructive heat wave. The fishing industry lost US$10 million and the sugar and cotton industry lost US$42 million (Thorp 1984: 100; Iguiñiz 1986: 317-321). This natural disaster also damaged the country's infrastructure. The manufacturing sector, which suffered the combined effects of a loss in purchasing power and unequal competition with foreign manufactured goods, registered the highest negative growth rates in the overall economy: -16 percent. The state's fiscal difficulties and a decline in the demand for private and public housing, led to a recession in construction. The banking system, which initially benefited from high interest rates and from profits accumulated by speculation with the exchange rate, became concerned with their clients' mounting debts. Some small banks (Surmebank, Banco de la Industria y la Construcción, Banco Comercial) went bankrupt as a result of a high level of concentration of credits to firms having economic difficulties. These bankruptcies, in turn, generated panic in the business sector (Sifuentes 1988: 50).

This unexpected turn of events made the weak national bourgeoisie politically powerful and the industrialists a key player in the political arena. The position of the different fractions of the national bourgeoisie started to change in this context. The recession was so deep, and its potential consequences so negative, that both the *grupos* and the mining industry stopped supporting orthodox policies. The *grupos'* position shifted because the costs of a generalized recession in all economic sectors was potentially more costly than the benefits obtained by currency speculation and takeovers of heavily indebted firms. The mining industry shifted because it needed an "emergency plan" from the government if it was to avoid economic collapse, a plan that the hardline orthodox economic team (headed by Rodríguez Pastor), and international financial organizations, were unwilling to support, because it demanded state subsidies and implied an interference with the laws of the market.

The Municipal Elections: A Plebiscite Against Orthodox Economic Policies

The municipal elections of November 1983 were seen by the opposition (APRA and the United Left) as a "plebiscite" against economic policies. A close look at the election reveals a clear shift of public opinion (Dietz 1987: 151-153). Whereas in the 1980 municipal elections Popular Action, Belaunde's party, obtained 35.86 percent of the votes, in 1983 the percentage had dropped drastically to 17.41. The votes for APRA and the United Left rose from 22.69 percent to 33.06 percent and 23.9 percent to 28.84 percent respectively (Tuesta 1987: 215-217). Independent voters and social groups dissatisfied with the government's economic performance moved over to the opposition. Both APRA and the United Left declared that the elections were a "plebiscite" on the government's "foreign oriented" economic policy orientation, an orientation that lacked "social sensitivity" to the poor and the unemployed. Both APRA and the United Left opposed the payment of the external debt and argued that the government's priority should be to promote economic growth rather than to meet financial obligations with foreign creditors. The government tried to adopt changes and recompose the relations with the national bourgeoisie before the opposition was able to profit politically from Belaunde's economic problems. This attempt failed and soon the government lost a clear sense of direction in terms of economic policies which, in turn, fueled the economic recession. It was at this point, in mid-1984, with the electoral campaign just beginning and the elections less than one year off, that the liberal-exporting coalition finally fell apart.

A few days after the close of the 1983 Annual Conference of Executives, Belaunde announced the probable resignation of his Minister of Economy and Finance. His own party had been pushing for the resignation. Senator Javier Alva Orlandini, a candidate campaigning for Popular Action's presidential nomination in the upcoming general elections, strongly criticized Rodríguez Pastor as a Minister too close to the International Monetary Fund and responsible for the adoption of severe austerity measures.[4] Political opposition to Rodríguez Pastor, both within and outside Popular Action party, intensified until he resigned on March 19, 1984. Neither Belaunde, Popular Action, the Christian Popular Party, nor any important fraction of the national bourgeoisie dared to defend him. Rodríguez Pastor's sole supporters seemed to be foreign capital and international financial organizations, but support from these quarters was neither active nor effective at this moment. By mid-1984, the opposition to orthodox policies was widespread. At this point, the government made one last but unsuccessful attempt to win the national bourgeoisie to its side.

A Failed Attempt of Concerted Action

The demands made by the national bourgeoisie for reactivation and *concertación* of economic policies could have been handled by Belaunde, but the government was internally divided and unable to make coherent policy decisions. After Rodríguez Pastor's resignation in March, 1984, an attempt was made to put the ruling coalition back together with the formation of a new cabinet headed by Sandro Mariátegui. Mariátegui's willingness to reactivate the economy, and adopt alternative economic policies through *concertación*, demonstrated the government's intention of reconstituting the coalition. The Prime Minister initially recognized the demands of the national bourgeoisie and showed a willingness to consider its participation in the governmental decision-making process. His performance was initially backed by the national bourgeoisie, now experiencing a unitary trend. A joint declaration of support to Mariátegui's initiative was signed by 11 trade associations and published in the press.[5]

But Mariátegui's attempt at *concertación* will soon come to an end. Instead of adopting policy measures through *concertación*, Mariátegui did the opposite, thereby setting himself on a collision course with the national bourgeoisie. Conflict broke out when the new Prime Minister, in a desperate attempt to control the fiscal deficit, adopted a legislative decree raising taxes on bank collections and interest to 17 percent. The decision, taken under international pressure, and without consulting the private sector, led to massive mobilization of the trade associations, which declared themselves "at war." Both the sectoral fractions and the *grupos* rejected the tax increase because it raised the financial costs of firms in all sectors and because the banks feared that firms would not be able to meet their financial obligations.

The tax increase affected the full spectrum of bourgeois fractions who reacted collectively and considerably strengthened their bargaining position. After some weeks of deliberation, opposition to the measure put forth by the national bourgeoisie was finally successful and the government had to lower the tax from 17 to eight percent. The tax reduction was an important political victory that will have lasting political consequences for the national bourgeoisie.

It was the first time a collective mobilization of trade associations, as an expression of widespread class unity, had obtained a concrete, immediate effect on a government decision. At this point, the national bourgeoisie discovered that collective actions, in some circumstances, are a prerequisite for successful political pressure on government. This time the national bourgeoisie was not internally divided, or willing to accommodate to the new cabinet. It was being politicized and the union of several trade associations made it politically stronger (Durand 1987a: 24).

From this point on, the government entered a period where policy decisions were oriented toward solving short term problems, without caring about the overall policy orientation. Certain short term decisions that favored the manufacturing industry (such as the protection of the domestic market, restriction on imports, and an *ad hoc* moratorium on the payment of the external debt), could not make the national bourgeoisie recover its lost confidence in Belaunde. In addition, the bourgeoisie became convinced that Popular Action and the Christian Popular Party had no chance in the upcoming elections and prepared itself to try to exert influence on the political party most likely to form a new government (APRA). Belaunde tried to reproduce the pattern of state/national bourgeoisie mediation by "slicing" apart the different dominant class fractions and maintain a policy orientation taken without much consultation with national investors, but in closed meetings with international financial organizations. But the isolation of the bourgeois fractions dissatisfied with orthodox policies did not last very long and, thanks to the economic recession and to the politicization of the national bourgeoisie, the process was reversed. The Belaunde government ended up being internally divided, isolated from public opinion and unable to reconstitute a governing coalition. Belaunde, and his Prime Minister, Mariátegui, miscalculated the political ability of the national bourgeoisie

A Trend Toward Internal Unity

In November 1984, the trend toward class unity took a step forward when the Confederation of Private Entrepreneurial Institutions (CON-FIEP) was created. Seven major trade associations (National Industrial Society, Association of Exporters, National Mining and Petroleum Society, Peruvian Chamber of Construction, National Confederation of Merchants, National Fishing Society, Association of Radio and Television) supported the initiative, thus ending independent action that had previously characterized internal relations between the sectoral fractions of the national bourgeoisie. Sensing the need to get organized but willing to maintain their independence, the *grupos*, rather than working through trade associations, attempted to create an organization composed of individuals.[6] But the plan to create a business confederation, led by "gremialistas" from the National Industrial Society, the Association of Exporters and the Peruvian Chamber of Constructors, competed successfully with the *grupos'* proposal. The idea of creating a business Confederation had stronger support in the private sector. It grouped organizations that were formally "representative" of economic sectors, including large and medium-sized firms, and was designed to enhance the bargaining power of the weak bourgeois fractions, and not that of the *grupos*. The *"gremialistas,"* to avoid confronting the powerful *grupos*, did not oppose the idea of creating a small group of entrepreneurs as an informal spokesman of the private sector and stated that this proposal was a complementary rather than a competitive one. Both organizations, according to the *"gremialistas,"* could exist at the same time and, therefore, decided to go on with their own plans and form the business confederation.[7] Once the *grupos* acknowledged the *"gremialistas"* determination to carry on their project, they decided to drop their proposal. But the two trade associations controlled by them (the Association of Banks and the Peruvian Association of Insurance Companies) did not participated in the formation of CONFIEP in 1984.

Initially, the newly formed Confederation was not very strong because it had not yet fully incorporated the majority of trade associations (the ones controlled by the *grupos*, as well as others). Their validity as an umbrella organization, to claim their role as a collective representative of the Peruvian private sector, was still relative. But once the confederation was organized (adoption of its internal statutes, formal recognition of the state, opening of the Confederation's headquarters), the next task of the "gremialistas" was to consolidate it by enhancing its membership. This would then demonstrate that the unity set in motion was strong enough to attract other members, sending a message to all business fractions, big and small, and to society as a whole, that the Confederation was being institutionalized and had started to obtain public recognition.[8]

At this critical moment, the Confederation received the unexpected backing of the U.S. Agency for International Development (AID). CONFIEP's formation coincided with a new policy plan of the U.S. government to provide support to business peak associations, recognizing their enhanced political role in the transitions to democracy and their potential influence on macroeconomic policy orientations and the external debt issue. The grant obtained from AID helped the Confederation make major expenses without requesting contributions from members. The resources were devoted to acquiring a new office in San Isidro, a Lima residential neighborhood, equip it, and pay a small staff.[9] This sudden interest of the U.S. governmental agency in the Confederation helped them to attract more members and the fact did not remain unnoticed by the *grupos*, the most reticent fraction. A step forward in that direction occurred in March 1985, when other trade associations joined the Confederation, raising total trade association membership to 16. Even trade associations controlled by the *grupos* (the Association of Banks and the Peruvian Association of Insurance Companies) joined the Confederation a year after its formation, when they finally decided it was better to be inside than out of it.

The need to get organized in order to participate more actively in the political decisions to be taken in the campaign period was not the only factor behind the trend toward business unification. Popular dissatisfaction, fueled by the growing economic crisis, and increased social tensions posed a potential threat to the national bourgeoisie and pushed undecided class fractions toward unification under an umbrella organization.

By 1984, the impact of recession on the population was apparent. Employment rates dropped from 41.8 percent in 1981 to 34.9 percent in 1984. Salaries declined from 70.8 in 1981 to 45.1 in 1985 (1973=100) (Balbi 1987: 21). By 1983, social unrest had become very active. Between 1983 and 1984, several national strikes took place both in the cities and the countryside. In March 1983, a national agrarian strike was organized. On September 27, 1983, March 22, 1984 and November 29, 1984, these strikes took place in the urban areas (Parodi 1988: 102). Trade unions demanded wage increases and policies to promote employment and protested the government's orthodox economic policies and foreign debt payments. Although the protests were organized by the United Left, complaints made in the course of these protests were the same as those voiced by the national bourgeoisie and APRA. During the last years of the Belaunde administration, the National Industrial Society proposed *concertación* aimed at increasing employment and wages. Despite their ideological differences, employers and employees became tactical allies in the fight against orthodox policies. This truce could only be sustained if an alternative governing coalition was formed agreeing on developmentalist policies that could, at least temporarily, fulfill the demands of the elites and the masses.[10]

Unity and political participation also seemed increasingly necessary to the national bourgeoisie because street crime and social and political violence were growing by leaps and bounds. Street crime rose from 123,230 reported crimes in 1980 to 152,561 in 1985. In addition, new types of crime began to be reported, in particular the kidnapping of businessmen and wealthy people. Political violence increased at a faster rate. In 1983, the military moved into Ayacucho, the center of Shining Path's armed revolution, but it was unable to halt the rebels. For the period between May 1980 and July 1985 the casualties included 6,697 dead and 1,354 injured. The number of terrorist attacks increased from 219 in 1980 (the year in which armed fighting started) to 2,050 in 1985. In a six year period, more than 6,000 terrorist attacks occurred, aimed at transportation and communications facilities, mining centers, electricity facilities as well as police stations and army barracks. By 1985, total economic losses were estimated at US$2,139,542.[11]

The national bourgeoisie saw these social and political problems as a social threat that generated a feeling of uncertainty about the future, a fact that accelerated the trend toward internal unity. The need to become organized grew stronger as an attempt to control uncertainty.

Rise of García's National-Developmentalist Coalition

The national-developmentalist coalition grew out of an alliance between APRA and most fractions of the national bourgeoisie. The partners based the alliance on their common interest in changing economic policies and the need to support each other in that critical economic situation. APRA and most bourgeois fractions rejected liberal-exporting policies and both adopted a nationalist stance toward the external debt problem. APRA was better positioned than any other party to form a new governing coalition. In addition, García launched a campaign to change the political stance of APRA as a radical party, moving it closer to the national bourgeoisie. APRA also needed the support of the national bourgeoisie (the *grupos* and the sectoral fractions linked to the domestic market), because the government could not use the state as a tool for economic development and the new policy orientation confronted foreign capital and international financial organizations. This peculiar situation enhanced the economic role of the national bourgeoisie as the government's most important economic partner. In 1985, no populist threat seemed to emerge from APRA and many business leaders thought that the days of nationalizations were definitely over.

The Nationalist Trend

The adoption of a nationalist, pro-domestic market policy, entailed a break in relations with such financial organizations as the International Monetary Fund and the World Bank. Foreign capital was already worried before the elections, sensing a new policy orientation in the making. This shift became apparent in July 1984, when the Council of the Americas, an organization of American corporations with interests in Latin America, declared that decisions about foreign investment or foreign debt should not be made before the outcome of upcoming elections had become clear. The Council calculated that the government might fall into the hands of APRA, a party heading opposition to Peru's doing business with the International Monetary Fund and to the Belaunde government's "good payer" policy (*Perú Económico*, July-August 1984: 4). By November 1984, the national bourgeoisie moved closer to APRA on issues such as limited payments of external debt and a nationalist (protectionist) economic alternative.

A survey taken at the Annual Conference of Executives in November 1984 unquestionably demonstrated the political inclinations of the national bourgeoisie. Only 8.1 percent of the business people surveyed considered that economic reactivation could be achieved by "increasing the competitiveness of market forces," that is, by applying macroeconomic policies favored by the International Monetary Fund. On the external debt question, 33 percent favored a payment moratorium, because debt payments created an "unsustainable situation for the economy and the country." It should be pointed out that the 62 percent of entrepreneurs surveyed that did not think the moratorium was a good idea took this position because they feared that economic sanctions could hurt their economic interests. Measures such as the closing of markets or the denial of credit were considered as possible consequences of a nationalist stance on the debt issue (*Quehacer*, December 1984: 31). The national bourgeoisie's support of APRA's nationalism, despite the risks, was becoming evident.

APRA and García

The alliance formed by APRA and the fractions of the national bourgeoisie linked to the domestic market had a better chance of becoming a new governing coalition. Both the United Left and the unions strongly opposed foreign capital and the influence of international financial organizations in economic policy-making. However, radicalism made it difficult, if not impossible, to form an alliance with the national bourgeoisie. The United Left supported the formation of a united front between the masses and the national bourgeoisie. This front did not include the *grupos*, who were considered as a "monopolic" fraction, allied to foreign capital. The United Left proposals were too narrow to include most of the business fractions as coalitional partners. Leftist policies, for example, considered necessary the nationalization of Banco de Crédito, Peru's leading private bank. In addition, their pro-labor policies were unpalatable for business because of their socialist leanings. The advantage of the political and policy alternative put forth by APRA was that it offered hope to several social classes at the same time. On this basis, APRA was able to compete successfully with the United Left, to win mass support and, also, to include most fractions of the national bourgeoisie as coalitional partners. To the national bourgeoisie, APRA held out the prospect of an improved economic situation; to the masses, better wages and more jobs.[12]

On the other side of the political spectrum, neither Popular Action nor the Christian Popular Party were able to articulate a multiclass alliance in 1985. After Belaunde's administration, both parties lost electoral support, not only among the poor, but also among the fractions of the national bourgeoisie most affected by the recession and orthodox policies.

The national bourgeoisie drew closer to APRA when it acknowledged that it was the only party capable of winning the elections. Political surveys clearly indicated that chances for election of either Popular Action or the Christian Popular Party were almost nil. The administration's disastrous management of the economy benefited APRA and the United Left, the major opposition parties. Of these two, however, APRA was better equipped to articulate a multiclass alliance.

García, APRA's candidate, according to a poll conducted by Apoyo in November 1984 about preferred presidential candidates, had the greatest support among many different income groups. His average of support was 40.1%, having a slightly lower preference among voters from upper income brackets (39.3%) and a higher support among voters of the "low" income category (42.3%). Javier Alva Orlandini, Popular Action's candidate, clearly lacked electoral support. His average was

4.1%. Luis Bedoya, from the Christian Popular Party, had a 12.9% of support and was doing well only among voters from the high-income strata (31.8%). Alfonso Barrantes, the United Left candidate, had a 21.8% average, and his support came primarily from lower-income groups (26% in the "low" income category and 29.3% in the "very low" category). The only candidate with support in all socio-economic groups was García (*Perú Económico*, November 1984: 3).

In order to succeed at governing, García needed to redirect the nations's economic resources, lowering the payment on the external debt and thereby freeing up resources to reactivate the domestic market and to support redistributive policies. It was possible, however, that this stance would have a negative impact on the flow of international credit. Given the potential consequences of the nationalist stance, the upcoming administration had to rely on domestic resources (mainly national private capital). APRA and the national bourgeoisie needed each other, at least for the time being.

The Renovation of APRA

García was one of the leaders of APRA's youth who formed part of the inner circle of Víctor Raul Haya de la Torre, the historical leader of the party (Becker 1983: 37). At age 30, García had been a member of the 1978 Constituent Assembly and, with the support of Haya de la Torre, he became APRA's Secretary of Organization. After Haya de la Torre's death in 1979, an intense struggle between Armando Villanueva and Andrés Townsend for party leadership cast APRA into a severe crisis.[13] Villanueva became APRA's presidential candidate in the 1980 general elections and he lost support within the party when he was defeated by Belaunde. In 1982, a scandal about Villanueva's dealings with a drug lord deepened APRA's internal crisis and opened the way for García. In February 1983, García became head of the party, appointed by APRA's XIV Congress. By then García had strengthened his position with the publication of *El Futuro Diferente*, a book in which he outlined a plan to update the political ideas of APRA left out by Haya de la Torre. The book, which was published in a moment of increasing tensions with the International Monetary Fund and foreign creditors, identified "new imperialism" with international financial capital. The book attracted the attention of party members around the time when Villanueva was discredited and Townsend was expelled from the party.[14] Not surprisingly, at the XIV Congress, García won the elections with 467 votes (55 percent of the total), thereby solving APRA's leadership crisis.[15]

A new generation had come to power within the party, headed by a charismatic leader not identified with APRA's past. Now in command of the party, García was intent on changing APRA's traditional image, a sectarian and violent image, an image that had alienated independent voters in past elections.[16] The new leader adopted a more open, less dogmatic position, stopped the use of para-military groups, and addressed his speeches not to the *apristas*, but to "all Peruvians."

In his political messages, he attempted to appeal to a variety of interests and thereby broaden his constituency. García's plan was to win the votes of the elites and the middle class by proposing a policy of economic recovery. Additionally, his promises to provide subsidies and to promote employment attracted voters from the working and non-working poor. García offered security to Peruvians in general at a time when insecurity was prevalent and widespread. He also offered hope in a country weighed down by deep pessimism.

Although one of the country's leading political analysts, Julio Cotler has stated that García's success was based on his outstanding ability to appeal to the masses,[17] it was García's ability to address the demands of a number of classes, and not simply those of the working and non-working poor, that explains his popularity in this period.

Limits and Potential of the Coalition

The working alliance between García's administration and the national bourgeoisie, (the industrialists and other sectoral fractions linked to the domestic market and the *grupos*), was the result of mutual convenience in given circumstances. This alliance was based more on a shared rejection of liberal-exporting policies and need of each other to achieve short-term goals, than on mutual trust, strong party-class linkages, or similarity of ideas and values. García was the only candidate capable of articulating a multiclass alliance at a time when the popular sector and the national bourgeoisie were both interested in economic reactivation. He was also the party leader in the best position to win the 1985 general elections. Pragmatism and short-term coincidences with APRA's program moved the national bourgeoisie to side with García.

Since the majority of business people were not APRA's members (or even sympathizers) and because García was a new, unknown figure in Peruvian politics, both partners eagerly approached each other during the campaign period and established a series of links. These links were initially built based on the following activities: (a) high-level meetings between party and business leaders, (b) business contributions to APRA's fund raising campaign; and (c) the inclusion of business leaders in the discussion and approval of APRA's official party platform. Despite the low numbers of business people in its membership ranks, APRA counted on the support of individuals who ensured García met often with business leaders. García even included several of the country's leading businessmen among his personal friends.[18] Both *grupos'* leaders and the heads of trade associations, were among those selected to meet García. His inner circle of business friends included *grupo* leaders such as Dionisio Romero, bankers such as Francisco Pardo (Banco Mercantil), and business leaders such as Julio Piccini (first President of Peru's business Confederation), Raymundo Duharte (former leader of the National Industrial Society), and Guillermo Arteaga (the industrialist who openly criticized orthodox policies in the 1983 Annual Conference of Executives). Manuel Moreyra, a consultant to the *grupos*, former President of the Central Reserve Bank and a small shareholder of a number of firms (including insurance companies), was also among those close to García.

APRA's electoral campaign, described as "the most expensive ever mounted in Peru," was partially financed by generous contributions from the national bourgeoisie, a fact kept for the records in a "Golden Book" that listed its major contributors (Becker 1985: 39). The following names appeared in the "Golden Book": Dionisio Romero, Pedro Brescia and Hugo Nicolini, all of them *grupos'* leaders.

Another important activity that formally linked APRA with business leaders was the party's National Commission of Government Planning. Members of the Commission included economists such as Felipe Ortiz de Zeballos, Moreyra and Manuel Romero Caro (all consultants to the *grupos*), as well as Ricardo Vega Llona, an emerging business leader with strong political ambitions who was to become President of the Association of Exporters and the third President of the Confederation of Private Entrepreneurial Institutions (Becker 1985: 41; CONFIEP 1987: 14).[19]

García's campaign speeches were quite revealing of the way he perceived the alliance with the national bourgeoisie. In *La revolución social es nuestro objetivo*, the most important campaign speech, García emphasized the need for a path to social reform which did not conflict with the interests of the national bourgeoisie. Although the publication was critical of those who were "privileged," its only real target among firms and financial institutions were the "external forces" (1985: 22). García's program emphasized the need to overcome Peru's income gap: 75 percent of the population received 23 percent of the national income, while the other 25 percent of the population controlled 77 percent of this income. Rather than confronting the "privileged" group against the "marginal" one, García promised to help the most needy asking the wealthy to contribute to narrow the income gap between Peruvians.

His nationalist speeches emphasized the need to "nationalize the decision making process" and to "reduce external debt payments." His guidelines for economic policy established "reactivation" as the basic short-term goal (through subsidies for private capital as well as promotion of internal demand). García's long-range plan was to transform Peru's economic structure in order to make the country self-sufficient.

In public, García always showed himself to be respectful of private sector interests, but he also emphasized the "social role" of private enterprise. The party's apparent official position emphasized redistributive policies and ruled out expropriations. However, secret party documents clearly stated APRA's plans to nationalize the banking system in order to obtain the financial resources necessary to carry on APRA's ambitious goals (Partido Aprista Peruano 1984).

With regard to business demands, García gave priority to reactivation rather than *concertación*. The alliance with the national bourgeoisie, in his vision, did not consider the inclusion of the national bourgeoisie in the government's decision-making process. The national bourgeoisie, however, demanded the "institutionalization" of *concertación*. It hoped that, once such a policy was institutionalized, the business sector would be in close touch with state affairs and capable of influencing economic policy-making in particular. The following statement made by industrialist Aguirre Roca, a "*gremialista*" leader, at the 1984 Annual Conference of Executives, is particularly revealing:

> The permanent divorce between politicians and entrepreneurs has created confusion rather than allowed collective initiatives. It is indispensable to give some thought to this separation and to promote, if not a formal wedding, at least a trial marriage, known in Peru as *servinacuy* (IPAE 1984: 35).

This demand for *servinacuy*[20] was, essentially, a call for some sort of political pact between the national bourgeoisie and the party in office, a pact that would create what the "*gremialista*" business leaders referred as the "stabilization of the rules of the game." *Concertación* was the national bourgeoisie's formula for actively participating in the governmental decision-making process. It was an attempt to go beyond participation in the governing coalition as supporters of the economic policy orientation adopted by state officials and to get involved in the policy-making process. But despite the national bourgeoisie's push for *concertación*, García's references to this were both vague and few in number. Instead, he spoke ambiguously of the need for "dialogue" between the state and the business sector.

When APRA won the election (3,457,030 votes, 53.11 percent of the total), García outlined the basis of the alliance in his inaugural speech on

July 28, 1985 (Tuesta 1987: 199). He made public his policy of the external debt problem (limiting payments to no more than 10 percent of export earnings), calling for direct negotiations with international banks and breaking off the dialogue with the International Monetary Fund. At the same time, several policy decisions were made with the aim of reactivating the domestic market. Exchange rates were frozen, bank accounts holding foreign currency were prohibited and dollar deposits in banks were frozen. The interest rate was lowered from more than 110 percent to an annual rate of 75 percent. In order to lower inflation rates, a temporary policy of price controls was put into effect. Taxes were also significantly lowered. Addressing the question of poverty, García announced that he would emphasize support for Andean agriculture, subsidization of massive job programs in urban areas and the "democratization" of the state through a program of regional administrative reforms. Trying to please union leaders, he also proposed a bill that reduced the probation period for workers from three years to three months. In general and from the outset, macroeconomic policies favored the economic interests of most fractions of the national bourgeoisie, particularly the interests of those fractions operating within the domestic market. However, the proposed labor bill and measures such as the freezing of dollar accounts did not coincide with business interests.

The coalition was, initially, a result of the government's need for private sector support. This support was necessary if the government was to successfully promote its program of economic reactivation. At this point, no other choice was available to García's government. Adopting a nationalist policy meant ruling out the possibility of counting on foreign capital investment and credit from international sources. García could not use the state as a "tool for development," as Velasco did in the 1970s, because public firms were facing financial and managerial difficulties. Adoption of a "statist" option, based on nationalizations, would have immediately alienated the national bourgeoisie and, consequently, would have undermined the consensus gluing together the governmental coalition. Therefore, the program of economic reactivation centered around the role of the national private sector as the key economic agent. In turn, the reactivation of the domestic market permitted García to maintain multiclass support. Only with economic success were increases in income and higher employment rates possible. To achieve those goals business support was critical.

APRA's large electoral victory and García's sudden popularity provided the government with ample room to maneuver. In 1985-1986, there was no significant opposition to García's government or policies. The challenge posed by the Shining Path's armed revolution could be controlled through a combination of repressive and populist policies.

Other guerrilla groups, such as the Tupac Amaru Revolutionary Movement, made a temporary truce with the García government, easing the tensions in the internal front. The primary forces of non-violent opposition were the United Left and the trade unions, but in the beginning both agreed to support García's policies.

Economically, the government's room to maneuver, was narrower. However, the foreign exchange problem, a critical element needed to initiate the process of economic reactivation, was solvable. Measures such as import restrictions, limited payment of the external debt, and reliance on foreign currency (dollars) obtained from informal sources (such as the cocaine industry), assured adequate foreign exchange reserves in the first years of García's administration. The manufacturing industry's idle productive capacity made a quick economic recovery possible thanks to the demand stimulation approach.

The Evolution of the Coalition: The Easy Phase

What was new, and unique indeed about García's governing coalition, compared to previous governments, was the government's choice of the national bourgeoisie as its most important coalitional partner. No other economic agent was capable of participating since foreign capital was ruled out and the state could not play a crucial role as a tool for economic development.

But despite the uniqueness of García's governing coalition, the traditional pattern of mediation between the state and the different fractions of the national bourgeoisie was not substantially altered. As did Velasco, Morales Bermúdez and Belaunde before him, García continued the pattern by siding with the most powerful fraction, the *grupos*, and making an alliance with bourgeois fractions operating in the domestic market. García attempted to divide them and to define the rules of the game. Even if the national bourgeoisie helped him win the elections and sustain his government, he was unwilling to share power with them and wanted no interference from his coalitional partners. As García said to Juan Francisco Raffo, a *grupo* leader close to him: "Leave politics to me." (*The Peru Report*, September 1987: A2). That is the reason why García avoided institutionalizing organs of *concertación* that would allowed the sectoral fractions to participate in the decision-making process.

During García's administration, particularly in his first two years, the *grupos* became his primary allies and the sectoral fractions the secondary allies. However, the power game between the national bourgeoisie and the state was under tension because the sectoral fractions were willing to redefine their relations with the state now that they were organized around the newly founded business Confederation. The tensions between García's government and the Confederation around the *concertación* issue surfaced even in the early stages of the alliance. And like Belaunde, García was about to make the same mistake, that is, to underestimate the political capabilities of the national bourgeoisie and its organizational developments.

During the first two years of the García administration there was an open confrontation with external forces and a sense of national unity. The rupture in relations with the International Monetary Fund and governmental policy on the external debt isolated the country from the international financial community. In November 1985, the U.S. Inter-Agency Review Committee ruled that the Peruvian debt was "value-impaired" and, a year later, the International Monetary Fund declared Peru "ineligible" as a borrower (Wise 1988: 26). The suspension of credit was the only severe consequence since other sanctions were not enforced by the international banks. And trade credits did not stop because the government opted to pay the private sector debt. However, as time passed, the external front became less significant as a unifying factor between the government and the majority of the population. External forces no longer interfered with national policies and neither the international banks, the International Monetary Fund, nor the U.S. government, wanted to run a collision course with García's nationalist government.

On the internal front, the government was able to achieve the goals outlined in the "emergency plan" and to move quickly to a adopt a "reactivation plan." But the engines of economic growth soon started to slow down. In July 1985, the overall economic situation was sound. Austerity measures enacted by the previous administration initially left García room to maneuver. There was a trade balance surplus of US$826 million, and imports were restricted to US$988 million. In addition, the external debt policy provided a larger amount of availability of foreign exchange (Iguíñiz 1988: 7). The government also obtained dollars from the illegal cocaine industry, estimated at US$700 million in 1986 (Thorp 1986: 7). However, as foreign exchange reserves gradually dwindled, the government was forced to adopt more extreme measures. Foreign currency reserves fell from US$346.2 million in 1985 to US$124.5 million in 1986. The recovery of the domestic economy implied a greater demand of imports (imports represented US$1,806 million dollars in 1985 and 2,597 million in 1986). The decline of export earnings, which fell from US$2,978 million in 1985 to US$2,531 in 1986, eroded the reserves and forced the regime to take restrictive measures (*Actualidad Económica del Perú*, May 1986: 34 and 39). In July 1986, the government suspended profit remittances for a two-year period (*Perú Económico* August 1986: 2). Later, in 1987, in an attempt to control the situation, the government decided to "rationalize" the use of foreign exchange and to limit the amount of dollars that the private sector could transfer abroad annually.

During García's first year, heterodox policies were quite successful. Price controls, interest rate reductions, tax reductions and the freezing of the exchange rate helped to defeat inflation. The annual rate of inflation fell from 163.5 percent in 1985 to 77.9 percent in 1986. Wages and salaries improved as a result of domestic market stimulation, going from 59 in August 1985 (1979=100) to 71 in February 1986, and to 87 in February 1987. The employment rate went up as well, thanks to a quick reactivation of the domestic market and massive government subsidization of employment. In Lima, the employment index was 92 in 1985 (1979=100) and went up to 96 in 1986 (Instituto Nacional de Estadística 1988: 99). In 1986, the economic growth rate averaged 8.6 percent, the highest in the last 25 years.[21]

Nevertheless, the economy began showing signs of economic decline in early 1987, when the fiscal deficit increased, prices started to rise again and foreign exchange reserves continued to decline. Faced with these problems, the government needed to take more effective measures to maintain economic growth. In order to assure the continuity of the economic recovery plan, from July 1986 to July 1987 the government sought to promote investments by the national private sector. The García administration was conscious of the fact that it was increasingly difficult to maintain the multiclass alliance. The easy phase was about to end.

The Logic of the Governing Coalition: Major and Minor Partners

In the first two years of the administration, the government's partnership with those fractions of the national bourgeoisie favored by economic policies was based on an asymmetrical relationship: The most powerful fraction of the national bourgeoisie became the government's major partner of the coalition and the sectoral fractions, those related to the domestic market, became the minor partners.

The Minor Partners. The sectoral fractions operating in the domestic market supported García's economic policies from the very beginning. Those linked to the world market, as was expected, soon complained about the "anti-export" governmental bias. However, despite the diversity of sectoral interests inside the business Confederation, a majority of members supported the government. The position of the different fractions of the national bourgeoisie toward García's government was reflected in the nature of the links between a particular trade association and the corresponding branch of the state apparatus, that is, the sectoral ministries.

Trade Associations' documents and interviews of heads of trade associations revealed that those sectoral fractions linked to the development of the domestic market enjoyed initially a very positive relationship with the state, while those fractions operating in the world market claimed to have a negative relationship.

In the first case, trade associations had close contact with both the Minister and high state officials. The majority of trade association leaders noted that to reach a government Minister, all they had to do was pick up the phone. The National Industrial Society, was clearly enthusiastic about its relations with García's government. A public communique dated January 1987, entitled "Our Cause is the Cause of Peru," declared that "all the private industrialists in Peru support President Alan García" (*El Comercio*, January 15, 1987: 7). The National Agrarian Organization and the Minister of Agriculture had excellent relations because of this Ministry's support of private farmers and its policy of generous subsidies to local agricultural producers. In the construction sector, the Peruvian Chamber of Construction also had a positive relationship with the state.[22]

This was not the case of the National Mining Society which claimed to be ignored because it "did not have any contact with the government's economic team."[23] Miners were politically isolated and, in general, exporters were in a very weak position. The state's relationship with the Association of Exporters and the National Fishing Society, for example, was different from that of the Mining Society, because in these two cases firms could easily shift toward production to the domestic market, instead of exporting to the world market. One of the members of the Association's Executive Committee admitted in an interview that:

> Few of the Association's members are true exporters. Only about five percent are clearly exporters and the majority operate in both markets. Now we are emphasizing business in the domestic market because it is more profitable. There is no exporting power in the country. It does not exist. If it existed, exporters would be truly able to change the government's economic policy.[24]

The same situation (the possibility of shifting emphasis to production for the domestic market instead of the world market), applies to the National Fishing Society. Left alone, without international support, exporters were easily isolated because they had become an economically and politically weak bourgeois fractions in the previous decade.

Relations between trade associations and the state regarding economic policies that regulated each economic sector were only one side of the problem. Other issues were at stake, both economic and political. Populist governmental policies generated uncertainty among business people, and access to the decision-making process was not granted to sectoral fractions in a clear way, as demanded by the business Confederation. For example, the Labor Stability Law proposed by García in his inaugural speech, was approved by Congress in June 1986, despite the opposition of trade associations and the business Confederation. Cases like this raised concern among the ranks of the national bourgeoisie. As a reaction to the new labor law, strong pressure from individual trade associations and the business Confederation was put on García's government, asking the executive branch to neutralize what the legislative branch just approved. As a result of business pressure, the Labor Stability law was essentially negated a month later when García issued a Supreme Decree and limited the scope of the law. The Supreme Decree enacted by the executive branch did not recognize employment stability for those workers employed under the "Temporary Income Support Program."

But despite that concession to trade associations and to the Confederation's demands, uncertainty continued to exist. The Peruvian Chamber of Construction criticized the government for implementing another of García's populist policies: a freeze on housing rents for an unspecified period. A number of trade associations, particularly associations related to the manufacturing industry, complained about price controls. In general, entrepreneurs saw populist policies as necessary to the maintenance of a multiclass alliance, but they lobbied to moderate them.

Trade associations and the Confederation also complained about the lack of any effective government measure toward *concertación*, and repeatedly called for "real concerted action." This opened a political opportunity for the business Confederation to play a major role. *Concertación*, according to the "*gremialista*" leadership, could give trade association access to the government policy-making process in the economic arena and it was one of the main issues raised by the Confederation since its formation.[25]

One of the advantages the Confederation had was a close contact between García and its leaders. The Presidents of the Confederation were all business leaders who had close ties either with the President or high level state officials. Julio Piccini, a businessman in the construction sector and the Confederation's first President (November 1984 to November 1985), considered himself to be a personal friend of President García.[26] Miguel Vega Alvear, a *grupo* Romero manager and the second President (November 1985 to November 1986), had close ties with the regime through his *grupo*. Ricardo Vega Llona, an exporter of manufactured goods and member of APRA's government planning commission as well as the Confederation's third President (November 1986 to November 1987), had also close ties with Prime Minister Alva Castro and APRA. It must be taken into account that in CONFIEP, Presidents were elected by unanimity. Thus, the sectoral fractions of the national bourgeoisie as a whole preferred to choose business leaders who had both personal ties and good relations with the government.[27] The Confederation maintained its stance on *concertación* repeatedly demanding the need to "institutionalize" relations between "representative business organizations" and the state. In its first formal contact with García in May 1985, the Confederation put forth the need to institutionalize *concertación* and suggested that an agreement be worked out among labor union confederations, the business Confederation and the state on how to address a specific set of problems (unemployment and the social security system). This proposal was politely rejected by García since he wanted to avoid any compromise that might reduce his room to maneuver. In August 1985, when García was formally elected President, the Confederation reaffirmed "the need for *concertación* in all sectors to be promoted and stimulated" (*La República*, August 5, 1985: 4). Shortly thereafter, working meetings were held between the Prime Minister and the Minister of Economy and Finance Luis Alva Castro, to promote "dialogue" between both partners (CONFIEP 1987: 50). In these meetings, the Confederation reiterated its demands for "permanent dialogue" and "effective *concertación*" (*Hoy*, August 8, 1985: 8).

The Confederation insisted on the need for *concertación* because it believed García's government was trying to reproduce the traditional pattern of relations between the state and the national bourgeoisie based on the lack of unity among bourgeois fractions. Indications that the government was indeed trying to reproduce such a pattern included: (a) the government's appointment of business leaders linked to the *grupos* as members of Advisory Committees, without taking into account the opinion of the Confederation; (b) the government's preference given to the Peruvian Institute of Business Administration as an entrepreneurial dialoguing group; and (c) the government's decision to establish a close relationship with individual trade associations rather than with the Confederation, the umbrella organization representing the private sector.

The appointment in September 1985 of an advisory committee to the Ministry of Economy and Finance confirmed the worries of the sectoral fractions. The government selected three business leaders (Piccini, Vega Alvear and Ortiz de Zeballos), but did so without formally consulting the Confederation. At that time, Piccini was President of the Confederation and accepted the appointment because he wanted to be in touch with the government and to avoid any confrontation; however, the Confederation made clear to García's government that business representatives should be appointed prior to consultation with trade associations.

The formation in January 1986 of the Advisory Committee on Planning, a new organization of the National Planning Institute, followed the same pattern. This Committee included representatives from all sectors: Eight out of 34 members were business people. From those, six were linked to the *grupos* and two to trade associations.

The formation of the Institute of Foreign Trade in December 1986 galvanized the Confederation. On this occasion, the Confederation also demanded the right to appoint the Institute's private sector representatives and, for the first and only time, the government appointed the individuals chosen by the Confederation.

In February 1987, the government created another organism, the National Investment Council, to promote national capital investment. The Council included 14 members from economic interest groups, ten of whom represented the national private sector and four the labor unions. Among the ten representatives of the private sector, six represented the *grupos*. Four were heads of the four most powerful *grupos* (Dionisio Romero, Mario Brescia, Gabriel Lanata Piaggio, Ernesto Nicolini) and one (Oscar Espinoza) was a manager of another *grupo* (Ferreyros). The other four were business leaders from different economic sectors and included Vega Llona, the newly-elected President of the Confederation and Piccini. The governmental predilection for the *grupos* was defended by Prime Minister Alva Castro when he stated that in the Council:

> The Executive Committee will select four Executive Directors. The first three will represent the twenty economic power groups with the highest investment capabilities and the fourth will be representative of medium-sized investors (*Gente*, February 26, 1986: 10).

García also established a privileged relationship with the Peruvian Institute of Business Administration in order to publicize the government's good will toward the business sector, but also to avoid dealing with the Confederation by emphasizing the need to dialogue with those businessmen that attended the Annual Conference of Executives. His intentions were clear since the very beginning. At the 1985 Annual Conference of Executives (CADE), only four months after his inaugural speech, García proposed a policy of *concertación* with the national bourgeoisie called "CADE permanente." The presidential proposal gave individual entrepreneurs who participated in the Conference a "permanent" status as government advisers. The idea of a "CADE permanente" was immediately accepted by Octavio Mavila, President of the Peruvian Institute of Business Administration. Mavila's decision led to a dispute between the Confederation and the Institute of Business Administration, because the Confederation was fighting for the institutionalization of dialogue with trade associations and its recognition as a valid spokesman of the private sector.[28] The Confederation bitterly criticized Mavila for playing the government's game and showed concern with divisions and disagreements within the national private sector, divisions and disagreements which increased as time went by. In May 1986, the Institute organized a forum on "Economic Reactivation and Price Controls," a forum attended by several ministers and by President García. The President of the Confederation was not invited.

The differences on *concertación* between the Confederation and García's government, at a moment when it was clear that the government was unwilling to recognize the role of CONFIEP as an umbrella organization of the business sector (capable of representing them in dialogues and negotiations), provoked a first although limited clash among them. On December 1986, without first consulting the Confederation, (or the business leaders who participated in "CADE permanente"), the government issued Supreme Decree 362, a tax norm that affected firms of all economic sectors, with the exception of those firms (mostly multinational corporations and firms that belonged to the *grupos*), which had signed "tax stability contracts" with the state. The Confederation decided to oppose the Supreme Decree but pointed out that opposition to the government's decision was the exception rather than the norm. The battle around Supreme Decree 362 was considered by the Confederation a "special case," because out of 20 policy decisions, Confederation leaders "only disagreed with one" (Supreme Decree 362). Despite its demands to change Supreme Decree 362, the Confederation was unable to obtain more than a few meetings with important members of the government. More specifically, it held meetings with a group of cabinet members and, eventually with García. These produced no results.

Even though there were open disagreements between the Confederation and García's government on certain issues as seen above, the Confederation policy was to avoid open conflict with García's closest allies (the Peruvian Institute of Business Administration and the *grupos*) and the government itself. The game was mostly defensive but proved to be highly effective. It was important for the Confederation to win time in order to strengthen its internal organization. Thus, the Confederation tried to coordinate with the government and, more importantly, with the *grupos* and the Institute, both of whom enjoyed a privileged relationship with the state. In the meantime, a short-term plan was approved to consolidate externally and internally the organization and prepare it for more decisive battles. The plan included the following initiatives: (a) to organize an annual congress (to be held every September,) (b) to enhance the Confederation's membership, and (c) to redesign its internal organization, creating special committees with the objective of incorporating well-known business leaders and the heads of the *grupos* into its ranks.[29]

The first Congress, held in September 1986, was a major success. It attracted approximately 450 business people, more than the attendance to the Annual Conference of Executives organized every year by IPAE. To avoid conflict, the Confederation leaders carefully selected themes that expressed the general concern of the national bourgeoisie, and left out those themes that provoked internal divisions (for example, the issue of trade tariffs). But the Confederation dared to point out, in the letter of invitation to the Congress, that the event was necessary to defend the general interests of the private sector, because, "for essentially political reasons, the private sector (the Confederation) has been minimized and criticized with the clear purpose of discrediting it." The message was clear. The government was trying to put aside the Confederation and play with the old rules of the game: to divide and conquer. And the Confederation, fully conscious of the game and its consequences, was challenging it.

The Confederation's cautious but firm tactic obtained some results. Instead of running into conflict with the Confederation, García, for the time being, adopted a conciliatory approach. The President invited Confederation leaders to the Government Palace and declared he would establish "contacts with national entrepreneurs so that meetings between his ministers and business representatives could be more frequent and useful" (*Caretas*, November 3, 1986: 26). At the beginning of 1987, state officials began meeting regularly with Confederation leaders. The meetings, as the Confederation soon learned, were, basically, a diversionary tactic; in the same period in which the government made moves to improve its relations with the Confederation, García selected a core group of *grupos*, whom he charged with the promotion of private investment. According to the 1987 Confederation Annual Report:

> In 1987, important steps were taken towards *concertación* with government representatives. Throughout January and February frequent meetings were held between Confederation leaders and the government's economic team. Unfortunately, the efforts at *concertación* were not very successful because the government limited itself to explaining measures it had already adopted, and did not listen to important practical suggestions presented by the Confederation leaders (CONFIEP 1987: 50).

Interviews held in 1986 and early 1987 with Confederation leaders depict the same scenario and clearly reveal their awareness of García's deliberate attempt to prevent the Confederation from playing a role as the main spokesman of the private sector. Therefore, the *"gremialistas"* were fully aware of the need to keep the Confederation's members united and of the critical importance to gradually increase its membership, while consolidating the presence of the Confederation in the political arena. Danger of internal divisions soon came when, in March 1986, one important trade association (the National Confederation of Merchants, CONACO) decided to split from the peak association. The *"gremialistas"* acknowledged in early 1987 the organization's precarious situation if other trade associations decided to follow the example of CONACO. Feeling the danger ahead, Edgardo Palza, a Confederation leader, described the institution at that moment as "a crystal" that could easily be broken by internal divisions.[30] Palza was right. The main danger of business collective organizations were lack of cohesion among members and intra-class conflicts.

The Major Partner: The "12 Apostles"

The privileged nature of the relationship between the state and the *grupos* was manifested in various and sometimes contradictory ways. The *grupos* were, undoubtedly, the government's major coalitional partner. García both took pleasure in showing off this special relationship and benefited politically from its being public knowledge. Because of his insatiable desire for publicity, he liked to declare to foreigners and Peruvians alike, that his government had the backing of the *grupos*. García went even further; he tried, for the first time, to institutionalize this special relationship by bringing together the 12 most powerful *grupos* for the purpose of promoting private investment.[31]

There was one problem with García's decision to make public the alliance. Publicity about a privileged relationship between the state and the *grupos* had a number of negative consequences in a society where rich people do not enjoy legitimacy and where the use of public resources for private purposes is a permanent source of political denunciations. It is not surprising then that Dionisio Romero, head of one of the wealthiest *grupos*, President of Banco de Crédito and García's personal friend, (he piloted the plane in which President García traveled to the 1986 Annual Conference of Executives), stated that "we participate in the process of *concertación* because we have to" (Reaño and Vasquez 1988: 125). The success of the special relationship between the *grupos* and the state depended heavily on the relationship remaining secret. When García ended this secrecy, he overexposed both himself and the *grupos* and the issue of a privileged relationship quickly became politicized.

García evidently attempted to reproduce the traditional pattern of state/national bourgeois relations (by establishing a privileged relationship with the *grupos*), but altered some of the conditions for its existence, because he broke the rule of secrecy. It is possible to think that García did it on purpose in order to force the *grupos* to invest more.

The privileged relationship between the *grupos* and the state is very difficult to prove systematically, but it can be exemplified by studying cases that fall into the following categories: (a) cases in which the *grupos* as a whole received special privileges from the state, (b) cases in which individual *grupos* received special treatment and, finally, (c) cases in which the *grupos* were able either to prevent laws unfavorable to them from being put into effect, or to introduce legislation beneficial for their firms.

With regard to the first group of cases, the *grupos* as a whole were generally benefited when the state granted credit of development banks, with subsidized interest rates, to their firms and, also, in the case of tax stability contracts signed only by a select group of firms.[32] In Peru, only a small portion of private savings are deposited in the country's banks. This enabled most *grupos*, who run very profitable firms, to be financially autonomous. However, the *grupos* normally obtained abundant credit from the state (through development banks) and from the private financial system (under their control).

A glance at the distribution of credit granted by the nation's financial institutions to the private sector shows the *grupos* as the country's biggest creditors. As shown on Table 6.1, in April 1987 the top 10 *grupos* concentrated 7.43 percent of the nation's credit. In the case of the Romero *grupo*, the *grupo* financing came from more than 20 different sources, with the state loaning 56.8 percent of the total.

Lower interest rates and long-term credit made state credit particularly tempting. Access to credit was not equally available to other firms, who usually complained about lack of credit. But both the state and other financial institutions gave preferential treatment to the *grupos*.

Tax stability contracts were approved by the Ministry of Industry, in accordance with the 1983 Industrial Law, in order to favor a selected group of firms. It was common to see a number of *grupo* firms enjoying tax stability contracts. Firms receiving such contracts included Universal Textil (Romero), Tejidos La Unión (Brescia), Compañía Nacional de Cerveza (Lanata Piaggio), Cervecería Backus y Johnston (Bentín), Hilos Cadena Llave (Brescia), Molitalia (Lanata Piaggio), Compañía Molinera del Peru (Nicolini).[33] In early 1987, Manuel Romero Caro, Minister of Industry, announced that the number of firms with tax stability contracts

TABLE 6.1   Bank Credit Given to the *Grupos* (Only Debts over 200 Million *Intis*)
As of April 30, 1987

Grupos	*Grupo's Credit as % of Total Credit*
Romero	1.57
Brescia	1.34
Nicolini	0.92
Lanata Piaggio	0.89
Ferreyros	0.65
Cilloniz	0.53
Benavides de la Quintana	0.45
Wiese	0.38
Bentín	0.37
Raffo	0.33

Source: The data in this table are drawn from *1/2 de Cambio* (September 1-15, 1987: 10).

had been broadened substantially since 1985 to include a number of big firms that were owned by the *grupos* in many cases: "The vast majority of large firms," Romero Caro noted, "signed tax stability contracts with us at the end of 1985, so later laws do not affect them" (*The Peru Report*, August 1987: A12).   The consequences of this policy that privileged a handful of firms, in isolating the demands of the Confederation against Supreme Decree 362, were obvious.   It was easy for the state to confront the Confederation's pressure to modify Supreme Decree 362, since the government knew that the *grupos* and a handful of other companies, (multinational corporations among them), would not be interested in joining the Confederation's protest.   By separating the *grupos* from the Confederation, the protest of the latter was already weakened, since the state knew that the national bourgeoisie could not act in a united fashion and since its strongest fraction was unwilling to back the Confederation's demands.   With regard to the second group of cases, there is also evidence that individual *grupos* obtained benefits as a result of their privileged relationship with the state.   The beef imports authorized by the Ministry of Agriculture in 1986 is just such an example.   In that year, 6,000 metric tons of beef above the scheduled amounts were imported. A select group of firms benefited from the Ministry's authorization. Ganadera Schilcayo, a powerful firm belonging to *grupo* Romero, obtained large profits from these imports (*Sí*, November 9, 1987: 16-17). The authorization to import larger-than-scheduled quantities of beef harmed the fishing industry, which favored a policy that gave priority to fresh and canned fish, rather than to beef. Beef, unlike fish, was consumed largely by upper-income and medium-income groups.

The case of wheat and corn imports by a state firm later sold to top milling firms, and in particular to the *grupo* Nicolini firms, is well known in Peru. The state firm currently buys wheat and corn on the international market and then sells it at subsidized prices to private mills. Final prices have been usually controlled by the state in order to make sure that the consumer is subsidized. Private mills profit from this business particularly from the sale of wheat by-products (pastry flour and bran), products not included on the official list of controlled prices during García's administration. The close ties between Remigio Morales Bermúdez, Minister of Agriculture, and the *grupos* who control this industry, were well-known. Morales Bermúdez had a particularly close relationship with the *grupo* Nicolini, which was regularly granted the right to buy 50 percent of the imported wheat and corn. In the late 1970s, when his father was President of Peru, he worked as a consultant for the *grupo*'s leading firm, Nicolini Hermanos.[34]

Another case where individual *grupos* were benefited was related to the allocation of foreign exchange quotas to importing firms, beginning in early 1987. The authorization of quotas was adopted by García's government as a way to stop the fall in international reserves. According to a manager of the Ferreyros *grupo*, they did not have any difficulty obtaining a generous quota, because of "the enormous political influence of the *grupo*."[35] The Romero, Nicolini and Ferreyros *grupos* were members of the group of "12 Apostles."

Finally, there were instances in which the *grupos* prevented enforcement of certain laws or pressured the state to introduce laws which benefited their own particular business activities (tailored legislation). The case of Inversiones Centenario is highly significant, because it illustrates how certain firms were not subject to the law. Inversiones Centenario was created in November 1986 by Banco de Crédito's four biggest stockholders who were, not incidentally, members of the "12 Apostles" (Romero, Raffo, Nicolini and Brescia). Only a month after Inversiones Centenario formed, it became an (illegal) owner of part of Banco de Crédito's buildings and land. In the process, assets belonging to thousands of Banco de Crédito shareholders were transferred into the hands of these four *grupos*. Although state agencies such as the Superintendency of Banks and the General Controllership of the Republic objected to the transfer, the state eventually turned a blind eye to it and the *grupos*' interests prevailed (*Actualidad Económica del Perú*, April 1987: 4-5; May 1987: 8 and 9).

The process in which quotas for cotton imports were set and adopted in May 1987 serves as an example of the successful promotion of legislation tailor-made to serve *grupos'* interests. Manufacturers of cotton products, largely controlled by *grupos* such as Romero, Nicolini, Brescia, Raffo and Gerbolini, demanded cotton imports. Because it lowered cotton prices, the measure was fiercely fought by cotton producers, who could not stop its adoption. Reflecting on this battle, Raul Chao, the head of the Committee of Cotton Producers, noted bitterly in an interview that "everybody steps on agriculture. We have no power, no influence."[36]

In cases like these, whether the *grupos* as a whole or individual firms owned by them benefited, the state protected *grupos'* interests and failed to protect the interests of less powerful fractions of the national bourgeoisie. However, in some instances regarding macroeconomic policies, *grupos'* influence was less strong or not evident.

Part of the anti-inflationary and anti-speculative schemes tried by García's government consisted of lowering interest rates and the financial spread. Both measures lowered bank profits. The first measure was initially accepted by the bankers but, by mid-1986, they began to demand an increase in interest rates. In the end, the bankers were unsuccessful in getting what they wanted because the government decided to maintain its policy. Nevertheless, there were limits on the government's ability to impose its will in the face of *grupos'* opposition. A quick look at another case of the government's attempts at policymaking in the banking sphere illustrates this. One of García's favorite projects was the decentralization of the state apparatus. The goal of this project was to reduce the concentration of credit in the hands of Lima's firms. Thus, the government adopted a policy of financial reform that included the formation of "financial districts" and required the recomposition of the boards of directors of the banks' regional branches. The recomposition process involved the inclusion of a third of the directors living in the corresponding financial district, removing those who resided in Lima.[37] The *grupos* opposed the reform because they did not want their bank executives to leave Lima, the capital. They successfully opposed the state's decentralization project although, in the process, this issue generated a new source of friction with high state officials.[38]

The complexity of state/*grupos'* alliance is further illustrated by a study of events which unfolded in the banking arena and in the flourishing informal (i.e. illegal) dollar exchange market. Initially, the illegal exchange market produced benefits for both the state and the *grupos* and the two entities closely coordinated exploitation of this business. Private banks actively participated in the capture of dollars from the cocaine industry, beginning in 1985. The government's urgent need for foreign exchange forced the Central Reserve Bank to authorize the purchase of dollars from "anywhere in the national territory" in order to accelerate the flow of coca dollars. With the informal government's approval, Banco de Crédito, Peru's largest private bank, flew a small aircraft which carried *intis* from Lima to the coca areas (the Upper Huallaga Valley) and returned with U.S. dollars. A majority of these dollars (80 percent) were used by Banco de Crédito for its own purposes and the rest were sold to the Central Reserve Bank at Lima's black market exchange rate (a rate always higher than that of the Huallaga's market). In addition, the Central Reserve Bank bought dollars from banks and Lima's Exchange Houses. According to Hector Neyra, Manager of the Central Reserve Bank, in 1986, the Central Reserve Bank made daily purchases of about US$2.5 million dollars from private banks.[39]

The Alliance with the "12 Apostles"

Initially, the existence of the alliance was kept quiet, but the relationship between the government and the *grupos* soon became public knowledge. The government wanted to promote private investment so that it could sustain growth rates and maintain its multiclass support. To do so, García considered it necessary to demonstrate publicly that it was capable of achieving its aim through a special relationship with the *grupos*, the nation's most powerful investors.

The privileged partnership was initiated in mid-1986 by García. The government judged that it was time to proceed with its plan of economic reactivation. According to this plan, the profits accumulated since the beginning of his administration should be invested in specific economic sectors in order to save foreign exchange, promote exports of manufactured goods and promote employment in rural areas.

It must be pointed out that the idea of formalizing an alliance with the *grupos* did not have internal consensus among APRA's hard-liners, but the party went ahead with it because President García convinced the radicals that the alliance was necessary to win time. The debate about the alliance with the *grupos* that took place inside APRA, and García's government, clearly revealed that the links among coalitional partners were fragile, that the governing coalition was built on weak foundations.

In June 1986, a debate broke out between several members of the President's inner circle. Hard-liners proposed ending the state's alliance with the *grupos*, by nationalizing the banking system, and redirecting the bank's resources toward restructuring the Peruvian economy and supporting the state's "regionalization" program.[40] The moderates proposed reinforcing the alliance with the national bourgeoisie in general and with the *grupos* in particular so as to give priority to private investment. García mediated between these two political factions and chose a middle course: It was necessary to formalize the alliance with the *grupos* to see if in a one-year period the private sector was willing to invest. García's official speech to Congress in July 28, 1986 reflected this middle course:

> One possibility for us, as some sectors propose it, is to proceed with the nationalization of firms owned by the *grupos*. However, that would generate the distrust and apprehension of the middle class, the economic agents, and would inevitably lead to a greater bureaucratization of our economy.... We offer a different alternative...[to] be achieved gradually, through productive investment of the *grupos'* economic surplus, according to national goals. In this way, they [the *grupos*] will not be the center of accumulation and power, or accomplices of dependence, but rather factors of support and stimuli to national development.[41]

Once APRA and García's government, as the presidential speech reveals, agreed on the policy toward national investors, this particular type of privileged relationship between the state and the *grupos* began. On July 26th, two days prior to the President's annual speech to Congress, García called a private meeting with 12 *grupos*. Business leaders from the Bentín, Romero, Brescia, Nicolini, Raffo and Lanata Piaggio *grupos* were among those invited. The remaining *grupos* sent their representatives because their leaders were out of town. The meeting was called to inform the *grupos* that, despite rumors, García did not intend to adopt radical measures. On the contrary, he intended to promote closer relations with "big investors" because the first issue on his agenda was that of private sector investment. In the meeting, the government agreed to propose broad policy guidelines in order to promote investment, and the *grupos*, in turn, agreed to propose investment projects in accordance with government policy priorities. Both parties also agreed to hold subsequent meetings between July and December (a total of three, in fact, occurred) and to arrive at agreement on ways to formalize the alliance.[42] One of the most important conclusions of the meeting between García and the "12 Apostles" was that a rapid investment pace could only occur if high state officials were in permanent touch with *grupos'* leaders and if both pragmatically agreed on concrete ways to promote investment.

The problem with this proposal, from a political standpoint, is that it excluded the rest of the private sector. The sectoral fractions and the Confederation were worried about being left out of this specific proposal of *concertación*. But the real problems came when high state officials began to have doubts about the feasibility of promoting investment. There were too many factors generating uncertainty in the mid-1980s to expect major investment proposals from the *grupos* or any other group of investors. Despite the alliance, García did not generate long-term confidence among investors. It was also unclear what would happen in the external front (international pressures) and how key internal macro-economic problems were going to be solved (inflation, fiscal deficit). In addition to that, big investors were mostly concentrated in speculative activities with the exchange rate.

When García formalized the alliance with the "12 Apostles" a number of problems emerged. The state's ability to insure that the *grupos* were investing according to policy guidelines was questionable. In addition, the state elites had no clear idea on how to institutionalize the alliance and on the type of policy decisions necessary to promote investment. From the *grupos'* point of view, García's proposal of *concertación* was worrying. They were about to accept political responsibility for making investments at a time when the government was losing its ability to maneuver both politically and economically. The *grupos* were also worried because a public discussion about investment, at a moment when it was clear that the government was granting them a privileged relationship, could be questioned by the opposition and by those left out of the alliance.

The alliance between García and the "12 Apostles" also posed a dilemma for the weaker sectoral fractions. They agreed that the state should promote investment and grant specific incentives to national investors, but they wanted a seat at the bargaining table. The alliance tended to weaken the Confederation's role as a representative business organization since García's proposal favored "big investors," not trade associations. In addition, the Confederation also saw the danger of the *grupos'* public commitment to invest. To the Confederation, the "12 Apostles" seemed more like the "12 hostages," because if the *grupos* did not comply with the agreements to invest profits, the government might try to strike back and nationalize their firms. The fact that this view was common among the Confederation's business members showed the latter's distrust of García. The Confederation's first reaction toward García's alliance with the "12 Apostles" was manifested in its first Congress, held in September 1986. Although the Confederation at that moment was lead by Vega Alvear (Romero *grupo*), the leadership agreed with most members that a policy of *concertación* open to all entrepreneurs and not limited to the *grupos* was necessary. Vega Alvear's strategy was to demand an inclusionary form of *concertación*, as demanded by trade associations, but avoided any criticism of the dealings between García and the "12 Apostles."

Once the issue of the alliance with the *grupos* became public, García had to decide how to formalize *concertación*: whether to bargain quietly with the *grupos*, to create a new bureaucratic entity that included *grupos* only, or to create an organization that included other members but privileging big investors. In the end, García's government chose the third option. This decision was good for the government's political image, but did not please the *grupos*, because the rule of secrecy was being broken. García's strategy was also problematic in the eyes of both the sectoral fractions and labor leaders, included as second-class partners only, with no decision-making capabilities.

One of the government's first steps included forming a top-level bureaucratic team, directly connected to the President, which would negotiate with the "12 Apostles." The team was headed by Daniel Carbonetto, García's primary economic adviser. Most of the top ranked state officials were also appointed to the team: Manuel Romero (Minister of Industry), Gustavo Saberbein (Vice-Minister of Economy and Finance), Javier Tantaleán (head of the National Planning Institute), Leonel Figueroa (President of the Central Reserve Bank) and José Salaverry (President of the Development Finance Corporation). By August 1986, the special team decided that incentives should be made to promote *grupos'* specific investment projects according to the following criteria: projects that emphasized production of basic-needs goods, exports of manufactured goods, production of industrial goods that substituted imports. Priority was to be given to investments in high poverty areas and in areas of widespread unemployment.

Despite the publicity about it, the bureaucratic team was not immediately put to work. Two reasons explain a slow start. First, not all *grupos* made detailed investment proposals for investment projects. Second, the government failed to decide how to specifically organize the *concertación* proposal. With regard to the first problem, lack of detailed investment proposals, only the Romero, Raffo and Bentín *grupos* (three out of the 12 the major investors) properly presented investment projects. The Romero *grupo* planned to invest US$38.5 million to expand the productive capacity of the palm oil and cotton spinning industry. The former aimed at saving imports and the latter at generating foreign exchange since the plant was designed to produce for the world market. The Raffo *grupo* made a proposal to invest US$5.1 million to expand the productive capacity of its knitwear plant, the products to be sold in the U.S market. The Bentín *grupo* made a proposal to invest US$21.7 million in the production of beer in a plant located on the Northern Coast of Peru and to produce asparagus and other agricultural products for the world market. Together, however, the proposed investment of these three *grupos* accounted for little more than US$63 million. According to the press, the proposed investment of all "12 Apostles," summed up a total of only US$120 million (*Caretas*, November 7, 1986: 20-21 and 70). The politicization of this economic issue now took a new turn: the big investors had little investment plans.

Sensing the government's indecisiveness and wanting to keep *concertación* as secret as possible, a last attempt was made to safeguard the *grupos'* rule of secrecy. In August 1987, the Romero *grupo* took the initiative at one of the meetings with García and suggested to the government that investment proposals should be promoted according to two legal formulas. "Alternative A," as it was called by the *grupo* experts, called for a law granting "special powers to the Executive." These "special powers" included the ability to sign investment contracts with private investors on "national interest projects." "Alternative B" called for signing a formal agreement, known as an "Act of Compromise," to be monitored directly by the President. As part of its "Alternative A" package, the Romero *grupo* even presented a draft of the proposed law.[43] The element common to both alternatives was the emphasis Romero placed on face to face dealings with the Executive, without forming any official organizations to negotiate private investment.

The debate among state officials as to how to proceed with *concertación* seriously delayed the government from making a final decision about Romero's proposal. Seven months after the first meeting between García and the "12 Apostles," the government finally agreed to create an official organization, the National Investment Council. The government designated that Council members include not only Peru's top business people and top ranked state officials, but, also, as a gesture toward the rest of Peruvian society, leaders of trade associations and labor unions. Their participation in the National Investment Council was mainly symbolic, since members representing state officials and the *grupos* formed the majority.

This experiment of *concertación* between the "12 Apostles" and García's government was short-lived. It became rapidly politicized, because the opposition openly criticized it. The politicization, in turn, added another negative factor affecting investment. The Council pleased only the government and none of the social actors who participated in it: i.e., the *grupos*, trade associations and union leaders. The *grupos* were dissatisfied because they preferred to deal secretly and not openly with the executive. The sectoral fractions were dissatisfied because they saw the alliance with the "12 Apostles" as a continuation of an unfair, discriminatory pattern of state/national bourgeoisie relations. The working class was also dissatisfied because they felt openly discriminated against. It should be noted that while García was dealing with the national bourgeoisie about how to promote private investment, the government avoided dealing with union leaders on labor matters. They, therefore, openly criticized the "class nature" of García's alliance with the "12 Apostles."

By early 1987, President García still enjoyed multiclass support and the governing coalition was still working, but at the same time it was evident that tensions within coalitional partners, and between the state and the popular sector, were growing. The government's ability to handle these tensions became increasingly limited as García moved into his third year in office.

Conclusion

A study of the demise of Belaunde's liberal-exporting governing coalition, and the rise of García's national-developmentalist coalition, reveals how the fractions of the national bourgeoisie have related to the state in given periods. In the mid-1980s, the pattern of relations between the state and the national bourgeoisie was being questioned by the sectoral fractions organized in the Confederation, demanding participation in the decision-making process as representatives of trade associations.

In the two governing coalitions analyzed, state elites attempted to take advantage of divisions within the national bourgeoisie. They sided with the *grupos*, who were permanent members of the governing coalitions. The economic policies adopted by the state, (liberal-exporting policies with Belaunde; national-developmentalist with García), benefited specific sectoral fractions that were incorporated into the governing coalition. At the same time, state elites sought to insulate those fractions harmed by its economic policies (industrialists in Belaunde's case and miners in García's case).

However, in the transition from one governing coalition to the next, political changes within the national bourgeoisie made it more difficult for state elites to continue with this pattern. The "*gremialista*" leaders took advantage of circumstances favorable to class solidarity at the end of Belaunde's administration and formed a business Confederation that made possible, at least potentially, class coordination and class unity on a permanent basis.

The impulse to form such an organization signaled the national bourgeoisie's decision to participate more actively in national and party politics. The bourgeoisie demanded that the state recognize the right of "representative" trade associations to bargain with state elites whenever collective interests were at stake.

The priority given by García's government to the *grupos* as his main coalitional partner, and his repeated attempts to ignore the Confederation as official spokesman of the private sector, revealed García's intention to reproduce the traditional pattern of mediation between the state and the national bourgeoisie. The Confederation continued to claim its right to be incorporated in state efforts toward *concertación*, despite the

fact that García considered sectoral fractions as minor coalitional partners. However, the politicization of the alliance between the state and
the "12 Apostles," designed to promote private investment, generated
increased political tensions at the level of the governing coalition and at
the level of society.

Notes

1. As a Minister, Puente y Lavalle strongly opposed Rodríguez Pastor in
cabinet meetings at a time (mid-1983) when his *grupo* was already questioning
orthodox policies. Other *grupos* had serious problems dealing with Rodríguez
Pastor because he was unwilling to grant them tailored legislation.

2. In an interview with Max Cameron in Lima, May 1986, Belaunde agreed
that insistence on "economic discipline" threatened the possibility of continuing
with public works.

3. This economic indicator was at that time the lowest of the twentieth
century. See Instituto Nacional de Estadística (1988: 6).

4. According to a member of Popular Action's Executive Committee, the
problem with Rodríguez Pastor was that he failed to take into consideration
changes in electoral behavior and the negative impact of economic policy on the
political future of the governing party. Interview with Edgardo Ochoa. Lima,
January 29, 1986.

5. Among the most important trade associations that openly backed Mariátegui were the National Industrial Society, the Association of Exporters and the
National Fishing Society. The joint declaration of support indicated that the
national bourgeoisie's trend toward unification was already in motion.

6. In Mexico the most powerful and successful businessmen are organized
in a group called Consejo Mexicano de Hombres de Negocios. The Consejo deals
behind closed doors with high state officials. Because of the existence of this
elite group, the Mexican political class did not care to establish formal relations
with trade associations. See Camp (1989: 169-169). In Brazil there is also the
"Group of Eight," composed of Sao Paulo top business people. The Peruvian
grupos attempted a similar formula in 1984 in order to monopolize dealings with
the state but they did not succeed.

7. Interview with Carlos Verme in Lima, September 1986; and Julio Piccini
in Lima, January 1988.

8. Interview with Edgardo Palza. Lima, November 20, 1986.

9. Interview with a former manager of CONFIEP. Lima, July 15, 1992.

10. On workers' attitudes, see Parodi (1988: 108-109). On entrepreneurs,
see IPAE (1983: 81-82).

11. For data on crime rates, see Senado de la República (1988: 246). Data
on terrorism were drawn from research done by Raúl Gonzáles. For an analysis

of the Shining Path and terrorism, see Degregori (1987), Favre (October 1984), Gonzáles (August 1984), Gianotten, de Wit and de Wit (1985) and Palmer (1992).

12. After all, this was the basis of early populist experiences in Latin America. However, populist movements have always faced the problem of being unable to maintain positive growth rates in the long run, because redistributive policies became contradictory with policies that favor continued capital accumulation. See Hirschman (1979). On the politics of redistribution in Latin America, see Ascher (1984).

13. García sided with that wing of the party that supported Villanueva, the wing that eventually gained control of the party machinery.

14. On García's book, see Gonzáles (1983) and Vergara (1983).

15. For comments about García's victory within the party, see Palmer (1984) and Sanborn (1989).

16. Traditionally, APRA was a party that received a third of the votes but was unable to move beyond this limit. García became the first party leader able to attract independent voters and, thus, to lead a coalition that included those fractions of the national bourgeoisie that had no strong identification with APRA and that generally voted for the Christian Popular Party or Popular Action. *El Zorro de Abajo*, a leftist magazine, did an interesting analysis of García's campaign in its June-July 1985 issue (pp. 15-16, 18-20).

17. See Cotler's comments in *El Zorro de Abajo* (June-July 1985: 18).

18. Interview with two entrepreneurial leaders in Lima, September 17, 1987.

19. Manuel Romero Caro, who became Minister of Industry in 1986, had a close relationship with the Brescia *grupo*, according to a high state official interviewed in December 1988.

20. The Quechua Indians define *servinacuy* as a trial marriage that lasts one year.

21. For more on the improvements that took place as a result of García's economic policies, see Thorp (1987: 8a) and Wise (1988: 29-30).

22. Interview with Julio Piccini, Lima, January 20, 1988.

23. A leading economic journal criticized the government's "anti-export bias." See *Perú Económico* (July 1986: 1-6).

24. Interview with Gastón Benza, Lima, December 18, 1987.

25. Interview with Edgardo Palza, Lima, December 20, 1986. See also *Presencia*, CONFIEP's monthly newspaper (December 1986: 27).

26. Interview with Julio Piccini, Lima, January 20, 1988.

27. Trade associations such as the National Mining Society and the Lima Chamber of Commerce, both among those members of the Confederation that criticized the so-called "anti-export bias" of the government's heterodox policy, never openly disagreed with the Confederation's position.

28. In the editorial page of *Gerencia* (December 1985: 2), the Institute's journal, Mavila attempted to justify himself, claiming that "CADE permanente"

did not interfere with the trade associations' attempt to institutionalize *concertación* with the government.

29. For information about the committee system, see CONFIEP's annual reports (1987: 38-39 and 1989: 36).

30. Interview with Edgardo Palza, Lima, January 20, 1987.

31. The press labeled the group of major investors the "12 Apostles."

32. Tax stability contracts began with the new industrial law of 1983 and ended in October 1990, when Fujimori suspended indefinitely these contracts (Supreme Decree 284-90-EF). A total of 189 industrial firms (118 located in Lima) benefited from this norm. Most contracts were signed during García's administration. Information obtained from the Ministry of Industry. According to a Vice Minister of Industry interviewed, the contract's proposals were first reviewed by his Ministry and then passed to the Ministry of Economy and Finance where firms used "political support" or "economic influence" to get them approved. This is one more example of clientelism as a factor shaping policy decisions. Interview in Lima, August 13, 1992.

33. The complete list of firms that received tax stability contracts was obtained from the Ministry of Industry. *Informativo Tagal*, a stock exchange publication, published information about some of the cases above mentioned (Nos. 1, 2, and 3, Serie Empresas, 1987).

34. Interview in Lima, July 10 1986. See also Malpica (1987). Remigio Morales Bermúdez was accused of corruption by the press and political leaders opposed to APRA. In 1992, he was expelled from APRA. This was not an isolated case. Several high state officials of the García administration had been involved in cases of corruption, including three from the Central Reserve Bank (Figueroa, Jensen and Neyra) who were involved in the BCCI (Bank of Commerce and Credit International) scandal. García himself has been involved in the BCCI scandal and was accused by Congress on charges of corruption in 1991.

35. Interview in Lima, February 18, 1987.

36. Interview with Raul Chao, Lima, May 3, 1987.

37. On the García government's financial reform proposal, see Salaverry (1987: 5-13). For more on the business sector's reaction to the reform, see *Perú Económico* (April 1987: 11-12).

38. Interview with José Salaverry, head of COFIDE. Huaraz, May 29, 1988.

39. Neyra made this statement at a forum organized by IPAE in May 25, 1987. For more on the "coca dollar" market, see *Actualidad Económica del Perú* (September 1988: 5-6), and *Semana Económica* (September 6, 1988: 3).

40. For more on this debate, see Cotler (1987: 95-96 and 113-114). APRA proposed radical policies against the *grupos* in a party document approved in 1984. See Partido Aprista Peruano (1984).

41. State of the Union address. July 28, 1986.

42. For more on the meetings between García and the "12 Apostles," see *Oiga* (April 26, 1986), *The Andean Report* (October 1986), *Caretas* (November 17,

1986) and *Sí* (April 27-May 4, 1987). In an interview with Francisco Durand and Alberto Graña, Manuel Romero Caro, Minister of Industry, outlined the conditions of the agreement between the government and the "12 Apostles."

43. The *grupos'* investment proposals were private documents obtained in 1987 from government sources.

7

A Leap Forward

The political advancements of the national bourgeoisie were most clearly manifested in its ability to become united and mobilized in critical circumstances and in the effective strengthening of the business peak association. These happened despite repeated governmental maneuvers to ignore the business Confederation and the dangers of internal business divisions. This process will acquire a more intense dynamic in the second half of the 1980s. The national bourgeoisie will pass a difficult test in mid-1987, when García threatened the private sector with the nationalization of the banking system. But the national bourgeoisie responded collectively, using all its economic, human and organizational resources and succeeded in stopping it.

The nationalization of the banks was a major event in Peru's political history because it provoked a process of business politicization and social polarization never seen before. In this key critical juncture, all fractions of the national bourgeoisie became united and were mobilized by the business Confederation. In addition to this extraordinary political behavior, the national bourgeoisie jumped forward, politically speaking. Business leaders became compelled to participate in party politics and helped to form a "new right" political movement. Business associations, for the first time, began to try to establish a link with civil society. The pattern of mediation established by the state during the Velasco administration were thus reversed. In the early 1970s, a passive, divided business class was manipulated by a strong state. In the mid-1980s, passing through a difficult and prolonged learning process, it became more active, capable of becoming united under an umbrella organization in critical junctures, less vulnerable to the political machinations of state elites, increasingly interested in party politics, and willing to establish contacts with other social groups. These developments did not transform the national bourgeoisie into a heroic class. They just strengthened its political capabilities in ways not seen before.

In that sense, the political process analyzed here sheds light on the complexities of Peruvian politics. This leap forward will be explained in detail in the following pages, beginning with the analysis of the factors that led to the rupture of the governing coalition, continuing with the political consequences that the nationalization of the banks generated and finalizing with an assessment of the legacy these changes have originated.

Problems within the Governing Coalition

At the 1986 Annual Conference of Executives, the partnership between the *grupos* and García was still solid but there were increasing tensions around a number of issues.[1] At the conference, and voicing the *grupos'* concerns, consultants such as Moreyra and Ortiz de Zeballos emphasized the need for the government to adopt measures to control the fiscal deficit and the drop in foreign exchange. They also demanded policy changes aimed at creating a climate of "confidence" for national investors and developing effective forms of *concertación* between the state and the private sector. Forecasting increasing economic problems, both Moreyra and Ortiz de Zeballos argued that coordination and consultation among coalitional partners was now absolutely necessary. The *grupos* were demanding, in their own peculiar, indirect way, to informally participate in the decision-making process and to be informed in advance about policy measures aimed at promoting private investment. But García was reluctant to share power decisions and to consider corrective measures to handle the economic problems.

In 1986, the GNP had expanded at the unparalleled rate of 6.9 percent and inflation declined from 158 percent to 63 percent. However, according to World Bank figures, the public sector deficit jumped from 5.6 percent in 1985 to 12.3 percent in 1986. Declining public revenues and increasing expenses stimulated economic reactivation, but it was predicted that economic growth would slow down and that an inflationary trend was underway. International reserves started to decrease dramatically since imports jumped from US$2,790 million in 1985 to US$3,625 million in 1986 and exports declined rapidly from US$3,792 million in 1985 to US$3,305 in 1986. In 1985 and 1986, direct investment of foreign capital was almost nonexistent and state investment decreased from 2.3 as a percentage of GNP in 1985 to 2.2 percent in 1986 (World Bank 1989: 40 and 55).

At the Conference, García did not listen to most of the suggestions made by business people. In his closing speech, the President offered only a limited number of concessions to the national bourgeoisie. For the most part, the state staunchly defended its right to decide what course of action to take and dismissed as unimportant the pessimistic predictions of the *grupo* consultants. *Grupo* demands to control the fiscal deficit, and their worries about falling international reserves, were considered exaggerated, unrealistic. García again appealed to the national bourgeoisie, and in particular to the "12 Apostles," to assume its political compromise and "invest for Peru." If he mentioned any policy decisions, it was not to change the policy orientation but to vaguely promise a set of initiatives to encourage private investment.

In November 1986, another event signaled the Confederation's decision to maintain good relations with García's government. Despite their condition of minor coalitional partners, the national bourgeoisie's sectoral fractions continued to support the government. That month, Vega Llona, President of the Association of Exporters, and well-known for his pro-government stance, was elected President of the Confederation. The sectoral fractions tried to establish a closer relationship with García by appointing a President considered to be a "friend" of APRA. But they also continued to insist on their demands for *concertación*.

A step toward improved relations with the private sector was taken by the government in February 1987, when the National Investment Council, an organization designed to promote private investment, was finally formed. The *grupos* and the sectoral fractions of the national bourgeoisie were represented in the Council in a fashion which reflected their respective statuses as primary and secondary partners of the coalition. For the *grupos*, their participation in the Council was problematic because it was a public bargaining table on private investment. For the sectoral fractions, their presence on the Council did not count because they had a minority of votes. In spite of the limitations of the government's most ambitious attempt at *concertación*, formal and informal means of dialogue and coordination were still viable ways of handling government policy changes on a number of specific issues. The government handled *grupos'* demands through informal channels. Relations with the sectoral fractions were based on meetings known as "*concertación* breakfasts" between state officials and the Confederation leaders.

The Debate on Accumulation and Redistribution

The main difficulty involved in promoting both capital accumulation and maintaining *dirigiste* and redistributive policies was that in early 1987 capital accumulation and resource redistribution were two processes at odds with each other.

Even if the various fractions of the national bourgeoisie disagreed among themselves about the merits of certain policies (policies which promoted certain fractions' interests but worked against the interest of other fractions), all business leaders coincided on the need to prioritize policies that promoted capital accumulation over redistributive policies.

The defense of specific economic interests followed a clear-cut pattern. Bourgeois fractions complained about regulations which adversely affected them, but kept quiet about those by which they benefited. Bankers wanted higher interest rates, but industrialists clearly favored a financial policy that subsidized interest rates.[2]   Miners and exporters demanded a devaluation of Peru's currency so as to bolster the export industry.   Those fractions doing business primarily in the domestic market, used and abused the "cheap dollar" policy.   They were fully aware of the fact that the situation could not last much longer and tried to take advantage of it by obtaining undervalued goods from the world market.   At the same time industrialists who sold final goods, bitterly complained about price controls, whereas merchants benefited from such a measure. On these matters, that is, the defense of particular interests, the Confederation left each trade association to battle for its own economic interests and did not intervene in the disputes over resource allocation.   However, despite the tremendous diversity of economic interests among various fractions, the national bourgeoisie agreed that emphasis on redistributive policies did not help foster capital accumulation at that time.[3]   The Confederation's main concern was the issue around which the fractions had stronger coincidences (criticism of redistributive policies) and where the danger of internal divisions was not present. The understandable differences of interests among sectoral fractions did not interfere with the ability of the Confederation to collectively mobilize the national bourgeoisie on questions concerning the general interest.

In early 1987, the national bourgeoisie's position on redistributive policies was made public at a time when the dangers of populism raised concern among their ranks. The most clear manifestations of their stance on this issue became apparent when the National Industrial Society published a series of public communiques in the press entitled "The Struggle Against Poverty in Peru" (*Industria Peruana*, June 1987: 62-67). The Society maintained that poverty could only be reduced if "wealth could be increased." In the Society's view, continued economic growth automatically spreads wealth throughout all of society. The Society argued that a number of conditions were necessary to promote capital accumulation in the private sector: the creation of a more efficient and less wasteful state, the de-politicization of the unions, policy stability, and the reinsertion of Peru into the world economy. The Society avoided any specific criticism on economic policies, (a cautious move given the division of interests within the national bourgeoisie), but was willing to send a message to the government about the principles that should guide future policy decisions.[4] What the industrialists and all the other fractions feared was a continuation of García's confrontational attitude with external forces (nationalism) and his willingness to retain popular sector support through redistributive measures despite the increasing fiscal deficit (populism). The classic Latin American conflict between redistribution and accumulation under populist regimes was beginning to unfold.[5]

At the heart of the policy debate was the question of what decisions should be adopted by the government in the future to promote long-term investment. It must be noted that promoting such investment had become a national priority when García declared 1987 the "Year of Investment," an announcement that helped to politicize the issue of private investment.

Carbonetto, President García's economic adviser, addressed this question in the following way in June 1987. After stating that a surplus of US$4,000 million had been generated by the private sector in 1986, he argued that:

> Reinvestment of the surplus is not a matter of the state, because it depends on private sector confidence in the Peruvian economy and society.... A businessman's decision to increase output when he can sell more is almost automatic, however, a long-term decision is another kettle of fish (*The Peru Report*, August 1987: A4).

The issue of surplus reinvestment, a surplus that García's government helped to generate by pursuing policies which stimulated the domestic economy, was seen from a different perspective by the national bourgeoisie. Business people believed it was the government's responsibility to create a favorable investment climate. In their version, "confidence" in the economy and society was generated by the state in order to stimulate private sector investment. The bourgeoisie recognized that surplus generated in the "easy phase" of the coalition was significant but it also believed that government figures were exaggerated by Carbonetto. The national bourgeoisie, worried about possible radical measures to be adopted by the state, argued that surplus was legitimate and that the state should not interfere with the right granted by the constitution to use the surplus according to its own goals. In their view, a confident investment climate could only be achieved if the government abandoned redistributive measures and promoted investment.

At a conference organized by the Confederation in March 1987 to discuss the investment issue with the government's economic team, the debate over accumulation and redistribution policies started to emerge.

On that occasion, one of the Confederation leaders dared to ask Carbonetto a critical question on economy and politics: "If it [investment] depends on us [the private sector], why does not the government let us establish the rules?" State officials answered back arguing that it was the state's function, not the bourgeoisie's, to adopt policies because it was the government's responsibility to look out for the general interest. When the debate became public, other officials intervened. Eduardo Bueno, Director of National Concertation, said that "national interests have priority over the interests of a group or sector." Bueno referred to entrepreneurs as the "impossible bourgeoisie," unable to create sustained economic growth or a decent standard of living for the general population. The Minister of Industry, Romero Caro, attempted another line of argumentation. He tried to convince the private sector to invest, referring to the urgent need to achieve economic growth in order to prevent the growth of guerrilla groups and to keep union activism and popular mobilization in check. He reminded the national bourgeoisie that investment "is not only a question of confidence but also of survival" (*Presencia* March 1987: 2).

It must be remembered that by 1987 the Shining Path had become increasingly active, and the Peruvian General Confederation of Workers (CGTP) had become more critical of García's government. In May 1987, CGTP called the first general strike of García's administration. Workers complained not only about labor issues, but also about the fact that unions were essentially unrepresented at *concertación* efforts. While the "12 Apostles" had on-going interactions with state officials, labor union demands were basically ignored. Business interests were given, according to CGTP, first priority treatment.[6] Fear of terrorism and union radicalism, however, were considered by the national bourgeoisie as a problem to be faced and solved by the government, not by business people. And the response to it had generally been capital flight. The debate about the roles and responsibilities of government and business continued until 1987. It revealed the unwillingness of the national bourgeoisie to simply accept passively more populist governmental policies. They simply assumed that the Velasco times were over and instead of fearing the government, the national bourgeoisie ran the risk and tried to exert influence on the government's policy decisions.

The conflicting goals of promoting accumulation and redistribution gradually increased. The President himself stepped into the fray when, on July 8th, 1987, in the last speech he made before he announced the nationalization of the banks, he openly criticized the national bourgeoisie. He declared that the business Confederation should be making proposals to favor the poor, rather than complaining about redistributive policies and demanding better investment conditions. The clash between the *aprista* political leadership and the bourgeoisie had already started.

Conflicting Policy Decisions and the Failure of Concertación

In this period, tensions within the governing coalition could have been channeled and handled through the existing mechanisms of *concertación*: the National Investment Council, the "concertation breakfasts" with the business Confederation, and informal meetings between the *grupos* and high state officials. However, in this critical moment policy decisions were taken by the government without consulting its allies. The "honeymoon" between García and the national bourgeoisie was over and divorce imminent. Which coalitional partner would prevail after the political storm that followed the rupture of García's governing coalition?

Policy decisions made between April 1st and July 5th, 1987 worried the national bourgeoisie for two reasons. First, the government did not inform or consult them, not even informally. Second, policy decisions were not clear; some policies stimulated private investment but others harmed the interests of the national bourgeoisie.

The government began to take the initiative by adopting a "package" of economic measures in April 1987, attempting to solve some critical economic problems. In response to the now dramatic decline of foreign exchange reserves, the government decided to "rationalize" the private sector's demand for foreign exchange by assigning priorities and fixing foreign exchange quotas for imports. But the government did not alter the exchange rate, thereby favoring firms operating in the domestic market and importing inputs from abroad. Since foreign exchange was getting scarce, the *grupos* and a handful of individual firms with permanent access to the state were the ones who could benefit from this policy change. Another governmental measure aimed at limiting the number of dollars that could be legally taken out of the country (through the banking system), from US$10,000 quarterly per person to 4,500 annually. This policy did hurt the major *grupos*, who seemed confused about these mixed policy signals.

To make things worse, in May 1987 a wave of dollar speculation was kicked off by expectations of a sudden devaluation of the *inti*, the national currency. The current official exchange rate was still 20 *intis* to the dollar, but the exchange rate on the informal (black) market jumped to 40 intis per dollar. Measures were taken to try to head off a "dollarization" of the economy but to no avail. The Central Reserve Bank sold US$50 million dollars at the official rate in order to stop dollar speculation, but instead of lowering the black market exchange rate, the sale refueled speculation. Customers bought dollars at a rate of 20 *intis* per dollar and sold them the same day on the black market at a rate of over 30 *intis* per dollar.

Other policy decisions taken in an attempt to lower the deficit were put into practice. The prices of some key commodities (gasoline and foodstuffs among others) were moderately raised and the government announced its decision to reduce the rate of wage increases for public employees. In addition, the government announced a tax increase on profits. A supreme decree authorized the government to issue "Public Treasury Investment Bonds" and to require that private firms operating in the most profitable sectors had to buy them with profits accumulated in 1986 (30 percent of the profits of banking and insurance companies, beverages and tobacco; 20 percent of other firms with profits exceeding 200 taxation units). This decision revealed that some state officials were angry because the private sector seemed to be delaying investment decisions.

Contradictorily, the government took a more positive approach toward the private sector on investment policies when it formed the "Investment and Employment Fund." This fund was meant to finance investment projects. The idea behind the Fund was that the state would provide one third of an investment project's funds, the project's minor shareholders would provide another third, and investors would provide the remaining third. The project's private promoters, who were allowed to have 51 percent of the shares, although they provided only a third of the total financing, retained control of property.[7] The "Investment and Employment Fund" proposal was strongly welcomed by the private sector, and in particular by the *grupos*, the most important potential promoters of investment projects.

The package of economic measures adopted in April revealed internal disagreements among policy makers, disagreements which continued to manifest throughout mid-1987. On July 5th, when García had just appointed a new cabinet, the government publicly announced the imminent implementation of another set of economic measures. If the measures adopted in April showed some willingness on the state's part to control the fiscal deficit, these July measures demonstrated the opposite. García raised the wages of unorganized workers by 25 percent, promised to maintain his program of subsidized massive employment and declared that interest rates should be lowered. He also insisted that the government would maintain its ten percent payment formula of the external debt and would not negotiate with the International Monetary Fund.

Populism and nationalism continued to inspire his actions despite business pressures to prioritize accumulation over redistribution. The

measures unveiled on July 5th were totally different from those suggested by the National Industrial Society when the debate about
redistribution and accumulation had started.

The reaction of the national bourgeoisie to some of these packages
of policy decisions was mostly negative. The increased limits on the
flow of dollars leaving the country were criticized by the *grupos* who
claimed that the government distrusted the private sector. In closed
meetings, the *grupos* demanded that the government ease currency
restrictions as a step to regain confidence and strengthen the coalition.[8]
This step, they argued, was essential to promote a proper climate for
investment. The obligation to purchase "Investment Bonds" was openly
rejected by the Confederation and the *grupos* and served as a point of
agreement around which all these class fractions were able to ally and to
unify. Even Vega Llona, the pro-government President of the Confederation stated that "the imposition of public bonds broke concertación
and had a negative effect on production" (*Presencia*, May 1987: 2). Some
trade associations even took the problem to the courts arguing that it
violated their constitutional rights. The national bourgeoisie's unified
opposition against the "Investment Bonds" proved to be effective because
it influenced the government's decision to rescind it. But the clash
created frictions between coalitional partners that eventually led to the
announcement of the nationalization of the banks.

Between April and July 1987, it was clear that the government
adopted policies which, as a whole, were not favorable to the national
bourgeoisie. García's July 5th speech revealed his disappointment with
the national bourgeoisie; *concertación* had not produced positive results,
private sector investment plans had been delayed and business openly
opposed redistributive policies.

APRA's Internal Disagreements

Rivalries between APRA leaders and a cabinet crisis also contributed to the growing tension within the governing coalition. A brief
look at the relationship between APRA as a party and García is necessary to understand the dynamics of these events (Ramos Tremolada
1988: 25).

When García was elected President, he successfully controlled
APRA and soon became the most influential leader within the party.
The fact that he was the first *aprista*, since the party's founding in 1924, to
ever become President of Peru enabled him to use his prestige to force
party leaders to create a new post (President of APRA) to which he was
elected. Following the 1985 general elections, *aprista* congressmen, and,

in fact, a major portion of the entire party, became subordinated to García.

Only young party radicals, and those who did not receive governmental appointments, remained independent, although all of them initially backed García and his government. García's unchallenged control of APRA lasted until early 1987.

Alva Castro's decision to resign his cabinet post and to become head of the Chamber of Deputies, (and, in time, head of APRA's party and presidential candidate for the 1990 elections), led to crises within APRA and within the government. Alva Castro was one of García's serious competitors within the party because of his intimate knowledge of the party machinery and his close relationship with party officials. As Prime Minister and Minister of Economy and Finance, Alva Castro wanted to use the cabinet's prestige to promote economic recovery and to lower inflation for his own political purposes, at a time when economic indicators were still positive. Alva Castro also conflicted with García's plan to modify the Constitution and thereby reassure himself of reelection in 1990.

García did everything possible to stop Alva Castro. First, he tried unsuccessfully to keep Alva Castro in the post of Prime Minister but on June 22, 1987, Alva Castro's resignation was officially accepted. Soon thereafter, García tried to prevent Alva Castro from being elected as President of the Chamber of Deputies. He failed as well. Contrary to what the President expected, Alva Castro was elected by a sizable majority. In fact, the congressional elections indicated a distrust of García on the part of many deputies.

Alva Castro's election was García's first political defeat as President. Alva's resignation also forced the government to appoint a new economic team at a time when internal disagreements about economic policies were open and the government was feeling trapped between business and popular demands. Before the cabinet crisis took place, there were two visible wings within the government: moderates and radicals. The moderates were willing to slow down domestic growth, promote export earnings and regulate the use of foreign exchange. This camp was closer to most fractions of the national bourgeoisie. Although Leonel Figueroa, President of the Central Reserve Bank, was the most visible leader of the moderates, Alva Castro was in fact the force behind the scenes. He was willing to comply with some demands of the national bourgeoisie in order to further his plans for becoming APRA's presidential candidate in 1990. In May 1987, when Figueroa was being pressed by García to resign, and made clear his position on accumulation and redistribution, he stated that:

A very intense increase in consumption could be dangerous since our productive apparatus would not be able to respond adequately. Such an
increase would affect our external front and would have a destabilizing
effect on prices. Such a course of action should be avoided. Our external
front is characterized by financial restrictions and with the inflow of foreign
currency depending on traditional export commodities, the search for formulas to solve the urgent current need for foreign exchange becomes a
clear priority (Banco Central de Reserva 1987: 5-7).

Figueroa, who was playing Alva Castro's game and had the support of
the national bourgeoisie, also became isolated from the most powerful
governmental faction and the President.[9]

The radicals, also known as "the audacious," rejected Figueroa's
position and accused him of being a "monetarist." This wing wanted to
continue to promote domestic growth, to maintain redistributive policies
and to accelerate the regionalization process. Carbonetto (adviser to the
presidency), Saberbein (Vice-Minister of Economy and Finance),
Tantaleán and César Ferrari (head of the National Planning Institute),
were the radical leaders. The "audacious" wanted to take control of positions that were becoming vacant because of the cabinet crisis and to
direct the economy toward "revolutionary" goals.

The national bourgeoisie, in this process, was not entirely absent
from the events that led to García's first cabinet crisis. The *grupos* and
the Confederation backed Figueroa and expected the government to
moderate its redistributive policies and strongly promote private investment. When rumors about Figueroa's resignation surfaced, both the
grupos and the Confederation openly defended him. Moreyra, former
head of the Central Reserve Bank and a *grupo* adviser, was an outspoken
critic of the candidate proposed by the "audacious" to lead the economic
team (Tantaleán). In mid-July, 1987, the dynamics of the internal political struggle taking place became clear during a televised debate between
Moreyra and Tantaleán. On this occasion, Moreyra took advantage of
his experience and publicly ridiculed Tantaleán (who was supposed to
replace Figueroa as President of the Central Reserve Bank), thereby
increasing political tensions between García and the national
bourgeoisie.

García, the dominant player in the decision-making process, finally
decided on a course of action. Appointments to the new cabinet were
completed by mid-July. Guillermo Larco, a moderate *aprista*, was designated the cabinet's leader, but all the key economic posts were filled by
radicals (Saberbein as Minister of Economy and Finance, Ferrari as General Manager of the Central Reserve Bank). Despite concessions to the
party hierarchy, which was allowed to select the Prime Minister, key

cabinet appointments went to the "audacious." As a result of this, the national bourgeoisie lost the chance of having an economic team sensitive to its demands and became alienated from the presidency. In this critical period, both the *grupos* and the Confederation criticized rather than supported the radicals and, by doing so, lost contact with García. A *grupo* spokesmen, Juan Francisco Raffo, later described this as a terrible political mistake (*The Peru Report*, October 1987: D3).

The Dynamics of Conflict

The rupture of the coalition came when García, supported by party radicals, decided to nationalize the banks in July 1987. The demands of the national bourgeoisie to force García to privilege capital accumulation over redistributive measures appeared at a moment when a cabinet crisis emerged and contributed to altering a delicate balance of forces between APRA's moderate and radical wings.

The Revival of a Radical Proposal

Within APRA's radicals, there were two main political enemies, one external and one internal. The radicals have always considered the possibility of attacking not only external forces (identified mainly with the International Monetary Fund), which they viewed as the main enemy from the early days of García's administration, but also the *grupos*, the most powerful internal enemy. Their plan was to reshuffle the governing coalition by siding with sectoral fractions and small-sized industrialists and use the banking resources to foster capital accumulation and maintain redistributive policies. It was a desperate and not well calculated attempt to restore Velasco's statist strategy.

In early 1985, before the elections, a proposal to form an alliance with the *grupos* gained momentum in APRA both because the party's conservative wing (headed by Second Vice-President Luis Alberto Sánchez) was still influential and because Garcia preferred to mediate conflicts between the two wings, emphasizing the importance of unity to win the elections. This delicate balance of power within the party was upset in early 1987 when the cabinet crisis gave party radicals an opportunity to side with the President and control the cabinet. During the crisis, the national bourgeoisie brought great pressure to bear on García, demanding both more concessions in the economic policy arena and a greater share of power. The national bourgeoisie also blocked and criticized García's populist and nationalist policies, claiming that accumulation (and confidence to invest) were to be the first policy priority. In doing so, the bourgeoisie contributed to alter García's role as mediator within the party, and pushed him, without knowing it, into abandoning his pragmatic posture toward the *grupos*.

For the radical wing of APRA, the *grupos* were an extremely powerful and unreliable ally. They were unreliable for two reasons: first, because they did not support nationalist policies and criticized the overtones of García's nationalist foreign policy;[10] and second, because although the *grupos* where the main beneficiaries of economic policies they were not investing their profits. The radicals suspected that the *grupos* were engaged in capital flight, were directly involved in speculation with the exchange rate and were provoking a shortage of goods and a black market. The *grupos* were seen as powerful because they controlled key resources, (most of the country's private credit and a large number of Peru's top firms), and exerted a silent but effective influence on both the state and the party (through clientelism). For the radicals, the *grupos'* power was most clearly demonstrated in their ability to resist reform projects such as financial decentralization and state regionalization. Both García and the radical wing of the party considered the projects crucial to transform Peru's economic and political structures.[11] The *grupos* were thus seen as an obstacle to achieve social justice and national development.

The nationalization project meant, for the party radicals and García, an open confrontation with the *grupos* but not necessarily a confrontation with the national bourgeoisie as a whole. The "audacious" considered the nationalization necessary because it gave the state resources to promote domestic growth and seemed a way to stop the growth of guerrilla groups and ease social tensions. A break with the *grupos* was possible if a new alliance could be arranged. The radicals' idea was to isolate the *grupos* and gain support from industrialists, the middle class, the informal sector, the urban poor, workers and peasants. The plan also included an alliance with the United Left, a coalition of socialist parties led by Alfonso Barrantes, who favored García's radical policies. For the radicals, the control of banking resources had the additional advantage of luring the weaker sectoral fractions with the idea of "democratizing" credit.

The adoption of such a tactic was considered off and on within APRA beginning in the early 1980s, but it truly reemerged as an option in the midst of the cabinet crisis. The plan to take over key resources and use them to harness development for national and social goals was already detailed in García's 1982 book *El futuro diferente*. The idea also appeared in a secret party proposal, prepared in 1984, entitled "*Plan Peru*." It should also be recalled that, in his July 1986 speech, García explicitly mentioned that "some sectors" demanded the nationalization of *grupos'* resources. In early 1987, the possibility of adopting such a strategy emerged again.

García decided to nationalize the financial system in May 1987, when he appointed a team to prepare a report and guidelines for his policy. The team included the "audacious" and García's main political adviser, Carlos Franco.[12] Research secretly conducted by the team seemed to confirm the supposition that the *grupos* were directly responsible for capital flight and currency speculation, two problems which worried policy makers considerably.[13] The research also led to the conclusion that credit was extremely concentrated in the hands of a small number of powerful firms, most of them operating in Lima, and that private investment projects were delayed by the *grupos*. Franco indirectly spoke of the need to change the alliance a few days before the nationalization was announced. In an editorial page published in the June 1987 issue of *Socialismo y Participación*, Franco's think tank criticized the government's alliance with the "12 Apostles" and proposed alternatives such as:

> Reformulating the strategy of economic policies, which have so far been based on an alliance between the state and large private firms. As things are nowadays, they [the *grupos*] gain and the state (that is, all Peruvians) loses (June 1987: ix).

Franco, who exerted an important intellectual influence upon García and the radicals as a former Velasco adviser, strongly argued that the alliance with the *grupos* had been turned into a zero sum game that could not continue any longer.

Chronology of the Nationalization

In this context, García made the final decision to nationalize the banking system the first week of July, with only three weeks left to announce it during the state of the union address of July 28th.[14] The project would affect 26 firms comprising the banking system (ten commercial banks, six finance firms and 17 insurance companies), but would not include the *grupos'* non-financial firms.[15]

The final steps toward the nationalization were carried out in five days. On Saturday the 23th, and Sunday the 24th, the government suspended telex and fax services to foreign countries. Monday the 27th, and Tuesday the 28th, were declared bank holidays and Lima's stock market and foreign exchange houses were ordered to close. On July

28th, leaders of the United Left (Barrantes and others) who had close ties with García were invited to the Presidential Palace and personally informed by García about the details of the project. An hour later, García drove to Plaza Bolívar, where Congress meets, to make his surprise announcement.

From the point of view of a surprise attack the nationalization project was initially successful. Very few party leaders were consulted.[16] Even cabinet members and the military were only informed of García's decision two days before García's speech. Despite having heard rumors, neither the *grupos* nor trade association leaders knew in advance what was actually happening and thus were totally unable to prevent the nationalization. Their ties to Prime Minister Larco and to Alva Castro, the newly elected President of the Chamber of Deputies, did not aid them in obtaining accurate information. By the time Larco and Alva Castro learned what was happening, it was too late. They possessed neither information nor access to the team that prepared the takeover. According to Piccini, one of García's friends and a former President of the Confederation:

> By Friday [July 22nd] rumors started circulating. The trade association's leaders met at CONFIEP on Friday night, Saturday and Sunday because there were people talking about a bank takeover. But we concluded that the government would lose on all counts (fall of investments, negative image, etc.) and that it was only a rumor. I left for vacations, as did many others, and learned the news while abroad.[17]

The decision was made without the cabinet, APRA or Congressional leaders knowing in advance about the specific details of the nationalization project and, once announced it, was imposed on APRA and its congressional delegation.[18] The chronology of events was as follows. Because Congress had to approve the draft law sent by the executive in order to carry out the expropriation, the government issued Supreme Decree No. 158-87 EF, intervening in the firms, dissolving the Board of Directors of all firms being nationalized and forbidding shareholder meetings. Alva Castro, President of the Chamber of Deputies, was caught off guard by García's move to the left. He had to approve the draft law in a single session (on August 13th) and pass it to the Senate.[19] But business reactions (to be explained in detail further on) were quick and effective. At the request of the Confederation, a court order declared the intervention unconstitutional because the state had not yet purchased the shares. This was a major setback because García was forced to withdraw the government-appointed managerial commissions, and the firms were once again administered by the private sector. In the meantime, Congress discussed it at length over the course of 20 sessions in a two-month period and finally approved a modified version on September 28th. García waited another two weeks, until October 11th, to officially approve the legislation now labeled Expropriation Law No. 24723.[20] The government then limited the takeover to two banks (Banco de Crédito and Banco Wiese) and one finance firm (Financiera de Crédito), but only for a short period of time, since the owners of these firms obtained injunctions ordering private administration of the firms. In the end, amidst a climate of national polarization, the national bourgeoisie fiercely attacked García and the nationalization law was never fully put into practice. The state was unable to take hold of Banco de Crédito, García's main target, because its owners agreed to transfer the *grupos'* shares to its 5,700 employees (an arrangement permitted by the law, as a result of modifications Congress had made). In 1988, the state withdrew the management commissions from Banco Wiese and Financiera de Crédito and did not show any further intention to buy the firms' shares and assume full control of the banking system. In a short period of time, García and the radicals were totally defeated and, since the governing coalition collapsed in the battle over the banks, they became increasingly isolated. Why was the government so rapidly and so badly defeated?

The Takeover Attempt

García's inability to takeover the banking system resulted in the most significant political victory of Peru's new bourgeoisie. The bourgeoisie's previous organizational and political developments, (consolidation of the Confederation and renewed efforts to achieve internal unity), together with the errors committed by García and party radicals, explain this victory. In order to fully understand it, it is necessary first to analyze García's nationalization program and focus on its inherent weaknesses.

In his July 28th speech, García spoke to the nation of the need for nationalization. His arguments had a radical populist overtone typical of APRA's political discourse of the 1930s. According to García:

> The financial system is both the most powerful instrument of economic power (and, therefore, of political influence), and the major obstacle to the democratization of production and surplus accumulation.... [With the nationalization] the state promotes an essentially democratizing function by opening credit to economic agents which, like small-sized and medium-sized private businesses, workers' associations, informal

producers and peasant communities, have been systematically discriminated against by the private financial system.

In order to justify the nationalization, the National Planning Institute
delivered a paper to *aprista*'s congressmen which offered more concrete
arguments for such a measure. In this document, the Institute argued
that the *grupos* had betrayed President García. They had accumulated
profits without having made big investments, and stimulated capital
flight using the banks, (in particular, Banco de Crédito Peru International, through its offices in Grand Cayman and the United States).
According to this governmental source, such deposits had reached
US$310 million dollars by September 1986. Additionally, money sent
out of the country by other means totaled US$298 million in 1985 and
US$206 million in 1986.

These arguments were soon corroborated by García. In an interview given to *The Peru Report*, he noted that "The mass of profits generated by the country's economic reactivation began to find its way into
dollars. Prices began rising and capital flight increased, in part through
the banks" (*The Peru Report*, September 1987: 2A).

Although the government's accusations seemed convincing, the
unity and conviction of the pro-nationalization coalition was weak from
the beginning because of the following factors: (a) the *apristas* were
divided over the issue. The radicals and García favored the nationalization but the conservative party wing opposed it. The conservatives
inside APRA argued that the measure was taken in secrecy and in a
short period of time, when the government and APRA could not carefully plan it; (b) García's allies, the United Left and the popular sector,
were not convinced that García and APRA were committed to carrying
out the nationalization to its end or to maintaining support for policies
giving priority to the poor and the unemployed. Despite the personal
support Barrantes expressed to the program, most of the left remained
undecided.

APRA's party discipline was tested during the battle of the banks.
When the nationalization program was first unveiled, party discipline
was stronger. Over time, however, it began to weaken. Both the party
and Prime Minister Larco, despite the fact that he opposed the program
in private, voiced its public support. In the Chamber of Deputies, Alva
Castro forced party deputies to approve it, without amendments, in only
one session. But in the Senate, APRA's moderate wing whose members
cultivated ties with the *grupos* and the private sector, began negotiating
with the *grupos* in an attempt to avoid a serious confrontation with this
most powerful bourgeois fraction. When the national bourgeoisie finally
mobilized all its resources against García and his program, the pace of

negotiations between APRA and the *grupos* speeded up. García's dissatisfaction with party members became evident when he bitterly spoke
of APRA's lack of conviction in his speech to APRA's 1988 Youth Congress:

> The hesitation came from the party, the hesitation came from parliament. If
> such a law would have been approved immediately, as I had thought
> would be the case, we would only have had to resist attacks by the right for
> four months (*Expreso*, July 4, 1988: 4).

Hesitation, however, was only part of the problem. It was difficult for
García and the *apristas* to accuse the *grupos* of being responsible for capital flight and currency speculation. The reason is evident since both
were at least partly the government's responsibility. During García's
administration the state was unable or unwilling to control the *grupos*.
The government was also partly responsible for letting the banks participate in the coca-dollar business, a business which brought with it the
chance to profit from in currency speculation. It is more than probable
that a number of powerful *apristas*, (particularly those in García's inner
circle), were themselves involved in transferring deposits abroad and/or
participating in some other form of businesses in partnership with the
private sector.

When Dionisio Romero, President of Banco de Crédito and leader
of his family *grupo*, was interviewed on television, he stated that the
transfer of deposits abroad was perfectly legal and that the government
was fully aware of all the details pertaining to such transfers and could,
if desired, easily investigate the practice (*La República*, August 14, 1987:
17-18). However, the government did not carry out such an investigation, nor did it make public any of the information it already had about
capital flight and currency speculation. Information on the *grupos*' property structure, their extensive use of governmental credit, and their failure to reinvest profits, was all leaked to the United Left and the press,
but a thorough investigation into the other grave issues, (the informal
exchange market), was never conducted, or at least made public.

In October 1987, when Congress approved the law, García tried to
negotiate its implementation with the *grupos*, calling for a meeting with
the *grupos* and state officials. He was retreating and trying to save face,
but the meeting had no positive results. The *grupos* were unwilling to
negotiate and already knew that García was in a weak position. Even if
García tried at one point to force the *grupos* to accept the law by threaten-
ing to make information about their activities public or leak to the press,
the *grupos* held their ground. The *grupos*, too, possessed damaging
information about García (and, in all likelihood, about a number of other

apristas), information in which they felt certain the press and public would be interested. In fact, when the President refused to approve a transfer of shares to Banco de Crédito employees, a proposal advocated by the *grupos* to avoid a governmental takeover, the bank leaked evidence to the press demonstrating García's involvement in questionable activities.[21] This evidence included a xerox copy of a check signed by the President and his wife in payment for an expensive house. The press printed a copy of the check and García, unable to prove if the money came from his own pockets, was publicly embarrassed. At this moment, García was losing control of the situation and showed signs of being in a desperate position. The following statement reveals his state of mind:

> The law says that everyone has to obey it, and by God they [the bankers] will have to obey it, because the law comes from the people and must be complied with.... Enough of concessions, enough of conversations, prudence and patience (*The Andean Report*, October 1987: 188).

But in the end the law was not carried out, because the *grupos*, together with most of the sectoral fractions of the national bourgeoisie, were unwilling to obey it. They had the power to stop its implementation and they used it exerting pressure on the APRA, mobilizing public opinion and, finally, fighting a successful legal battle in which the courts essentially ruled the intervention of the banks unconstitutional.[22]

The nationalization program forced the García government to try to redefine its alliances with the national bourgeoisie and with other social groups as well. García tried to isolate the *grupos* and to side with the weaker fractions of the national bourgeoisie, fractions that he expected would back a demand for the "democratization of credit." He tried to form what he described as "a solid alliance of peasants, workers and the informal sector, with the middle class and national industry" (*El Comercio*, January 10: 2).

But the recomposition of political alliances with the popular sectors and the left did not work out. Labor unions did not fully understand García's shift to the left; why he had suddenly broken off his alliance with the "12 Apostles." The policy changes adopted by the government beginning in December 1987 to cope with a deep recession and an inflationary crisis, had alienated the popular sectors, whose standard of living had been declining since 1988. According to World Bank figures, in the first quarter of 1988 alone, the cumulative inflation rate stood at 54.6 percent, between January and August 1988 (base year 1985), real wages decreased from 138 in 1987 to 125 (World Bank 1989: 93 and 121). Both the concessions APRA and García made to the *grupos* during the congressional debate over the draft law, and García's inability to enforce the law, weakened support from the United Left, the labor unions and the popular sectors.

García's attempt to appeal to "national industry" and "small businessmen," and to isolate the *grupos*, also ran into obstacles. García's improvised decision to nationalize the banks created a climate of class solidarity among its various fractions. It must be noted that since the early 1980s the national bourgeoisie was experiencing a unitary trend and made recent demonstrations of cohesive action, when the Bond Law was nullified in April 1987. These developments were unnoticed by APRA and García, who were used to underestimate the "weak bourgeoisie." By nationalizing the banking system, the government moved against not only the interests of *grupo*-owned firms, but also the interests of thousands of shareholders, thus creating the conditions for class unity.

The *grupos* owned only 53.3 percent of Banco de Crédito's shares, 49.05 percent of Banco Regional del Norte's shares, 39.68 percent of Banco del Sur del Peru's shares, and 12.59 percent of Banco de Lima's shares. The remaining shares were owned by thousands of shareholders. Only in four banks (Latino, Mercantil, Financiero and de Comercio) were at least 92 percent of the bank's shares owned by the *grupos*. Furthermore, as shown in Table 7.1 insurance companies owned, in turn, a number of firms and were minority stockholders in various companies so their nationalization would have given the state control of several firms.

The extent of bourgeois interests adversely affected went far beyond those of the *grupos*, even more so since the program originally planned to nationalize all property, including that of minority shareholders. The government intended to nationalize all firms and all shareholders, a decision that proved to be improvised and imprudent. García's actions, rather than isolating the *grupos*, contributed to the growth of class solidarity.

In addition, and most important in understanding the developments of state/bourgeoisie relations in contemporary Peru, García's actions planted the seeds of fear at the prospects of a renewed statist threat, a fear that the national bourgeoisie had nurtured under Velasco's regime. Trade associations such as the National Agrarian Organization, the National Fishing Society, the Association of Radio and Television Companies as well as certain committees of the National Industrial Society suffered nationalizations under Velasco. All of these organizations condemned the nationalization program and supported the owners of firms that had been threatened by nationalization, despite the fact that they had been enjoying a positive, close relationship with the state. If, during the García administration a move toward unification was rapidly

TABLE 7.1 Investment of Insurance Companies in Other Firms in Cases Where Shares Represent More Than Five Percent of the Total, 1986

Economic Sector	% of shares
Real Estate:	
Inmobiliaria Bravo	90.55
Inmobiliaria Los Portales	15.64
Inmobiliaria Beta	20.20
Inmobiliaria Peret	99.00
Inmobiliaria Deinpesa	99.90
Manufacturing Industries:	
Backus and Johnston Brewery	18.37
Textil Piura	04.42
Universal Textil	27.56
Tejidos La Union	05.54
Peru Pacifico	08.00
Prolansa	11.54
Indunor	06.48
Automotriz Andina	05.37
Inca Motors	05.38
Reparaciones Automotrices	07.27
Explosivos SA	21.09
Construction:	
Constructora Montevideo	99.99
Constructora San Alberto	99.99
Constructora Muñoz	07.46
Other:	
Inversion Nacional de Turismo	17.60
Inversiones Centenario	10.00
Isisa	99.99
Segus	24.56
Plan Invest	23.40
Cia. Internacional	42.84
Cons. Depos SA	33.33
Fenper SA	99.99
Mercantil Cayma	20.00
Inversiones Cosepa	95.78

Source: The data in this table are drawn from 1/2 de Cambio (September 1987: 12).

and effectively set in motion, this was because the national bourgeoisie now had an umbrella organization, the Confederation, ready to be used for collective mobilization, and had finally become conscious of the fact that an attempt at unified action was necessary in some instances and should supersede the pursuit of fractional interests. All bourgeois fractions fought against nationalization, considering it a violation of property rights guaranteed by the constitution. To the private sector as a whole, the nationalization program was seen simply as a "first step" in the state's far reaching plans for nationalization. Likewise, leaders of the Confederation seemed completely convinced that García had devised a large-scale "plan to eliminate private enterprise."[23] The threat factor against private property as a whole was rapidly becoming a political reality, a key element of the political agenda.

García's improvised decision generated an opposite reaction to his government; it intensified and prolonged the conflict and instead of dividing and neutralizing the national bourgeoisie it fostered their internal unity and pushed them toward an intense process of politicization against his administration. The President, the "audacious" and their allies, were generating the opposite political results. García's comments on the nationalization program are particularly revealing of his errors:

> It was a big mistake to try to alter the distribution of wealth without first succeeding in isolating those few *grupos* negatively affected from the industrialists and the middle class (*El Comercio*, January 10, 1988: 2).

It must be noted that certain segments of the business community supported García, although in the end their support made little difference in the outcome of the struggle. The National Federation of Small Industry and a small number of trade associations representing businesses operating in the informal sector openly backed the government. They did so largely because they hoped to trade support for increased access to credit (Durand 1987b). The merchants' trade association (CONACO), which decided to leave the Confederation (CONFIEP) in early 1987, criticized the nationalization as an attack against private property but pointed out that García's goal to democratize credit was correct. However, these organizations were politically unimportant and their support was relatively meaningless. Most fractions of the national bourgeoisie which opposed the program wielded enough power to defeat García in a very short period of time. The allies García had with isolated organizations of the business class did not have any effect in terms of dividing the national bourgeoisie.

Internal Unity and Organizational Strength

A comparison of two periods, the early 1970s and the late 1980s, is necessary to understand the national bourgeoisie's process of political formation. From 1968 to 1975, Velasco adopted a series of nationalizations that negatively affected foreign capital, fishing industrialists, the landed oligarchy and certain manufacturing industrialists. Velasco also introduced a reform to gradually socialize private property in a number of economic sectors (*comunidades laborales*). Throughout this eight-year period the national bourgeoisie was unable to prevent or reverse these state initiatives. It was a sign that during the Velasco regime the balance of power between the national bourgeoisie and the state was not favorable to business interests. Velasco's military regime was strong and internally unified. It controlled public opinion and was able to neutralize the opposition, the national bourgeoisie included. It also enjoyed popular support, particularly at the beginning of his regime.[24] The national bourgeoisie was organizationally and politically weak. It had no ties with any of the major political parties or civil society and was accustomed to accommodate itself to shifting circumstances instead of acting publicly in defense of its interests. Trade associations were at that time feeble, fearful and lacked an umbrella organization.

In 1987, a little over ten years later, much had changed, and the political power of the national bourgeoisie was now something to be reckoned with. This change was brought about by developments experienced by the national bourgeoisie and by the fact that democracy helped it to defend itself against nationalizations. But the crucial factor was that the events took place at a moment when the process of political formation was already maturing. The Velasco administration, according to García, could carry out the nationalizations because:

> These kinds of measures were taken during dictatorships. In Peru the military carried out an agrarian reform with a silenced press and acting against second-rate adversaries, who no longer had real power, with no Congress and no real trade unions. Anybody can make a revolution under those conditions (*The Peru Report*, September 1987: A2-A8).

In fact, what García was learning was that the national bourgeoisie could not be considered any longer a "second-rate adversary."

During the Velasco administration, a new pattern of mediation between the state and the national bourgeoisie was established, based on a strong state that had a close and hidden relationship with emerging *grupos*, and the capability to isolate trade associations that opposed its reforms. The "sausage policy," of slicing apart the different bourgeois fractions, proved to be effective and continued in the next administrations (Morales Bermúdez, Belaunde). Under the García administration, the government made a sudden and imprudent attempt to nationalize the *grupos*, trying unsuccessfully to appeal for support to those fractions of the national bourgeoisie (industrialists, builders, merchants) that had until then been second-tier allies. In 1987, unity among bourgeois fractions was maintained, and the Confederation became an important factor in achieving internal cohesion, a factor that led to a political victory against García.

This new factor influenced events in the following way. The Confederation was presented with a perfect opportunity to attract the *grupos*, and the *grupos* found in the Confederation and organization through which they could mount a unified, effective, public defense of their interests. Before July 1987, the *grupos* had tried to influence events silently, by using the firm as a vehicle of political penetration of the state and by acting behind the scenes. These tactics showed their limits when the state attempted to nationalize them. The defense of the banks was more effective if trade associations, and not individuals (or firms), publicly attacked the nationalization. This could have been achieved at least in part through the Association of Banks, but its role would have been limited. The Association of Banks was the *grupos'* association and the situation called for a general defense of private property rights. Additionally, the public was unfamiliar with it, since the association always kept a low profile. Most Peruvians did not know that such an organization existed. But the defense of the banks was more effective if the *grupos* worked in conjunction with the Confederation.[25] In fact, the Confederation agreed to defend the *grupos* both as a matter of principle and because the Association of Banks was a Confederation's member.[26] Cooperation and teamwork gave the national bourgeoisie an unusual strength, a necessary condition to defeat García. In this confrontation between economic and political power, most forms of influence available to both the *grupos* and the national bourgeoisie were used. The Confederation enjoyed the support of its members, including the trade association of the media business (radio, television, newspapers and magazines) and the *grupos* mobilized their economic resources to influence APRA's leaders, congressmen and judges.

With all the organizational and economic resources at hand, the Confederation organized and led a campaign against the nationalization program. Confederation allies in this campaign included political parties such as Popular Action and the Popular Christian Party (and the newly formed political movement "Libertad"). The first two parties mentioned above were eager to establish ties with the national bourgeoisie and seize the opportunity to reenter the political arena in a stronger position after their electoral defeat of 1985. Other interest groups (the Association of Lawyers, members of conservative think tanks, right wing intellectuals and even conservative Catholic groups) also joined the campaign.

The Confederation's role was crucial. It held various fractions of the national bourgeoisie together and acted as public spokesman for the private sector. By doing so, the Confederation was also able to counterbalance the ads published by small businessmen and business people operating in the informal sector in support of the nationalization. The Confederation organized a public campaign and coordinated the publication of ads to maximize the use of resources to maintain pressure on government and mobilize public opinion (already polarized in two camps, in favor of and against the nationalization). Between July 31 and August 16, the nation's leading newspapers published 75 ads, all paid for by firms and trade associations; the newspapers published an average of 4.4 ads a day at a total cost of US$700,000.

The Confederation was also important in coordinating the legal defense of firms threatened by nationalizations. The measure was considered "unconstitutional" and individual firms affected agreed with Confederation leaders to challenge García's decision in the courts. This legal battle was also supported by Lima's Bar Association and it was carried out by the best law firms in the country.[27] In the end, García could not resist the counterattack and the government was forced to withdraw government-appointed management commissions twice (once on August 1987, before Congress had approved the law; and again on September 1987, because García intervened once more in the firms without compensating stockholders).

On the whole, García's defeat began with Congress's amendments to the original draft law. It should be noted that a shift in García's strategy occurred when he finally realized that he was unable to take over the whole financial system. At the beginning, when García sent to Congress a draft law, the goal was to convert all banks, insurance companies and financial firms into public firms. But when he saw that this goal was impossible to achieve, he retreated and proposed a partial nationalization to be initiated with a major private bank. The amendments introduced in Congress kept stockholders (each individual representing less than one percent of the bank's property) but the state could exert control over the administration of the nationalized firms as the major shareholder if it acquired the *grupos'* shares. The assumption was that only the state could buy those shares.

This formula, however, was cleverly used by the *grupos* who owned Banco de Crédito to defeat García and publicly embarrass him, converting the retreat into a major defeat. The *grupos'* scheme was simple but effective. They worked out an agreement with bank employees to sell them their shares on credit the same day the law was approved. In this way, banks employees, together with other small shareholders, became the legal owners of more than 51 percent of the shares, enough to control the bank. With this scheme, Banco de Crédito became a worker-owned bank that was neither in the hands of the state nor in the hands of the *grupos*. To make matters worse for the government, the *grupos* who used to control Banco de Crédito (Romero, Raffo, Brescia, Nicolini) managed to retain control of Banco de Crédito Peru International, with offices located in Miami, New York and Grand Cayman.[28] Sometime before July 28th 1987, the *grupos* decided to separate the international section of the bank from its Peruvian subsidiary. These *grupos* also continued to operate in the financial market since they were able to organize an "informal banking system" (*mesa de dinero*) through Inversiones Centenario.

The consequences of these critical events went even beyond a major business political victory and signaled the beginning of a new period of state/national bourgeoisie relations. Not only did a united bourgeoisie badly defeat the government but the rupture of the coalition led to a more complex business politicization process, to a new stage of political activism that was totally unknown to the national bourgeoisie. For the first time, the business class was becoming seriously concerned about such things as political parties, ideology, political alliances with the informal sector and, more generally, in the national political agenda. In that sense, 1987 can be considered a historical turning point and, if the legacy of this key critical juncture prevails, a major event in Peruvian political history.

The Legacy

The battle over the banks brought about a number of significant changes in the political organization and the type of behavior of the national bourgeoisie, changes that altered its pattern of mediation with the state. These changes are specified in the following way: (a) the internal consolidation of the business peak association and the social recognition of its role as spokesman of the private sector granted by the state and other institutions of civil society, (b) new initiatives of business trade associations to link themselves with the informal sector and to influence public opinion, and (c) the participation of business leaders in party politics.

The Confederation came out of this battle with a new sense of confidence and a larger membership. If in mid-1986 Confederation leaders seemed preoccupied with the fragility of their organization, a year and a half later their confidence in it had grown. Vega Llona, the Confederation's President at the time of the nationalization, remarked that "at the beginning, CONFIEP was a crystal. Now it is a rock."[29] The successful defense of private property and business fear of further nationalizations drove up significantly the number of members. Soon after the government's nationalization plans were announced, ten new trade associations signed up for membership (*Presencia*, November 1987: 1-2). Their victory over García helped to consolidate the Confederation both in terms of new members and in terms of a closer, more frequent relationship between the *grupos* and the sectoral fractions.

The Confederation had become the private sector's undisputed peak association, displacing in the process the Peruvian Institute of Business Administration and being recognized as a true representative of business interests not only by the new administration but also by political parties, labor unions and other interest groups, who granted the Confederation recognition of its importance. On this basis, the Confederation was able to establish contact with the Fujimori administration in 1990, an administration that did not attempt to play with their internal divisions or ignore business demands.[30]

This consolidation does not mean that internal divisions do not exist or that the Confederation does not have problems. It basically means that, despite a number of problems that are normal in business life, the Confederation exists as a permanent organization that is "ready to be used" whenever the circumstances force business people to speak with a single voice and defend the general interest.[31] For example, the grant from the U.S. Agency for International Development came to an end in 1990 and the Confederation was forced to stop publishing *Presencia*, its monthly newspaper, but it kept coordinating the defense of the general interest with trade associations' members. The Confederation had a weaker, less experienced leadership in the 1990-1991 period, but in 1992 elected as its President Aguirre Roca, one of the most distinguished members of the "*gremialista*" leadership.

The Confederation also played a leading role in terms of establishing a new and broader consensus over trade liberalization policies adopted by Fujimori's government in 1990. By doing so, the Confederation was sending signals to society about their position on a key policy issue in a clear, definite way. Despite the fact that the larger membership made it more difficult to reach a consensus, and that individual businessman and some trade associations tended to disagree on economic policies, the Confederation was able to express publicly a support to liberal-exporting policies as an expression of the will of the majority of trade associations. This decision did not provoke a rupture or paralyze its activities. The formation of business consensus and business ability to communicate its position on key political issues to the rest of society was one main legacy of the key critical juncture of 1987. This new business liberal consensus of the 1990s was also visible among the *grupos*. A number of major exporters, who split from the Association of Exporters, organized a new trade association, the Society of Exporters, led by *grupo* leader Juan Francisco Raffo (Castillo 1990 and 1991). Despite the rivalry between the two business organizations, the Confederation decided to incorporate the Society of Exporters as a new member while maintaining a seat for the Association of Exporters. The emergence of this new trade association, signaled the *grupos'* public compromise in favor of liberal-exporting policies.

The Confederation became a key political player in another critical juncture. Most business trade associations and the Confederation agreed to support Fujimori's decision to close Congress and the court system in April 5, 1992.[32] Soon after, as a recognition of the Confederation's crucial role in supporting the governmental coalition, Jorge Camet, former President of the Confederation (1990-1991), became an important cabinet member as Ministry of Industry. It was the first cabinet position held by a business leader representing the Confederation. As part of this trend, the Confederation also played a major role in the downfall of Carlos Boloña, the Ministry of Economy, in January 4, 1993, by openly criticizing him at the CADE 92 Conference (*Oiga*, December 7, 1992: 38-41). The presence of business leaders at the cabinet level was reinforced in September 1993, when Camet continued as Minister of Economy, Alfonso Bustamante, another *gremialista* leader, became Prime Minister and a third businessman, Efraín Goldenberg, was nominated Ministry of Foreign Affairs.

The national bourgeoisie's attempt to develop ties with other social groups was another important dimension of political change. The Confederation's goal was to initiate an alliance with its poor brothers, business owners operating in the informal sector. To this end, the Confederation signed a contract with Hernando de Soto's think tank, the Institute of Liberty and Democracy, to promote unity between "the formal sector" and "the informal sector." In early 1988, the "Formal-Informal Union" was created to defend the "economic rights" of the "business class" (ILD 1988). Other trade associations, in particular the National Industrial Society, also became very active in terms of providing advice and support to informal industrialists. These activities were limited and reached only the informals. Nevertheless, despite the little impact it had on the majorities, it was a significant departure from past practices, practices that emphasized isolation and lack of concern about Peru's serious national problems. The social gap between the economic elites and the masses continued to exist, but it was the first attempt of business leaders to build a bridge between the two. Their electoral experience in the 1990 elections (when the elite's candidate Mario Vargas Llosa lost to Fujimori), helped them to discover the importance of this issue and to realize the fact that the process was slow and complicated. It is part of the learning process of another, new dimension of politics. Whether the lessons will be assimilated and the business class will be able to make a great leap forward, that is to break with social isolation and to gain cultural hegemony, remains to be seen.

Compared to the bourgeoisie's self-perception in the 1970s, trade associations and their leaders adopted a more affirmative attitude in the late 1980s and early 1990s. In this new period business people began to openly advocate the idea that the private sector could play a positive role in the country's economic and social life. A campaign on television and radio was carried out during the battle over the banks and afterwards, in order to sway public opinion that private property could not play a positive role because *dirigiste* and redistributionist policies were preventing it from making a more significant contribution to the country's economy and society. Emphasis was now placed on establishing and disseminating the "liberal" economic doctrine.

The 1992 elections were the first to witness an active participation of business leaders in party politics, a process initiated as a result of the rupture of García's governing coalition. The dissolution of the alliance forced the national bourgeoisie to redefine its relationship to the state. This political crisis created the need to "conquer" the state and keep the political coalition against García united. The parties (Popular Action and the Christian Popular Party) were told that no economic collaboration would be given if they did not unite, a condition necessary to compete successfully in the 1990 general elections. The new alliance, whose members included the national bourgeoisie, Popular Action, the Christian Popular Party and "Libertad," the movement founded by Vargas Llosa, was formed not only as a defensive maneuver in response to attacks on private property, but also as a tool with which the national bourgeoisie could participate as active members of a ruling elite. The formation of the Democratic Front in January 1988 expressed the unity among conservative political parties, formed with the support of the national bourgeoisie.

The politicization of the national bourgeoisie became apparent in November 1987. A survey of members attending the 1987 Annual Conference of Executives revealed that 48 percent of those present did not participate actively in politics, 26 percent considered themselves party sympathizers, and only 24 percent were members of a political party. However, 76 percent concluded that their level of political participation "was insufficient" and felt they, "should participate more" (IPAE 1987). In addition to the rupture in the national bourgeoisie's relationship with the state, a general crisis in Peruvian society also forced the national bourgeoisie to seek control of the state. This crisis manifested in key economic indicators at the time when García ended his period. The economic recession in July 1990 reached a record rate of -19.4 percent and hyperinflation went over 4,000 percent a year; political violence also reached record rates in 1990, a year when the highest number of deaths occurred: 3,452 (*Oiga*, August 5, 1991: 5; *Caretas*, December 30, 1991: 26). This situation accelerated the business politicization process.

Before the takeover attempt, a *grupo* leader once stated that the alliance with García was based on the assumption that politics was a matter left to political parties and the President, not to business people: "when we [the "12 Apostles"] first talked to President García about the alliance with the big investors he said, 'leave politics to me'" (*The Peru Report*, September 1987: A-2). After the takeover, and when the general crisis broke out, the idea of "leaving politics" to some one else seemed dangerous. From 1987 on, pragmatism and accommodation were openly criticized as typical businessman attitudes toward politics. Many business leaders who politicized themselves during the battle over the banks, and acquired name recognition, decided to run for office. Some became candidates on an independent list, Somos Libres, mainly composed of business people. Somos Libres was headed by Francisco Pardo, leader of the Association of Banks at that time, and included such prominent leaders as Julio Piccini, first President of the business Confederation and Eduardo Iriarte from the Lima Chamber of Commerce. Other business leaders decided to join the Democratic Front. Miguel Vega Alvear, also a former President of the Confederation, became one of the founders of Libertad and a member of its Central Committee. Vega Alvear ran for a senatorial position, together with two other leaders: Ricardo Vega Llona and Rafael Villegas (third and fourth Presidents of CONFIEP).

The 1992 elections proved to be a painful learning experience for the new right and the business elites because Vargas Llosa lost in the runoff elections (32.5 percent of the votes, compared to 62.5 percent for Fujimori). The new right was defeated because of its inability to establish a closer link to the majorities and because all other parties (APRA, United Left) united against the new right.[33] But many business leaders, those who ran with the Democratic Front, were elected and began to learn the art of congressional politics. As part of this learning experience with party politics, businessmen also began to understand about the complexities of national politics and the need to maintain a difference between a political representation (through parties) and the organizational representation (through trade associations). In April 1992, the political representatives of businessmen fought against Fujimori's presidential coup but the Confederation and most trade associations backed the President. Despite the tensions generated between representatives and those being represented, the national bourgeoisie's more intense and direct participation in the political process proved to be a new, more complex and exciting learning process. The new right did not become the party in government in 1990 and the connection with business people became difficult in 1992, but the national bourgeoisie could manage to maintain influence on the political process. It was not possible to consider it any longer an "invisible class," or a minor player of the political system.

Conclusion

The national bourgeoisie shaped itself into an important political actor in the years 1987 and 1988, years marked by the nationalization of the banking system. García's move to the left came out at a moment when increasing tensions between the national bourgeoisie and the government appeared as a result of their differences in terms of economic policy changes to be adopted. García emphasized the need to maintain redistributionist policies and encouraged the national bourgeoisie to invest, in order to keep the pace of economic growth. The national bourgeoisie demanded that the government deemphasize redistributionist policies and promote private investment by adopting measures previously in accordance with it.

These tensions among coalitional partners occurred when a government internal crisis was taking place. Between April and July 1987, a power struggle broke out between radicals and moderate policy makers, supported by the national bourgeoisie, at a time when García had to form a new cabinet. In the end, García supported the radicals and decided to adopt a new course of action.

The decision to nationalize the banking system, a decision which terminated the governing coalition formed in 1985, was made rapidly and imprudently by García and the party radicals. García attempted to make the nationalization program possible by isolating the *grupos* and allying himself with the industrialists, the middle class, the popular sectors and the United Left. However, disunity between APRA's allies as well as the government's inability to ward off a counteroffensive by a strongly united national bourgeoisie, all contributed to García's defeat.

García's defeat had a number of short-term and long-term consequences. In the battle over the banks, the links between the Confederation and the *grupos* were strengthened, the Confederation consolidated its role as an umbrella organization and started to seek allies among businessmen participating in the informal sector. The political crisis of the relationship between the state and the national bourgeoisie generated by the rupture in the coalition, added to the larger crisis then plaguing Peruvian society, forcing the national bourgeoisie to attempt to participate in party politics. Business people, for the first time, decided to participate in the battle of ideas. The legacy of the 1987 key critical juncture was visible in the years that followed. A more active, better organized, more politically sophisticated national bourgeoisie became a primary political actor.

Notes

1. The relationship was a positive one, despite the fact that García forced the *grupo* leaders to attend the Conference and exposed the alliance to public opinion. Once the opposition learned about the "wedding" between García and the *grupos*, attacks became common.

2. On the negative effect of the defense of specific economic interests, see comments made by Chlimper at the 1987 Annual Conference of Executives (IPAE 1987: 294-295).

3. The national bourgeoisie knew that the government would soon be unable to maintain its redistributive policies. Demands to control the fiscal deficit were raised in order to avoid a tax increase on profits.

4. The concern felt by Peru's business world about "delinking" the Peruvian economy from the world market was expressed in *Perú Económico* (August 1986: 1-2). Most business people interviewed in 1986-1988 felt that García's stance toward the International Monetary Fund was unnecessarily aggressive. However, they supported García's external debt policy, and expected that, despite his radicalism, both the international banks and international financial organizations would be tolerant of Peru's problems.

5. On the problems of combining redistribution and capital accumulation in early Latin American populism, see Hirschman (1979 : 61-98). On García's populism, see Sachs (1989) and Paredes and Sachs (1991).

6. See the pro-labor journal *Coyuntura Laboral* (May 1987).

7. For an analysis of the "Investment and Employment Fund," see Campodónico (1987a and 1987b).

8. According to a highly-placed government official (interviewed in Lima, August 8, 1987), this reduction was strongly criticized by the *grupos*, particularly by those linked to Banco de Crédito. According to the same source, in private meetings between the *grupos* and state officials, the *grupos* claimed that if the measure was rescinded, most probably the exchange rate on the informal (black) exchange market would stabilize because "confidence" would be restored. Some

state officials suspected that there was some sort of connection between coca-dollars, the informal exchange market, and capital flight, and that the *grupos* were behind these activities. See *Semana Económica* (September 26, 1987). An interesting analysis on the political manipulation of the informal exchange market is found in *Actualidad Económica del Perú* (September 1988).

9. A manager of the Central Reserve Bank, close to Figueroa, confirmed that his resignation was a direct consequence of the struggle between García and Alva Castro. Interview in Lima, December 4, 1987.

10. In several interviews, *grupos'* managers and trade association leaders constantly mentioned that García's external debt policy was "necessary" to promote domestic growth but the attacks on the International Monetary Fund were seen as negative. Excessive nationalism caused concern because it made the national bourgeoisie more politically vulnerable if the private sector as a whole was attacked. Interviews with Luis Paredes, a member of the board of Banco Mercantil, and Edgardo Palza manager of the business confederation. Lima, November 5, 1987 and December 13, 1986 respectively.

11. In closed meetings held at the Development Finance Corporation in Lima, (November 1986), the representative of Banco de Crédito rejected the idea of opening bank agencies in poor areas of the country. However, he added that this bank was willing to open branches in the Upper Huallaga Valley, the coca-growing area. Interview with Alberto Graña, an economist who attended one of these meetings. Lima, January 5, 1987.

12. In May 1986, Franco, former adviser to President Velasco, a political adviser to García, argued for the need to break the alliance with the *grupos*, because they "make an articulation of interests with other social groups and classes impossible." See Cotler (1987: 95-96).

13. Portions of this research were published. See Alarcón (1987) and Anaya (1988a).

14. García decided that the plans for the nationalization had to be announced on July 28th, the date on which, according to a political tradition, an administration's plans for the coming year are set forth.

15. Detailed chronologies of the nationalization of the Peruvian banking system were published in several journals. See *Perú Económico* (August 1987: 1-2), *Quehacer* (August 1987: 15-19) and *The Peru Report* (August 1987). *The Andean Report* also published a chronology in several issues, between August 1987 and February 1988.

16. Those consulted included Villanueva and Negreiros, the two General Secretaries. García did not consult with APRA's National Executive Committee, headed by Sánchez, García's Second Vice President and leader of APRA's moderate wing. Alva Castro, the President of the Chamber of Deputies and García's main political adversary within APRA, was also not informed. Interview with a member of García's takeover team, Lima, August 10, 1987.

17. Interview, Lima, December 10, 1988.

18. According to Vega Llona, at that time President of the Confederation, he called his friends in the government and in APRA, but none of them knew what was happening. They informed him that there were only rumors. Interview, Lima, January 20, 1988.

19. By doing so, Alva Castro alienated himself from the national bourgeoisie.

20. On the several modifications of the draft law, see *Hoy* (August 1, 1987), *El Comercio* (August 14 and September 29, 1987) and *Sí* (August 17, 1987).

21. The proposal was sponsored by the *grupos* who control Banco de Crédito and supported by minor shareholders and most of the bank's employees.

22. García was defeated, but this does not mean that the *grupos* were unaffected. For the first time in Peru's post-oligarchical period, the Peruvian public learned of the enormous concentrations of wealth in *grupo* hands. Articles and books about "The New Owners of Peru" began to appear and were read avidly by the public. See Durand (1988b) and Malpica (1987, 1990).

23. The fear of nationalization prompted several trade associations to become members of CONFIEP. See *Presencia* (August 15, 1987), p. 8.

24. Velasco went on with nationalizations until the end of his period. In July 1974, he nationalized the newspapers, and, in 1975, the Marcona Mining Company, a U.S, multinational corporation, two measures that generated tensions within the military government. See Pease (1978).

25. Industrialist Carlos Verme once declared that the *grupos* saw the Confederation as an "inexpensive shield," an opinion that proved justified. The *grupos* put no effort into creating the Confederation, but once formed, they used it to their advantage.

26. A quick look at the ads placed by the *grupos* in *Presencia*, the Confederation's monthly journal, indicates how the *grupos* began to support the Confederation. In the journal's first eight issues (published between November 1986 and June 1987) financial-sector firms placed only ten ads. But in subsequent issues (published between July 1987 and September 1987), the number rose to 20.

27. Bribery, a common phenomenon in Peru, might also explain the fact that bankers' lawyers obtained an injunction in a remarkably short period of time. Corruption was one of the main reasons why Fujimori closed the judicial system on April 5, 1992.

28. According to a report on Latin banks in New York, Banco de Crédito Peru International was ranked number 33 (by assets) in 1988. See *Latin Finance* (July-August 1989: 26).

29. Interview, Lima, January 10, 1988.

30. On Fujimori's victory in the 1992 general elections, see Salcedo (1990) and Schmidt (1991). On Vargas Llosa and the role of the new right see Klaiber (1990: 133-135), Vargas Llosa, M. (1991: 15-75) and Vargas Llosa, A. (1991).

31. Interview with Edgardo Palza. Lima, June 12, 1992.

32. For comments on business continuing and generalized support to

Fujimori's presidential coup, see Pásara (1992: 53) and *Caretas* (April 20, 1992: 28-30).

33. A survey conducted in June 1989 revealed that the Democratic Front was seen as a party representing the elites, not the masses. Fifty-two percent of the respondents answered that Vargas Llosa's political organization "represented the business sector" *Caretas* (June 19, 1989: 16).

8

The Political "Making" of the National Bourgeoisie

The study of the national bourgeoisie as a political actor is based on a class analysis perspective, where economic and political power relations are understood as a complex, changing mediation between the state and the national bourgeoisie. This mediation is determined by the bourgeoisie's control of economic resources, a fact that helps to establish a special relationship with the state, particularly for the most powerful class fractions. Political factors such as the nature of the political system, the type of business political culture and the national bourgeoisie's organizational achievements also have to be considered to explain this relationship.

This comprehensive, dynamic, class approach is particularly important in Latin America, a region that experienced late industrialization, and where the domestic industrial elites are known to be economically weak. In Latin America, the political activation of the national bourgeoisie is, historically speaking, a more recent phenomenon that has been frequently misunderstood and not adequately studied.

At the beginning of the century, when the first manufacturing industries began to appear, the national bourgeoisie, as Haya de la Torre liked to describe it, was seen as an "invisible class." Since the 1930s, when the process of industrialization and urbanization speeded up, the perception changed. An overextended set of expectations about its political role led different schools of thought to view the national bourgeoisie as conquering the heights of political power beginning in the 1930s, when the first phase of industrialization and the political phenomenon of populism emerged. The studies on the national bourgeoisie, focused on countries that initiated earlier the process of industrialization and the opening of the political system (Brazil, Mexico, Argentina) and based their analysis on the assumption that the national bourgeoisie was the driving force of change.

In the late 1960s and 1970s, this optimistic vision was gradually replaced by a pessimistic outlook. Foreign capital penetrated so deeply into the domestic market, and became so influential in determining the pace and character of industrialization, that the national bourgeoisie seemed to be an irrelevant actor, lacking the qualities of its European counterpart. The early image of a "conquering bourgeoisie" was followed by that of a non-actor, a puppet class in a period where multinational corporations predominated as economic agents and military governments imposed their rule over society.

In the 1980s this image began to change. A new realist approach that moved away from the optimistic and pessimistic visions developed in Latin America and focused on the national bourgeoisie as a political actor. This realist approach recognized the importance of the national bourgeoisie in forming and sustaining governing coalitions and did not consider its "economic weakness" as a crucial independent variable. The study of the process of democratization initiated in the 1980s revealed that the national bourgeoisie played a critical role in influencing the areas's regime transition. The national bourgeoisie also began to actively participate in the debate over economic policy changes. In this period, governments needed to adopt liberal-exporting policies in order to cope with the debt crisis and continued gaps in the balance of trade. Despite internal divisions between class fractions still attached to the model of import substitution industrialization and those who favored integration into the world economy, the national bourgeoisie became capable of developing new organizational and political capabilities and of actively participating in the political process in response to changing circumstances. This political activation might not be so spectacular as to convert business people into a ruling, hegemonic elite, but it shows that the actor itself has changed in terms of its organizational and mobilizational capabilities. The economically "weak" national bourgeoisie compensated for the limitations posed by structural factors by becoming politically activated. Internal divisions were being compensated for by unified actions and trade associations were being coordinated by business peak associations. The bourgeoisie's traditional attitude of accommodating itself to the party in office, and of being isolated from the rest of society, was also fading away.

Peru is, within this context, an important case to be studied. The analysis of the bourgeoisie shows that both structural and organizational developments have been taking place in the 1980s, and that the challenges posed by the second Great Depression of the century, democratization and economic liberalization have forced the national bourgeoisie to politicize itself and actively respond to changing circumstances.

The analysis of the economic power structure in three distinct periods (prior to 1968, the 1968-1975 Velasco period, and the post-1975 period) showed a complex process of structural change. This recomposition occurred both in terms of the economic areas where capital was located and in the relative weight of national private capital vis-à-vis foreign capital and non-private forms of capital. Before 1968, prior to Velasco's revolution, the landed-exporting oligarchy still was the strongest national bourgeois fraction, but a number of changes were taking place that weakened its long-time predominance. These changes were occurring within the realm of the private sector, affecting the relative position of national and foreign private capital only. Both the rise of native industrialists in the urban-industrial area, and the stronger position of foreign capital in the manufacturing sector and export activities, eroded the landed oligarchy's economic hegemony. In this first period, the economy was still geared toward the primary-exporting area but the urban-industrial area showed signs of stronger dynamism.

In the 1968-1975 period, the property structure was radically altered in two ways. First, Velasco sponsored "structural changes" by eliminating the landed oligarchy, nationalizing foreign firms and introducing a number of socialist oriented reforms. The emergence of new types of property (state and worker-owned firms) diminished the role of private property. Second, the urban-industrial area developed rapidly and the economic structure was considerably modernized.

In the post-Velasco period (1975 onwards), attempts to change the property structure and reprivatize the economy were gradually achieved. Private capital was given priority over state-owned and worker-owned firms while state-owned firms were considerably weakened or sold out. The urban-industrial area of the economy lost its dynamism, but governmental attempts to dismantle the manufacturing sector and to reinforce the primary-exporting area made very slow progress. The third period seemed similar to the first but in fact Peru had not only a new structure of economic power but also a legacy of development oriented toward the urban-industrial area. Both factors made it initially difficult to reorient the economy toward exports and to allow the private sector to reign again as the predominant form of capital.

Deep changes in the economic power structure also occurred within the national private sector, an alteration that has been adequately analyzed thanks to a comprehensive, long-term approach. This approach has permitted a drawing of a more accurate map of the contemporary economic power structure, identifying class fractions with different power resources and sectoral location. A new bourgeoisie, known as *grupos*, emerged as the dominant class fraction that now occupies the upper ranks of the economic power structure. The *grupos* own and manage firms in various economic sectors as well as banks. Because of their diversified investment portfolio, and their privileged position in the private banking system, the *grupos* had become the most versatile and modern bourgeois fraction, with a vision of the economy as a whole and interests in both the urban-industrial and primary-exporting area. Below them are the weaker sectoral fractions of the national bourgeoisie, which have interests in specific economic sectors. The industrialists, as well as the miners, are part of this strata and do not constitute leading bourgeois fractions as some scholars claimed in the late 1970s and early 1980s, when the process of change was still unclear and the *grupo* phenomenon not well known.

Once Velasco abolished the old oligarchy in 1968-1969, the *grupos* and the sectoral fractions developed peculiar types of organization to mediate with the state. While the *grupos* used their firms' economic power to defend particular, selfish interests, the weaker sectoral fractions operated basically through trade associations. A pattern of mediation between the state and the national bourgeoisie evolved in the Velasco period. In the 1970s, the different fractions of the bourgeoisie were fragmented, and trade associations accustomed to act separately, each one struggling to defend its particular interests. In addition, business people in Peru had a very low propensity for participating in party politics, and were accustomed to accommodating themselves to the swings of the pendulum, in terms of political regime and economic policies. Politically and socially, the national bourgeoisie was isolated from the rest of society and concerned only with having access to the executive branch of government, the center of the decision-making process. The state elites (the political class) enjoyed ample room to maneuver in policy-making, because their alliance with the *grupos* and the sectoral fractions favored by economic policies made it easier to isolate those fractions negatively affected by policy changes. Lacking an umbrella organization, and being internally divided, the national bourgeoisie was indeed a weak political actor. Nationalizations of national private capital during Velasco's period, and the economic policy changes initiated in 1975, were taken without an active, effective involvement of the national bourgeoisie in the decision-making process.

The analysis of two governing coalitions, Belaunde (1980-1985) and García (1985-1990), demonstrates that the pattern of mediation between the national bourgeoisie and the state began to change. In the 1980s, the national bourgeoisie, despite differences of economic interests, became increasingly united and achieved outstanding organizational developments. As an umbrella organization, the Confederation of Private Entrepreneurial Institutions was formed in 1984 in an attempt to foster internal unity among class fractions. The emergence of the Confederation revealed the willingness of a new generation of trade association leaders, the *gremialistas*, to become more active politically. During Belaunde's government, policy decisions were made with disregard for the opinion and demands of trade associations negatively affected by its liberal-exporting economic policies. His government, which initially enjoyed the support of the *grupos* and exporters, became unstable when an economic recession weakened the governing coalition and the national bourgeoisie decided to promote policy changes. The national bourgeoisie was able to reverse some policy decisions and began to learn about the significance of unitary actions. In 1985, García formed a nationalist-developmentalist coalition in an attempt to establish an alliance with the *grupos* and those sectoral fractions favored by economic policies. García, however, tried to ignore the demands of the Confederation to participate in the decision-making process and attempted, as did his predecessors, to exploit the bourgeoisie's internal divisions.

In mid-1987, the situation dramatically changed when García broke the governing coalition by attempting to nationalize the banking system. Tensions among coalitional partners appeared in 1987, because of disagreements about the need to emphasize either capital accumulation (a position favored by the national bourgeoisie), or redistribution (a position favored by García and the party radicals). The alliance between García and the *grupos* was based on the assumption that private investment was critical to continue economic growth. But the *grupos* did not massively invest because they were expecting García to deemphasize redistributionist policies and to grant new economic incentives. In addition, they were involved in speculative practices with the exchange rate and capital flight. The coalition came under greater pressure when a political struggle within APRA broke out and ended up in the formation of a new cabinet willing to promote social reforms by nationalizing the banks. The national bourgeoisie actively participated in this political struggle but sided with the losing faction, the moderates, and became isolated from the presidency.

When the battle over the banks broke out, all bourgeois fractions were united under a single leadership and the Confederation successfully organized the defense of the banking system. In this key critical juncture, García tried to divide the fractions of the national bourgeoisie in order to isolate the *grupos*, the ones most affected by the nationalization program. In addition, García attempted to side with the industrialists and the informal sector who were in need of banking credit. But García failed to do so because solidarity among class fractions soon developed and the Confederation mobilized all fractions in the defense of private property. In this context, a remarkable degree of internal cohesion was achieved, particularly between the *grupos* and the sectoral fractions, and the Confederation strengthened its role as spokesman of the private sector.

One remarkable outcome of this period of conflict between the state and the national bourgeoisie was the defeat of García's nationalization program, the first major political victory of the Peruvian bourgeoisie in the post-1968 period, a victory that had long-lasting consequences. Soon after, as part of this process of backlash politics, the Confederation became internally consolidated when a number of trade associations joined its ranks, enhancing its representational role. In this process, the national bourgeoisie, through the Confederation, made its first albeit modest attempts to establish a bridge with informal entrepreneurs and break with social isolation. Attempts to disseminate ideas to influence public opinion about the positive role that the private sector could play to solve Peru's numerous and serious problems also became another significant initiative. Other political and organizational developments occurred. The national bourgeoisie actively contributed to the formation of a new political movement, Libertad. In this period, business leaders began to get successfully involved in party politics and were willing to put an end to the "politics of accommodation." During the Fujimori administration, despite internal tensions, the national bourgeoisie in general, and the business Confederation in particular, continued to play an enhanced role both in terms of supporting the pro liberal-exporting policy-orientation and backing the presidential coup of April 5, 1992.

As it had been observed, a remarkable process of political activation occurred. This process developed from within the national bourgeoisie, when a new generation of bourgeois leaders learned from failed unitary experiences of the 1970s and decided to promote internal unity among trade associations. This project was concurrently accelerated in critical junctures (1984, 1987-1988), which triggered the process of unitary action, giving impulse to the need of linking business people with the majorities and influencing the formation of a political movement closely identified with the national bourgeoisie.

The importance of these political developments to understand the process of political change are quite evident. In the 1970s and early 1980s, the state elites used to adopt public policy decisions (expropriations, macroeconomic policy changes) without facing a strong, organized pressure from the private sector. They could always count on their ability to isolate the bourgeois fractions affected by policy decisions and to neutralize their protest. Today, despite internal economic differences between dominant-class fractions (between the *grupos* and sectoral fractions, between exporters and manufacturing industrialists), the Confederation plays an effective role to defend business collective interests and to neutralize the effect of the bourgeoisie's economic differences by mediating their internal disputes. The national bourgeoisie's newly acquired ability to defend general business interests, its commitment to overcome social isolation, to participate in the "battle of ideas" and to become directly involved in party politics, indicates a political trans-formation. The organizational developments accomplished with the consolidation of the Confederation are a significant legacy of the key critical juncture of 1987, as is the politicization of the national bourgeoisie and its crucial role played in major political decisions taken by the Fujimori administration.

The "making" of the national bourgeoisie into a primary political actor, however, does not mean that a new ruling elite has emerged. The changes experienced by the national bourgeoisie have occurred mainly in terms of an economic internal restructuring that makes the *grupos* the most powerful national class fraction and in terms of being capable of acquiring an enhanced collective political capability that empowers it as a political actor. It must be remembered that its economic limitations are still present and condition its role in politics. The national bourgeoisie's structural weakness constrains its ability to influence society and politics and to bargain with other social actors because of its limited control of economic resources. But this limitation is one factor among others, a fac-tor that does not block its ability to play an enhanced role in politics. In addition, its condition as an economic agent changes over time and can-not be considered a permanent, immutable factor. In the 1980s and 1990s, the fact that the state could not be any longer an economic agent and that foreign capital became less active in the Peruvian economy enhanced its relative economic importance.

The economically weak national bourgeoisie is not any more a minor political player. Both Belaunde in 1984 and García in 1987 learned bitter lessons when they underestimated the national bourgeoisie's col-lective ability to defend its interests. Their governments ended up politi-cally isolated and considerably weakened. Neither as an economic agent, nor as a political agent, can the national bourgeoisie be ignored or underestimated. The lesson was learned by President Fujimori in 1990. Fujimori understood from the very beginning the changing balance of forces of interest groups in Peru in favor of the national bourgeoisie. Since the first months of his administration he bargained for their sup-port and established a solid alliance symbolized by the incorporation of several of the *gremialista* leaders as cabinet members. In fact, the national bourgeoisie, better coordinated and less divided over policy (the liberal consensus) and political issues (need of law and order above all), has become Fujimori's most reliable coalitional partner. At the turn of the twentieth century, in the final days of the populist era and the dawn of neo-liberalism, the national bourgeoisie has been a key player in the political arena, strengthening its political position compared to other players (labor unions) and maintaining, despite the conflicts and shifting circumstances, more stable forms of access to political power.

What remains to be seen in the last half of the 1990s and the twenty-first century is the national bourgeoisie's ability to break with social isolation, assume a social responsibility and contribute to the establishment of stable governing coalitions in the long run. The ability to defend business interests is then different than the ability to become a "hegemonic class." The national bourgeoisie has learned defensive tactics in difficult times. It remains to be seen if it can play offensive tactics, that is to take initiatives and build durable coalitions to defend them, and to be a stabilizing factor of Peruvian society and not merely one more element of the country's chronic political instability. At least its performance during the Fujimori administration show signs that they head in that direction. The fact that in 1993 the Peruvian economy has been stabilized, that foreign capital begins, timidly, to invest again in Peru and that the phenomenon of terrorism fades away (with Abimael Guzman's capture and surrender), may be other factors that enhance the chances of building up durable coalitions.

The making of the national bourgeoisie is relative but its political and organizational advancements cannot and should not be ignored. It is not, properly speaking, a "ruling class," a permanent, powerful and dominant actor of the political process, but politics in contemporary Peru cannot be understood without considering the role played by business. The national bourgeoisie and all its distinct fractions has to be studied because it has proved itself able to collectively defend its interests, to transform the system of interest representation and to affect the political process in key moments. Most likely, the neither invisible nor heroic national bourgeoisie will continue to do so in the next century.

Bibliography

Abuggatas, Luis. 1986. "Crisis de transición, asociaciones empresariales y partidos políticos: El caso peruano." Paper presented at the meetings of the Latin American Studies Association, Boston, Massachusetts, October.

Acedo, Henry Machado de. 1981. *Estado y grupos económicos en Venezuela.* Caracas: Editorial Ateneo.

Actualidad Económica del Perú. 1987. "36 años de economía peruana: 1950-1986." *Especial Estadístico* No. 11, (July).

Acuña, Carlos. 1985. "The Importance of the Industrial Bourgeoisie as a Political Actor." Unpublished paper. Department of Political Science, The University of Chicago.

Alarco T., Germán. 1987. "Fuga de capitales en el Perú. Destino del excedente." *Actualidad Económica del Perú*, No. 92 (August), pp. 36-40 and 49.

Alarcón Aliaga, Carlos. 1986. *Privilegios y capital transnacional.* Lima: Instituto José María Arguedas.

Alayza, Rosa. 1981. "Constitución económica y comportamiento político del empresariado industrial en la década del 70." Bachelor's Thesis, Departamento de Ciencias Sociales, Pontificia Universidad Católica del Perú.

Alberti, Giorgio and Luis Pásara. 1976. *Estado y clase: La comunidad industrial.* Pp. 5-43. Lima: Instituto de Estudios Peruanos.

_____. 1985. "Desarrollo y democracia: Algunas reflexiones sobre el caso peruano." In Gino Germani, ed. *Los límites de la democracia.* Pp. 203-208. Buenos Aires: Consejo Latinoamericano de las Ciencias Sociales.

Alcorta, Ludovico. 1987. *Concentración y centralización del capital en el Perú.* Lima: Fundación Friedrich Ebert.

_____. 1992. *El nuevo capital financiero: Grupos financieros y ganancias monopólicas en el Perú.* Lima: Fundación Friedrich Ebert.

Alva Castro, Luis. 1985. *La nueva empresa pública*. Lima: Imprenta del Ministerio de Economía y Finanzas.

_____. 1987. "El desafío del cambio." *Gente*, (February 26), pp. 35-42.

Anaya Franco, Eduardo. 1974. *Imperialismo, industrialización y transferencia de tecnología en el Perú*. Lima: Editorial Horizonte.

_____. 1987a. "Estudio de los grupos económicos en el Perú." Unpublished paper. Universidad Nacional Mayor de San Marcos.

_____. 1987b. "El grupo Banco de Crédito." Unpublished paper. Universidad Nacional Mayor de San Marcos.

_____. 1988a. "Banco Mercantil: Grandes intereses de un banco pequeño." *Actualidad Económica del Perú*, No. 96 (January), pp. 12-15.

_____. 1988b. "La inversión extranjera directa en el Perú." *Actualidad Económica del Perú*, No. 100 (June), pp. 23-30.

_____. 1991. *Los grupos de poder económico*. Lima: Editorial Horizonte.

Asborno, Martín. 1988. "Grupos económicos y estado." Buenos Aires: CICSO, Serie Estudios No. 59.

Ascher, William. 1984. *Scheming for the Poor: The Politics of Redistribution in Latin America*. Cambridge: Harvard University Press.

Aste, Daffós, Juan. 1984. "Southern: Sus tácticas de defensa." *Actualidad Económica del Perú*, No. 71 (November), pp. 16-18.

Aste Daffós, Juan and Alfonso Obando M. 1987. *Crisis y reactivación en la minería peruana 1971-1985: El caso de la pequeña y mediana minería*. Lima: Fundación Friedrich Ebert.

Astiz, Carlos. 1969. *Pressure Groups and Power Elites in Peruvian Politics*. Ithaca: Cornell University Press.

Azpiazu, D., E.M. Basualdo and M. Khavisse. 1986. *El nuevo poder económico en la Argentina de los años 80*. Buenos Aires: Editorial Legasa.

Azpiazu, Daniel and Eduardo M. Basualdo. 1989. *Cara y contracara de los grupos económicos*. Buenos Aires: Cántaro Editores.

Bagley, Bruce Michael. 1988. "The Hundred Years War? U.S. National Security and the War on Drugs in Latin America." *Journal of Inter-American Studies and World Affairs* 30, No. 1 (Spring), pp. 161-182.

Balbi, Carmen Rosa. 1987. "Sindicalismo y concertación." Unpublished paper. Centro de Estudios y Promoción del Desarrollo-DESCO, Lima.

Balbi, Carmen Rosa, et al, 1990. *Movimientos sociales: Elementos para una relectura*. Lima: Centro de Estudios y Promoción del Desarrollo-DESCO.

Bamat, Thomas Patrick. 1978. "From Plan Inca to Plan Tupac Amaru: The Recomposition of the Peruvian Power Bloc." Doctoral Dissertation, Department of Sociology, Rutgers University-The State University of New Jersey (New Brunswick).

Bambirra, Vania. 1973. *Capitalismo dependiente latinoamericano*. Santiago de Chile: Centro de Estudios Sociales.

Banco Central de Reserva del Perú. 1983. "El proceso de liberalización de importaciones: Perú 1979-1982." Banco Central de Reserva del Perú, Lima.

Banco Central de Reserva del Perú. 1987. "Memoria." Banco Central de Reserva del Perú, Lima.

Banco Continental. 1988. "La situación económica del Perú. Primer trimestre." Banco Continental, Lima.

Banco Mundial. 1981. "Perú: Principales cuestiones y recomendaciones en materia de desarrollo." Banco Mundial: Washington D.C.

Baran, Paul. 1957. *The Political Economy of Growth*. New York: Monthly Review Press.

Basadre, Jorge and Rómulo Ferrero. 1964. *Historia de la Cámara de Comercio de Lima*. Lima: Cámara de Comercio de Lima.

Beaulne, Marie. 1975. *Industrialización por sustitución de importaciones*. Lima: Escuela Superior de Administración de Empresas.

Becker, David G. 1983. *The New Bourgeoisie and the Limits of Dependency: Mining, Class, and Power in "Revolutionary Peru."* Princeton: Princeton University Press.

_____. 1985. "Bourgeois Hegemony and Political Institutions in Latin America: The Peruvian Case." Paper presented at the Annual Meeting of the

American Political Science Association, New Orleans, Louisiana, August-September.

_____. 1991. "Business Associations in Latin America." *Comparative Political Studies* 22, No. 1, pp. 114-138.

Bernales B., Enrique and Marcial Rubio C. 1981. *Perú: Constitución y sociedad política*. Lima: Centro de Estudios Promoción y Desarrollo-DESCO.

Blackbourn, David and Geoff Eley. 1984. *The Peculiarities of German History: Bourgeois Society and Politics in Nineteenth-Century Germany*. New York and Oxford: Oxford University Press.

Bonilla, Heraclio and Paul W. Drake, eds. 1989. *El APRA: De la ideología a la praxis*. Lima: Centro Latinoamericano de Historia Económica y Social and San Diego: Center for Iberian and Latin American Studies, University of California at San Diego.

Bottomore, Tom and Robert Brym, eds. 1989. *The Capitalist Class*. New York: New York University Press.

Bourricaud, Francois, et al. 1971. *La oligarquía en el Perú*. 2nd Edition. Lima: Instituto de Estudios Peruanos.

Bresser Pereira, Luiz Carlos. 1978. *O colapso de uma alliança de clases*. Sao Paulo: Editora Brasiliense.

Brown, Lawrence A. 1988. "Reflections on Third World Development: Ground Level Reality, Exogenous Forces, and Conventional Paradigms." *Economic Geography* 3, No. 64 (July), pp. 255-278.

Burgos, Hernando. 1988. "Industria: El dólar nuestro de cada día." *Quehacer*, No. 53 (July-August), pp. 49-62.

Caballero, José María. 1977. "Sobre el carácter de la reforma agraria." *Latin American Perspectives* IV, No. 3 (Summer), pp. 146-159.

Calderón, Fernando. 1988. *Búsquedas y bloqueos*. La Paz: Centro de Estudios de la Realidad Social.

Cámara de Comercio e Industria de Arequipa. 1972. *Guía 72*. Cámara de Comercio e Industria de Arequipa, Arequipa.

Cámara Peruana de los Constructores. 1986. *Annuarium '86*. 2 volumes. Cámara Peruana de los Constructores, Lima.

Cámara Peruana de los Constructores. 1986. "Memoria 1985-1986." Cámara Peruana de los Constructores, Lima.

Cameron, Maxwell A. 1989. "Cycles of Class Conflict and Regime Change: The Case of Peru." Doctoral dissertation, Department of Political Science, University of California at Berkeley.

Camp, Roderic A. 1989. *Entrepreneurs and Politics in Twentieth Century Mexico*. New York: Oxford University Press.

Campero, Guillermo. 1988. "Los empresarios ante la alternativa democrática: El caso de Chile." In Celso Garrido, ed., *Empresarios y estado en América Latina*. Pp. 245- 266. Mexico City: CIDE-UAM-UNAM/Instituto de Investigaciones Sociales-Fundación Friedrich Ebert.

Campodónico, Humberto. 1986. *La política petrolera*. Lima: Centro de Estudios Promoción y Desarrollo-DESCO.

_____. 1987a. "¿Adónde va el fondo de inversión?" *Actualidad Económica del Perú*, No. 90 (May), pp. 20-21.

_____. 1987b. "Los secretos del FIE." *Actualidad Económica del Perú*, No. 91 (June), pp. 4-6.

Canak, William L. 1984. "The Peripheral State Debate: State Capitalism and Bureaucratic-Authoritarian Regimes in Latin America." *Latin American Research Review* 19, No. 1, pp. 3-36.

Caravedo Molinari, Baltazar. 1979. *Estado, pesca y burguesía. 1979-1973*. Lima: Ediciones Teoría y Realidad.

Carbonetto, Daniel. 1983. "Las opciones para un nuevo modelo de acumulación: Sus límites." In Carlos Franco, ed., *El Perú de Velasco*. Vol. 2. Pp. 29-98. Lima: Ediciones Centro de Estudios y Participación.

_____. 1987. "Plan de inversiones para 1987." Paper presented at the forum "Encuentro Empresarial," organized by the Confederation of Private Entrepreneurial Institutions. Lima, March 18-19.

Carbonetto, Daniel, ed. 1987. *Un modelo económico heterodoxo: El caso peruano*. Lima: Instituto Nacional de Planificación.

Cárdenas, Gerardo. 1983. *El sector de economía social en el Perú: Cooperativas y empresas autogestionarias.* Lima: Centro de Estudios y Participación.

Cardero, María and Lilian Domínguez. 1982. "Grupo financiero y crisis actual del capitalismo." *Revista Mexicana de Sociología* (México), XLIX, No. 3 (July-September), pp. 887-926.

Cardoso, Fernando Henrique. 1972. *Las ideologías de la burguesía industrial en sociedades dependientes (Argentina y Brasil.)* 2nd Edition. Mexico City: Siglo Ventiuno Editores.

_____. 1973. "The Industrial Elite." In Seymour Martin Lipset and Aldo Solari, eds. *Elites in Latin America.* Pp. 94-115. New York: Oxford University Press.

_____. 1977a. "The Originality of the Copy: CEPAL and the Idea of Development." *CEPAL Review* No. 4, pp. 7-40.

_____. 1977b. "The Consumption of Dependency Theory in the United States." *Latin American Research Review* 12, No. 3, pp. 7-24.

_____. 1977c. "Las clases sociales y la crisis política de América Latina." In Instituto de Investigaciones Sociales-UNAM, eds., *Clases sociales y crisis política en América Latina.* Mexico City: Siglo Veintiuno Editores.

_____. 1979. "Teoria da dependencia ou analises concretas de situaçoes da dependencia?" *Estudos CEBRAP* (Sao Paulo), No. 1, pp. 25-33.

_____. 1981. "El desarrollo en capilla." Instituto Latinoamericano de Planificación Social, Boletín de Planificación No. 12 (Junio), Santiago de Chile.

_____. nd. "La cuestión del estado en Brasil." Mimeo. Departamento de Ciencias Sociales, Pontificia Universidad Católica del Perú.

Cardoso, Fernando Henrique and Enzo Faletto. 1979. *Dependency and Development in Latin America.* Translated by Marjory Mattingly Urquidi. Berkeley: University of California Press.

Casar, María Amparo. 1988. "Los empresarios y el estado en México: Un análisis político." In Celso Garrido, ed., *Empresarios y estado en América Latina.* Pp. 207-228. Mexico City: CIDE-UAM/UNAM/Instituto de Investigaciones Sociales-Fundación Friedrich Ebert.

Castillo Aramburú, Melba. 1988. "El papel de los empresarios industriales en la economía nicaragüense." In Celso Garrido, ed., *Empresarios y estado en América*

Latina. Pp. 97-120. Mexico City: CIDE-UAM-UNAM/Instituto de Investigaciones Sociales-Fundación Friedrich Ebert.

Castillo Ochoa, Manuel. 1981. "Proceso político y comportamiento del empresariado industrial: 68-75." Master Dissertation, Departamento de Ciencias Sociales, Pontificia Universidad Católica del Perú.

_____. 1986. "Identidad confundida: El movimiento empresarial en la crisis reciente." In Eduardo Ballón, ed., *Movimientos sociales y crisis: El caso peruano.* Pp. 69-164. Lima: Centro de Estudios Promoción y Desarrollo-DESCO.

_____. 1988. "¿La formación de una clase? Empresarios, política y estado en el Perú." In Celso Garrido, ed., *Empresarios y estado en América Latina.* Pp. 185-205. Mexico City: CIDE-UAM-UNAM/Instituto de Investigaciones Sociales-Fundación Friedrich Ebert.

_____. 1990. "Realineamientos, sorpresas y responsabilidades de la clase empresarial." *Quehacer*, No. 66 (September-October), pp. 46-52.

_____. 1991. "Empresarios: Promesas incumplidas." *Quehacer*, No. 70 (March-April), pp. 20-23.

Cavanagh, Jonathan. 1980. "Reflections on Class Theory Suggested by Analyses of the Peruvian Military Regime, 1968-1979." Doctoral Dissertation, Social Science Faculty, University of Gottingen.

Centro de Estudios y Difusión Social-CEDIS. 1988. *Los grupos monopólicos en el Ecuador.* Serie La economía ecuatoriana en los últimos años, No. 4, Centro de Estudios y Difusión Social, Quito.

Centro de Estudios y Promoción del Desarrollo-DESCO. 1981. *Estrategias y políticas de industrialización.* Lima: Centro de Estudios y Promoción del Desarrollo-DESCO.

_____. nd. "Estado y empresas públicas." Unpublished paper. Centro de Estudios y Promoción del Desarrollo-DESCO, Lima.

Centro de Informaciones y Estudios del Uruguay, ed. 1991. *Organizaciones empresariales y políticas públicas.* Montevideo: Ediciones Trilce.

Centro de Investigación Económica de América Latina-CIEDLA. 1984. "El empresariado latinoamericano." Centro de Investigación Económica de América Latina-Fundación Konrad Adenauer, Buenos Aires.

Centro Peruano de Estudios Internacionales-CEPEI. 1988. "La economía peruana en el contexto internacional." Informe de Coyuntura 1, No. 1 (June), Centro Peruano de Estudios Internacionales, Lima.

Chalmers, Douglas. 1972. "Parties and Society in Latin America." *Studies in Comparative International Development* 7, No. 2, pp. 102-130.

Chueca Posadas, Susana and Florinda Julia Alfaro Vallejos. 1974. "El proceso de 'hacer la América': Una familia italiana en el Perú." Masters Dissertation, Departamento de Ciencias Sociales, Pontificia Universidad Católica del Perú.

Claudín, Fernando. 1975. *The Communist Movement: From Comintern to Cominform.* New York: Monthly Review Press.

Coleman, William and Wynn Grant, eds. 1988. "The Organizational Cohesion and Political Access of Business: A Study of Comprehensive Associations." *European Journal of Politics and Research* 16, pp. 467-487.

Collier, David. 1979. *The New Authoritarianism in Latin America.* Princeton: Princeton University Press.

Collier, Ruth Behrins and David Collier. 1991. *Shaping the Political Arena: Critical Junctures, the Labor Movement, and Regime Dynamics in Latin America.* Princeton: Princeton University Press.

Conaghan, Catherine M. 1988a. *Restructuring Domination: Industrialists and the State in Ecuador.* Pittsburgh: University of Pittsburgh Press.

_____. 1988b. "Capitalists, Technocrats, and Politicians: Economic Policy-Making and Democracy in the Central Andes." The Kellogg Institute for International Studies, University of Notre Dame, Working Paper # 109.

Confederación de Instituciones Empresariales Privadas del Perú-CONFIEP. 1987. "Memoria 1986-87." CONFIEP, Lima.

_____. 1990. "Memoria 1990." CONFIEP, Lima.

Confederación Nacional de Comerciantes-CONACO. 1988. "Pese a las dificultades empresarios alientan recuperación." *Síntesis Semanal de CONACO*, No. 1592 (January 9), pp. 1-4.

Conniff, Michael L. 1982. *Latin American Populism in Comparative Perspective.* Albuquerque: University of New Mexico Press.

Cordero, Salvador H. and Rafel Santín, eds. 1986. "Concentración, grupos monopólicos y capital financiero del sector privado en México." In Julio Labastida, ed., *Grupos económicos y organizaciones empresariales en México*. Pp. 164-216. Mexico City: Alianza Editorial Mexicana-UNAM.

Cotler, Julio. 1975. "The New Mode of Political Domination in Peru." In Abraham Lowenthal ed., *The Peruvian Experiment*. Princeton: Princeton University Press.

————. 1978. *Clases, estado y nación en el Perú*. Lima: Instituto de Estudios Peruanos.

————. "Los partidos políticos en la democracia peruana." In Luis Pásara and Jorge Parodi, eds., *Democracia, sociedad y gobierno en el Perú*. Pp. 151-192. Lima: Centro de Estudios Democracia y Sociedad.

Cotler, Julio, ed. 1987. *Para afirmar la democracia*. Lima: Instituto de Estudios Peruanos.

Council of the Americas. 1980. "Country Risk Analysis: Peru." Washington D.C. Seminar Report, (December 17).

Cueva, Agustín. 1988. *Las democracias restringidas de América Latina*. Quito: Editorial Planeta.

Dahse, Fernando. 1979. *El mapa de la extrema riqueza: Los grupos económicos y el proceso de concentración de capitales*. Santiago de Chile: Editorial Aconcagua.

————. 1983. "El poder de los grandes grupos económicos nacionales." Contribuciones No. 18 (June), Facultad Latinoamericana de las Ciencias Sociales, Santiago de Chile.

Degregori, Carlos Iván. 1987. *Sendero Luminoso: I. Los hondos y profundos desencuentros. II. Lucha armada y utopía autoritaria*. Lima: Instituto de Estudios Peruanos, Documento de trabajo No. 4 and 6.

Demaison, Alejandro. 1985. "Las instituciones empresariales en el Perú." *Análisis Laboral*, (October), pp. 47-48.

Derossi, Flavia. 1971. *The Mexican Entrepreneur*. Paris: OCDE-Development Centre Studies.

Deuschter, Isaac. 1968. *El profeta desarmado*. Mexico City: Editorial Era.

Dietz, Henry. 1987. "Aspects of Peruvian Electoral Politics in Peru, 1976-86." *Journal of Inter-American Studies and World Affairs* 28, No. 4 (Winter), pp. 139-164.

Diniz, Eli and Renato R. Boschi. 1988. "Empresarios y constituyente: Continuidad y ruptura en el modelo de desarrollo capitalista en Brasil." In Celso Garrido, ed., *Empresarios y estado en América Latina.* Pp. 307-325. Mexico City: CIDE-UAM-UNAM/Instituto de Investigaciones Sociales-Fundación F. Ebert.

Domínguez, Jorge I. 1982. "Business Nationalism: Latin American National Business Attitudes and Behavior Toward Multinational Enterprises." In Jorge I. Domínguez, ed., *Economic Issues and Political Conflict: US-Latin American Relations.* Pp. 16-68. London and Boston: Butterworth Scientific.

Dore, Elizabeth. 1980. "La burguesía nacional y la revolución en el Perú." *Estudios Andinos,* No. 16, pp. 115-125.

Dos Santos, Mario. 1987. *Concertación y democratización en América Latina.* Buenos Aires: Centro Latinoamericano de las Ciencias Sociales-CLACSO.

Durand, Francisco. 1977. "Estudio de las relaciones sociales en el marco de la reforma de la empresa industrial, 1970-1976." Master Dissertation, Departamento de Ciencias Sociales, Pontificia Universidad Católica del Perú.

_____. 1981. "Empresarios y política: Ser o no ser." *Debate,* No. 16, pp. 47-48.

_____. 1982a. "Estado, capital y trabajo en el Perú." *Análisis,* No 10 (January-April), pp. 43-79.

_____. 1982b. *La década frustrada: Los industriales y el poder, 1979-1980.* Lima: Centro de Estudios y Promoción del Desarrollo-DESCO.

_____. 1984. *Los industriales, el liberalismo y la democracia.* Lima: Centro de Estudios y Promoción del Desarrollo-DESCO and Fundación Friedrich Ebert.

_____. 1987a. *Los empresarios y la concertación.* Lima: Fundación Friedrich Ebert.
_____. 1987b. "¿Y el pequeño capital?" *Quehacer,* No. 48 (September-October), pp. 32-36.

_____. 1987c. "La pequeña industria: Otro mundo." *Quehacer,* No. 49 (November-December), pp. 24-31.

_____. 1988a. "La nueva derecha se organiza." *Quehacer,* No. 50 (January-February), pp. 20-23.

_____. 1988b. "Los nuevos grupos de poder." *Actualidad Económica del Perú*, No. 100 (June), pp. 40-45.

_____. 1989. "La 'batalla' de los empresarios." *Quehacer*, No. 56 (January), pp. 24-34.

Eckstein, Harry. 1960. *Pressure Group Politics*. Stanford: Stanford University Press.

Encuentro Nacional de Autogestión-ENDA. 1986. *ENDA '86*. Lima: Centro de Estudios de Participación-Centro de Investigación para la Acción-Centro de Estudios y Promoción del Desarrollo/DESCO-Instituto de Empresas de Propiedad Exclusiva de los Trabajadores.

Espinoza Uriarte, Humberto and Jorge Osorio Torres. 1972. *El poder económico en la industria*. Lima: Universidad Nacional Federico Villareal.

Evans, Peter. 1979. *Dependent Development: The Alliance of Multinational Capital, State and Local Capital in Brazil*. Princeton: Princeton University Press.

_____. 1982. "Reinventing the Bourgeoisie: State Entrepreneurship and Class Formation in Dependent Capitalist Development." In Michael Burawoy and Theda Skocpol, *Marxist Inquiries: Studies of Labor, Class, and States*. Chicago: The University of Chicago Press.

_____. 1983. "State, Local and Multinational Capital in Brazil: Prospects for the Stability of the 'Triple Alliance' in the Eighties." In Diana Tussie, ed., *Latin America in the World Economy: New Perspectives*. Pp. 139-168. New York: St. Martin's Press.

Evans, Peter. 1986. *Ari: The Life & Times of Aristotle Socrates Onassis*. 2nd Edition. New York: Charter Books.

Expreso. 1989. "Entrevista exclusiva de *Expreso* al candidato a la presidencia de la República por el Frente Democrático." Suplemento Extraordinario (August 27).

Farnsworth, Elizabeth. 1988. "Peru: A Nation in Crisis." In *World Policy Journal* (Fall), pp. 725-746.

Favre, Henry. 1971. "El desarrollo y las formas del poder oligárquico en el Perú." In Francois Bourricaud, et al., *La oligarquía en el Perú*. 2nd Edition. Lima: Instituto de Estudios Peruanos.

_____. 1984. "Perú: Sendero Luminoso y horizontes oscuros." *Quehacer*, No. 31 (October), pp. 25-35.

Ferner, Anthony. 1981. "Clase dominante y desarrollo industrial en el Perú." *Estudios Andinos* 9, No. 17-18, pp. 75-102.

_____. 1982. *La burguesía industrial en el desarrollo peruano*. Lima: Escuela Superior de Administración de Empresas.

Figallo, Flavio. 1987. "La parcelación y los problemas de la agricultura costeña." *Debate Agrario*, No. 1 (October-December), pp. 10-17.

Fishlow, Albert. 1983. "The Great Latin American Depression of 1979." Unpublished paper. Department of Economics, University of California at Berkeley.

FitzGerald, E.V.K. 1981. *La economía política del Perú, 1956-1978*. Lima: Instituto de Estudios Peruanos.

Flores Galindo, Alberto. 1980. *La agonía de Mariátegui: La polémica con la Komintern*. Lima: Centro de Estudios y Promoción del Desarrollo-DESCO.

Franco, Carlos. 1983. "Los significados de la experiencia velasquista: Forma política y contenido social." In Carlos Franco, ed., *El Perú de Velasco*. Pp. 249-422. Lima: Ediciones Centro de Estudios y Participación.

_____. 1992. *El Perú de los 90: Un camino posible*. Lima: Centro de Estudios y Participación.

Frank, Andre Gunder. 1969. *Capitalism and Underdevelopment in Latin America: Historical Studies of Chile and Brazil*. Revised and Enlarged. New York: Monthly Review Press.

_____. 1972. *Lumpenbourgeoisie: Lumpendevelopment*. Translated by Marion Davis Berdecio. New York and London: Monthly Review Press.

Gallegos, Armando. 1985. *Mapa económico financiero de la actividad empresarial del estado peruano*. Lima: Escuela Superior de Administración de Empresas.

Gallón Giraldo, Gustavo. 1982. "Concertación simple y concertación ampliada." Serie Controversia No. 15., Centro de Investigación y Educación Popular, Bogotá.

García, Alan. 1982. *El futuro diferente*. Lima: Editorial Imprenta D.E.S.A.

_____. 1985. "La revolución social es nuestro objetivo." Sistema Nacional de Comunicación Social, Lima.

_____. 1986. "Mensaje a la nación." Sistema Nacional de Comunicación Social (July 28), Lima.

_____. 1989. "Reflexiones para nuestra burguesía nacional." *Caretas*, (October 16), pp. 18-19 and 24.

_____. 1991. *El nuevo totalitarismo*. Lima: Instituto de la Deuda Externa Latino-americana.

García de Romaña, Alberto. 1975. "Comportamiento gremial y político de los empresarios industriales, 1968-1973." Mimeo. Departamento de Ciencias Sociales, Pontificia Universidad Católica del Perú.

Garrido N., Celso, ed., 1988. *Empresarios y estado en América Latina*. Mexico City: CIDE-UAM-UNAM/Instituto de Investigaciones Sociales-Fundación Friedrich Ebert.

Germaná, César. 1981. "La oposición burguesa: ¿Hasta dónde va?" *Sociedad y Política*, No. 12 (August), pp. 7-19.

Germani, Gino, ed. 1985. 2 volumes. *Los límites de la democracia*. Buenos Aires: Consejo Latinoamericano de las Ciencias Sociales.

Gianotten, Vera, Tom de Wit and Hans de Wit. 1985. "The Impact of Sendero Luminoso on Regional and National Politics in Peru." In David Slater, ed., *The New Social Movements and the State in Latin America*. Pp. 171-202. Amsterdam: CEDLA.

Gibson, Edward L. 1989. "Democracy and the New Electoral Right in Argentina." Columbia University, Institute of Latin American and Iberian Studies, Papers on Latin America # 12.

Giddens, Anthony. 1975. "Elites in the British Class Structure." In Philip Stanworth and Anthony Giddens, eds., *Elites and Power in British Society*. Pp. 1-21. Cambridge: Cambridge University Press.

Gilbert, Dennis. 1977. *The Oligarchy and the Old Regime in Peru*. Cornell University, Latin American Studies Program.

Glade, William, ed. 1991. *Privatization of Public Enterprises in Latin America*. San Francisco: ICS Press.

Glewwe, Paul and Dennis de Tray. 1989. "The Poor in Latin America During Adjustment: A Case Study of Peru." Washington D.C.: The World Bank, LSMS Working Paper No. 56.

Gonzales, Raul. 1983. "Los secretos del señor García." *Quehacer*, No. 21 (February), pp. 14-27.

_____. 1984. "El despertar de Ayacucho." *Quehacer*, No. 31 (August), pp. 20-21.

Gonzales de Olarte, Efraín and Lilian Samamé. 1991. *El péndulo peruano*. Lima: Consorcio de Investigación Económica/Instituto de Estudios Peruanos.

Gonzales Vigil, Fernando, Carlos Parodi and Fabián Tume. 1980. *Alimentos y transnacionales*. Lima: Centro de Estudios Promoción y Desarrollo-DESCO.

Goodsell, Charles T. 1974. *American Corporations and Peruvian Politics*. Cambridge: Harvard University Press.

Gorriti, Gustavo. 1988. "Democracia, narcotráfico y la insurrección de Sendero Luminoso." In Luis Pásara and Jorge Parodi, eds., *Democracia, sociedad y gobierno en el Perú*. Pp. 193-212. Lima: Centro de Estudios de Democracia y Sociedad.

Graciarena, Jorge. 1967. *Poder y clases sociales en el desarrollo latinoamericano*. Buenos Aires: Paidos.

Gramsci, Antonio. 1983. *Selections from the Prison Notebooks*. 7th Edition. Edited and Translated by Quintin Hoare and Geoffrey Wowell Smith. New York: International Publishers.

Grant, Wyn and Wolfgang Streek. 1985. "Large Firms and the Representation of Business Interests in the UK and West German Construction Industry." In Alan Cawson, ed., *Organized Interests and the State*, pp. 145-173. London: SAGE Publications.

Green, Raul H. and Catherine Laurent. 1988. *El poder de Bunge & Born*. Buenos Aires: Editorial Legasa.

Guasti, Laura. 1983. "The Peruvian Military and the International Corporations." In Abraham Lowenthal and Cynthia McClintock, eds., *The Peruvian Experiment Reconsidered*. Pp. 181-207. Princeton: Princeton University Press.

Gutierrez Aparicio, Luis. 1981. "La promoción de las exportaciones no tradicionales en el Perú." In Centro de Estudios y Promoción del Desarrollo-

DESCO, ed., *Estrategias y políticas de industrialización*. Pp. 248-271. Lima: Centro de Estudios y Promoción del Desarrollo-DESCO.

Harbrom, John D. 1965. "The Dilemma of an Elite Group: The Industrialist in Latin America." *Journal of Inter-American Studies and World Affairs* 19, No. 2 (Autumn), pp. 43-62.

Hartlyn, Jonathan and S. Morley, eds., 1986. *Latin American Political Economy: Financial Crisis and Political Change*. Boulder: Westview Press.

Haya de la Torre, Víctor Raul. 1985. *El antimperialismo y el APRA*. 7th Edition. Lima: Ediciones Cultura Marfil.

Hazari, R.K. 1966. *The Structure of the Corporate Private Sector*. Bombay: Asia Publishing House.

Hernández Rodríguez, Rogelio. 1988. *Empresarios, banca y estado: El conflicto durante el gobierno de José López Portillo. 1976-1982*. Mexico City: Facultad Latinoamericana de las Ciencias Sociales.

Hiller, Barbara. 1979. "External Debt and Economic Development: The Debt Crisis in Peru." Doctoral dissertation, Department of Economics, University of California at Berkeley.

Hirschman, Albert O. 1961. "Ideologies of Economic Development in Latin America." In Albert O. Hirschman, ed., *Latin American Issues: Essays and Comments*. Pp. 3-42. New York: The Twentieth Century Fund.

_____ 1979. "The Turn to Authoritarianism in Latin America and the Search for Economic Determinants." In David Collier, ed., *The New Authoritarianism in Latin America*. Pp. 61-98. Princeton: Princeton University Press.

Hobsbawn, Eric J. 1971. "Peru: The Peculiar Revolution." *New York Review of Books* (December 16), pp 33-34.

Hughes, William R. and Iván A. Quintero, eds. 1987. ¿Quiénes son los dueños de Panamá?" Panamá City: CEASPA.

Hunt, Shane. 1975. "Direct Foreign Investment in Peru: New Rules for an Old Game." In Abraham Lowenthal, ed., *The Peruvian Experiment: Continuity and Change Under Military Rule*. Pp. 302-349. Princeton: Princeton University Press.

Iguiñiz, Javier. 1986. "La crisis peruana actual: Esquema para una interpretación." In Heraclio Bonilla, ed., *Las crisis económicas en la historia del Perú*. Pp.

299-364. Lima: Centro Latinoamericano de Historia Económica y Social-Fundación Friedrich Ebert.

_____. 1987. "Estatización de la banca: Lo que está en juego." *Quehacer*, No. 48 (September-October), pp. 15-19.

_____. 1988.   "Perú: Crisis, política microinstitucional y empresarios." Unpublished paper. Centro de Estudios y Promoción del Desarrollo-DESCO, Lima.

Imaz, José Luis de. 1970. *Los que mandan (Those who Rule.)* Translated and with and introduction by Carlos A. Astiz. Albany: State University of New York Press.

Instituto de Investigaciones Sociales de la Universidad Nacional Autónoma de México. 1977. *Clases sociales y crisis política en América Latina.* Mexico City: Siglo Ventiuno Editores.

Instituto Libertad y Democracia-ILD. 1988. "Los fundamentos para la integración de productores formales e informales." Mimeo. Instituto Libertad y Democracia (February), Lima.

Instituto Peruano de Administración de Empresas-IPAE. 1984. *CADE 84. Anales de la XXII conferencia anual de ejecutivos.* Lima: Instituto Peruano de Administración de Empresas.

_____. 1985. *CADE 85. Anales de la XXIII conferencia anual de ejecutivos.* Lima: Instituto Peruano de Administración de Empresas.

_____. 1986. *CADE 86. Anales de la XXIV conferencia anual de ejecutivos.* Lima: Instituto Peruano de Administración de Empresas.

_____. 1987. *CADE 87. Anales de la XXV conferencia anual de ejecutivos.* Lima: Instituto Peruano de Administración de Empresas.

_____. 1990. *CADE 90. Anales de la XXVIII conferencia anual de ejecutivos.* Lima: Instituto Peruano de Administración de Empresas.

_____. 1991. *CADE 91. Anales de la XXIX conferencia anual de ejecutivos.* Lima: Instituto Peruano de Administración de Empresas.

Instituto Peruano de Empresas de Propiedad Exclusiva de sus Trabajadores-INPET. 1985. *La autogestión empresarial urbana: Seminario taller, informe final.* Lima: Instituto Peruano de Propiedad de sus Trabajadores.

Inter-American Development Bank. 1987. *Economic and Social Progress in Latin America: 1987 Report.* Washington, D.C.: Inter-American Development Bank.

_____. 1990. *Economic and Social Progress in Latin America: 1990 Report.* Washington, D.C.: Inter-American Development Bank.

Jaquette, Jane and Abraham F. Lowenthal. January 1987. "The Peruvian Experiment in Retrospect." *World Politics* 39, No. 2. pp. 280-296.

Janvry, Alain de. 1981. *The Agrarian Question and Reformism in Latin America.* Baltimore: The John Hopkins University Press.

Jessop, Bob. 1982. *The Capitalist State.* New York and London: New York University Press.

Johnson, John J. 1966. *Political Change in Latin America: The Emergence of the Middle Sectors.* 5th Edition. Stanford: Stanford University Press.

Kafka, Folke. 1983. "Competencia y poder en el Perú: Ideas teóricas y aproximación empírica." Fundación Friedrich Ebert, Documento de Base para el Conversatorio.

Kenworthy, Eldon. 1970a. "The Formation of the Peronist Coalition." Doctoral Dissertation, Department of Political Science, Yale University.

_____. 1970b. "Coalitions in the Political Development of Latin America." In Sven Groennings, E.W. Kelley and Michael Leiserson, eds., *The Study of Coalition Behavior.* Pp. 103-140. New York: Holt, Rinehart and Winston, Inc.

Klarén, Peter and Thomas Bossert, eds., 1986. *Promise of Development.* Boulder: Westview Press.

Kong Torres, Walter. 1984. "Southern: Recursos necesarios que se 'remesan'." *Actualidad Económica del Perú*, No. 70 (October), pp. 19-20.

Kostova, Teminka. 1992. "Leaders in a Transitional Period: Risk and Adaptation." Paper presented at the international conference "Liberal Strategies of Refoundation: Contemporary Dilemmas of Development" organized by IUPERJ/Centro Latinoamerican de las Ciencias Sociales/International Sociological Association, Rio de Janeiro, August 19-21.

Laclau, Ernesto. 1979. *Politics and Ideology in Marxist Theory.* London: Verso Editions.

Lagos Escobar, Ricardo. 1965. *La concentración del poder económico.* 5th Edition. Santiago de Chile: Editorial del Pacífico.

Lee III, Reinsslaer. 1988. "Dimensions of the South American Cocaine Industry." *Journal of Inter-American Studies and World Affairs* 30, No. 2-3 (Summer/Fall), pp. 87-104.

Leff, Nathaniel H. 1974. "El espíritu de empresa y la organización industrial en los paises menos desarrollados: Los 'grupos'." *El Trimestre Económico* (Mexico City), 41, No. 163 (July-September), pp. 521-541.

_____. 1976. "Capital Markets in the Less Developed Countries: The Group Principle." In R. McKinon, ed., *Money and Finance in Economic Growth and Development.* Pp. 97-122. New York: Marcel Dekker Inc.

_____. 1986. "Trust, Envy, and the Political Economy of Industrial Development: Economic Groups in Developing Countries." Cornell University, First Boston Working Paper Series FB-86-38.

Lindblom, Charles. 1977. *Politics and Markets.* New York: Basic Books Inc.

Lipset, Seymour Martin. 1967. "Values, Education and Entrepreneurship." In Seymour Martin Lipset and Aldo Solari, eds., *Elites in Latin America.* Pp. 3-60. Oxford, London and New York: Oxford University Press.

_____. 1985. *Consensus and Conflict: Essays in Political Sociology.* New Brunswick and Oxford: Transaction Books.

Lopez, Sinesio. 1985. "Perú 1985: Entre la moderación y la realidad." *El Zorro de Abajo*, No. 1 (June-July), pp. 9-10.

Lowenthal, Abraham F. 1975. *The Peruvian Experiment: Continuity and Change Under Military Rule.* Princeton: Princeton University Press.

Lowenthal, Abraham F. 1983. "Peru's Ambiguous Revolution." In Abraham F. Lowenthal and Cynthia McClintock eds., *The Peruvian Experiment Reconsidered.* Pp. 3-43. Princeton: Princeton University Press.

Lowenthal, Abraham F. and Cynthia McClintock, eds. 1983. *The Peruvian Experiment Reconsidered.* Princeton: Princeton University Press.

Luna, Matilde and Ricardo Tirado. 1992. *El Consejo Coordinador Empresarial: Una radiografía.* México: Instituto de Investigaciones Sociales / Universidad Nacional Autónoma de México, Proyecto Organizaciones Empresariales en México, No. 1.

Malloy, James M. 1988. "The Politics of Transition in Latin America." In James M. Malloy and Mitchell A. Seligson, eds., *Authoritarians and Democrats*. Pp. 235-258. Pittsburgh: Pittsburgh University Press.

Malloy, James M. and Mitchell A. Seligson, eds. 1988. *Authoritarians and Democrats*. Pittsburgh: Pittsburgh University Press.

Malpica, Carlos. 1968. *Los dueños del Perú*. 3rd Edition. Lima: Ediciones Ensayos Sociales.

_____. 1976. *Anchovetas y tiburones*. Lima: Editorial Runamarka.

_____. 1987. "Los nuevos dueños del Perú." Fascículos de la *La Voz* (September-November.)

_____. 1990. *El poder económico en el Perú: Los bancos y sus filiales*. Volume I. Lima: Mosca Azul Editores.

_____. 1990. "Los ricos no pagan impuestos." Lima: Ediciones Amauta.

Mamalakis, Marcos. 1969. "The Theory of Sectoral Clashes." *Latin American Research Review*, No. 3 (Fall), pp. 9-46.

Mao, TseTung. 1951. *The Chinese Revolution and the Communist Party of China*. New York: Committee for a Democratic Far Eastern Policy.

_____. 1985. *Analysis of the Classes in Chinese Society*. Amsterdam: University of Amsterdam, Asia Studies No. 53.

Mariátegui, José Carlos. 1975. *Ideología y política*. 7th Edition. Lima: Editorial Amauta.

Marceau, Jane. 1989. "France." In Tom Bottomore and Robert J. Brym, eds., *The Capitalist Class*. Pp. 46-72. New York: New York University Press.

Martinelli, Alberto and Antonio M. Chiesi. 1989. "Italy." In Tom Bottomore and Robert J. Brym, eds., *The Capitalist Class*. Pp. 109-139. New York: New York University Press.

Marx, Karl. 1955. "The Eighteen Brumaire of Louis Bonaparte." In Karl Marx and

Friedrich Engels, *Selected Works.* Pp. 243-344. 2 volumes. Moscow: Foreign Languages Publishing House.

Marx, Karl and Friedrich Engels. 1955. "Manifesto of the Communist Party." In Karl Marx and Friedrich Engels, *Selected Works.* Pp. 21-65. 2 volumes. Moscow: Foreign Languages Publishing House.

Maxfield, Sylvia. 1988. "Internacionalización de las finanzas y concentración de la industria: México en una perspectiva comparativa." In Celso Garrido, ed., *Empresarios y estado en América Latina.* Mexico City: CIDE-UAM-UNAM/Instituto de Investigaciones Sociales-Fundación Friedrich Ebert.

_____. 1988. "National Business, Debt-Led Growth and Political Transition in Latin America." In Barbara Stallings and Robert Kauffman. 1989. *Debt and Democracy in Latin America.* Pp. 75- 90. Boulder and San Francisco: Westview Press.

Maxfield, Sylvia and Ricardo Anzaldúa Montoya, eds. 1987. "Government and Private Sector in Contemporary Mexico." Center for U.S.-Mexican Studies, University of California at San Diego, Monograph Series 20.

McClintock, Cynthia. 1988. "The War on Drugs: The Peruvian Case." *Journal of Inter-American Studies and World Affairs* 30, No. 2-3 (Summer/Fall), pp. 127-142.

Meisel, James H. 1962. *The Myth of the Ruling Class: Gaetano Mosca and the Elite.* Ann Arbor: The University of Michigan Press.

Mendez, María Julia. 1982. "Las cooperativas agrarias de producción y las parcelaciones: Situación actual y perspectivas." In Fernando Eguren, ed., *Situación actual y perspectivas del problema agrario en el Perú.* Pp. 95-136. Lima: Centro de Estudios y Promoción del Desarrollo-DESCO

Menshikov, S. 1973. *Millionaires and Managers.* 2nd Edition. Moscow: Progress Publishers.

Miliband, Ralph. 1969. *The State in Capitalist Society.* London: Wenfield & Nicholson.

Mills, C. Wright. 1956. *The Power Elite.* New York: Oxford University Press.

Minella, Ari Cesar. 1988. *Banqueiros.* Rio de Janeiro: Espaco e Tempo.

Minsburg, Naúm. 1987. *Capitales extranjeros y grupos dominantes argentinos/2 (análisis histórico y contemporáneo)*. Buenos Aires: Centro Editor de América Latina.

Moncada, Samuel. 1985. *Los huevos de la serpiente: Fedecamaras por dentro*. Caracas: Alianza Gráfica.

Monge, Carlos. 1988. "Características y representatividad de los gremios empresariales agrarios." *Debate Agrario*, No. 2 (April-June), pp. 25-50.

Mosca, Gaetano. 1939. *The Ruling Class*. Translation by Hannah D. Kahn. New York and London: McGraw-Hill Book Company, Inc.

Muñoz G. Oscar. 1988. "El papel de los empresarios en el desarrollo: Enfoques, problemas y experiencias." *Colección de Estudios de la CIEPLAN* (Santiago de Chile), No. 20 (December), pp. 95-120.

Murillo, Gustavo. 1986. "Hacia una ley de pequeña empresa." *Revista Peruana de Derecho de la Empresa*, No. 26, pp. 3-25.

Nuncio, Abraham. 1982. *El grupo Monterrey*. Mexico City: Editorial Nueva Imagen.

O'Donnell, Guillermo A. 1978a. "State and Alliances in Argentina, 1956-1976." *Journal of Development Studies* 15, No. 1 (October), pp. 3-33.

_____. 1978b. "Burguesía local, capital transnacional y aparato estatal: Notas para su estudio." Mexico City: Instituto Latinoamericano de Estudios Transnacionales, DEE/D/2 (July).

_____. 1979. *Modernization and Bureaucratic-Authoritarianism. Studies in South American Politics*. Berkeley, CA: Institute of International Studies.

Offe, Claus. 1981. "The Attributions of Public Status to Interest Groups: Observations on the West German Case." In Suzanne Berger, ed., *Organizing Interests in Western Europe*. Cambridge and London: Cambridge University Press.

Ogata Shimokawa, Clara. 1981. *Políticas explícitas de tratamiento al capital extranjero en el Perú*. Lima: Centro de Estudios y Promoción del Desarrollo-DESCO.

Ominami, Carlos. 1988. "Desindustrialización y restructuración industrial en América Latina." *Colección Estudios CIEPLAN* (Santiago de Chile), No. 23 (March), pp. 87-115.

O'Phelan, Fernando. 1988. "Marco jurídico en el Perú." *Actualidad Económica del Perú*, No. 100 (June), pp. 61-65.

Organización Nacional Agraria-ONA. 1986. *Directorio 1986*. Lima: Organización Nacional Agraria.

Ortiz de Zeballos, Felipe. 1989. *The Peruvian Puzzle*. New York: A Twentieth Century Fund Paper, Priority Press Publications.

Paix, Catherine. 1990. "Les Bourgeoisies des Tiers Mondes D'Hier a Aujourd'hui." In *Tiers Monde* (Paris), 31, No. 124 (October-December), pp. 725-734.

Palmer, David Scott. 1984. "The Changing Political Economy of Peru Under Civilian and Military Rules." *Journal of Inter-American Studies and World Affairs* 37, No. 4 (Spring), pp. 37-62.

_____. 1992. *Shining Path of Peru*. New York: Saint Martin's Press.

Paredes, Carlos and Jeffrey Sachs, eds. 1991. *Estabilización y crecimiento en el Perú*. Lima: Grupo de Estudios del Desarrollo-GRADE.

Pareto, Vilfredo. 1935. *The Mind and Society*. Edited by Arthur Livingston, translated by Andrew Bongiorno. New York: Harcourt Brace and Co.

Partido Aprista Peruano. 1984. "Plan del Perú." 2 Volumes. Partido Aprista Peruano-Secretaría Nacional de Sindicatos, Lima.

Parodi, Jorge. 1988. "Los sindicatos en la democracia vacía." In Luis Pásara and Jorge Parodi eds., *Democracia, sociedad y gobierno en el Perú*. Pp 95-136. Lima: Centro de Estudios de Democracia y Sociedad.

Patiño Guardiola, Bolívar. 1986. "Estado, empresarios y revolución." *Industria y Exportación*, No. 5 (April 1-May 15), pp. 20-21.

Pease García, Henry. 1977. *El ocaso del poder oligárquico: Lucha política en la escena oficial, 1968-1975*. Lima: Centro de Estudios y Promoción del Desarrollo-DESCO.

Perú-Contraloría General de la República. 1985. "Las Empresas estatales." Contraloría General de la República, Lima.

Perú-Instituto Nacional de Estadística. 1988. "Informe estadístico." Instituto Nacional de Estadística-Dirección General de Indicadores Económicos y Sociales, Lima.

Perú-Instituto Nacional de Planificación. 1971. *Plan del Perú*. Instituto Nacional de Planificación, Lima.

_____. 1977. "Concentración de la producción y estructura de la propiedad." Cuadernos de la Planificación No. 3, Instituto Nacional de Planificación, Lima.

_____. 1980. "Diagnóstico de la realidad nacional." Volume 1. Instituto Nacional de Planificación, Lima.

_____. 1986. "Plan nacional de desarrollo 1986-1990." 2 volumes. Mimeo. Instituto Nacional de Planificación, Lima.

Perú-Ministerio de Economía y Finanzas. 1987. "Principales indicadores económicos de las 250 empresas más importantes." Dirección General de Asuntos Económicos, Lima.

Perú-Ministerio de Industria, Comercio, Turismo e Integración. 1987. "Establecimientos informantes y omisos de 5 a más personas ocupadas." Dirección de Estadística, Lima.

Perú-Ministerio de Industria, Turismo e Integración. 1985. *Desarrollo y planeamiento industrial*. Ministerio de Industria, Turismo e Integración, Lima.

Perú-Senado de la República. 1988. "Violencia y pacificación: Informe general." Senado de la República, Lima.

The Perú Report. 1987. "The Peruvian Financial System at the Time of the Expropriation." Perú Reporting E.I.R.L.

_____. 1988. "The Top One-Thousand Five Hundred Companies in Perú." Perú Reporting, E.I.R.L.

Pfaller, Alfred, et al. 1989. *Perú frente a la economía internacional*. Lima: Fundación Friedrich Ebert.

Pinilla Cisneros, Susana. 1988. "Políticas y programas de promoción de empleo. El PAIT y el IDESI." In Heraclio Bonilla and Paul W. Drake, eds. *El APRA: De la ideología a la praxis*. Lima: Centro Latinoamericano de Historia Económica y Social, and San Diego: Center for Iberian and Latin American Studies, University of California at San Diego.

Porter, Roger B. "The Enterprise for the Americas Initiative: A New Approach to Economic Growth." *Journal of Interamerican Studies and World Affairs* 32, No. 4 (Winter 1990), pp. 1-12.

Portes, Alejandro. 1985. "Latin American Class Structure: Their Composition and Change During the Last Decades." *Latin American Research Review* 20, No. 3, pp. 7-38.

Portocarrero, Felipe. 1976. "El gobierno militar y el capital imperialista." Cuadernos de Sociedad y Política No. 1 (January), Lima.

Portocarrero, Filix. 1980. "Crisis y centralización del capital." *Quehacer*, No. 4 (April), pp. 50-59.

Portocarrero, Gonzalo. 1978. "Empresarios, Sociedad Nacional de Industrias y proceso político." Mimeo. Departamento de Ciencias Sociales, Pontificia Universidad Católica del Perú.

Prebisch, Raul. 1962. "El desarrollo económico de la América Latina y algunos de sus principales problemas." Comisión Económica Para América Latina, Boletín de América Latina 60, Santiago de Chile.

Prieto, Alberto. 1983. *La burguesía latinoamericana comtemporánea.* La Habana: Casa de las Américas.

Przeworski, Adam. 1977. "Proletariat into a Class: The Process of Class Formation from Karl Kautsky's 'The Class Struggle' to Recent Controversies." In *Politics and Society* 7, no. 4, pp. 343-401.

Quijano Obregón, Aníbal. 1971. *Nacionalismo, neo-imperialismo y militarismo en el Perú.* Buenos Aires: Ediciones Periferia.

_____. 1972. "Imperialismo y capitalismo de estado." *Sociedad y Política*, No. 1 (June), pp. 5-18.

_____. 1973. "La respuesta de los trabajadores." *Sociedad y Política*, No. 4 (September), p. 1.

Ramos Tremolada, Ricardo. 1988. "El APRA en vísperas de su XIV congreso." *Quehacer*, No. 53 (July-August), pp. 24-33.

Reaño, Germán and Enrique Vásquez. 1986. "Origen y evolución de los grupos económicos en el Perú: El caso Romero (1890-1985). Bachellor thesis, Departamento de Economía, Universidad del Pacífico.

_____. 1988. *El grupo Romero: Del algodón a la banca.* Lima: Centro de Investigación y Promoción del Campesinado-Centro de Investigaciones de la Universidad el Pacífico.

Rocca Torres, Luis. 1973. *Imperialismo en el Perú: Viejos ataduras y nuevos nudos.* Lima: Imprenta Ramos.

Roncagliolo, Rafael. 1987. "De espinazos y libertades." *Quehacer*, No. 48 (September-October), pp. 29-31.

Rospigliosi, Fernando. 1991. "Empresarios en política." *Caretas* (November 4), p. 25.

Rozas, Patricio and Gustavo Marín. 1989. *1988: El "mapa de la extrema riqueza" 10 años después.* Santiago de Chile: Ediciones Chile América Centro de Estudios de Sociedad.

Rubio Correa, Marcial. 1974. "Evolución de la legislación de las comunidades laborales." Cuadernos DESCO, Lima.

Saberbein Chevalier, Gustavo. 1981. "Políticas de tratamiento al capital extranjero en el grupo andino: El caso del Perú." In DESCO-Centro de Estudios y Promoción del Desarrollo, *Estrategias y políticas de industrialización.* Pp.195-205. Lima: Centro de Estudios y Promoción del Desarrollo-DESCO.

Sachs, Jeffrey D. 1989. "Social Conflict and Populist Policies in Latin America." National Bureau of Economic Research, Inc., Working Paper No. 2897.

Salaverry, José. 1987. "La reforma del sistema financiero peruano." *Banca*, Nos. 21-22 (August-December), pp. 5-13.

Salcedo, José María. 1990. "Tsunami Fujimori." Lima: *La República.*

Salgado, René. 1987. "Economic Pressure Groups and Policy-Making in Venezuela: The Case of FEDECAMARAS." *Latin American Research Review* 22, No. 3, pp. 91-105

Sanborn, Cynthia. 1989. "El APRA en un contexto de cambio, 1968-1988." In Heraclio Bonilla and Paul W. Drake, eds., *El APRA: De la ideología a la praxis.* Pp. 91-123. Lima: Centro Latinoamericano de Historia Económica y Social and Center for Iberian and Latin American Studies/University of California at San Diego.

Sánchez Alvabera, Fernando. 1981. *Minería, capital transnacional y poder en el Perú.* Lima: Centro de Estudios y Promoción del Desarrollo-DESCO.

_____. 1984. "El capital extranjero en la economía Perúana." Comisión Económica Para América Latina, United Nations, E/CEPAL/G.1300 (March), Santiago de Chile.

_____. 1987. "Ajustones y desafios." *Quehacer*, No. 46 (April-May), pp. 8-11.

_____. 1978. *Historia de una industria peruana*. Lima: Empresa Editorial Científica.

Sanfuentes, Andrés. 1984. "Los grupos económicos: Control y políticas." *Estudios CIEPLAN* (Santiago de Chile), No. 15 (December), pp. 131-169.

Saragoza, Alex M. 1989. *The Monterrey Elite and the Mexican State, 1880-1940*. Austin: University of Texas Press.

Saulniers, Alfred H. 1988. *Public Enterprises in Perú: Public Sector Growth and Reform*. Boulder: Westview Press.

Schattschneider, E.E. 1956. *The Semi Sovereign People*. New York: Holt, Rinehart and Winston.

Scheetz, Thomas. 1986. *Perú and the International Monetary Fund*. Pittsburgh: Pittsburg University Press.

Schmidt, Gregory D. 1991. "Electoral Earthquake in Perú: Understanding the Fujimori Phenomenon." Paper presented at the Annual Meeting of the Illinois Conference for Latin American Studies, Loyola University of Chicago, Lake Shore campus, November 1-2, 1991.

Schmitter, Philippe C. and Wolfgang Streek, eds. 1985. *Private Interest Government*. London: SAGE Publications.

Schuldt, Jurgen. 1986. "Desinflación y restructuración económica en el Perú: Modelo para armar." In Persio Arida, et al., *Inflación cero*. Pp. 119-199. Bogotá: Editorial Oveja Negra.

Schvarzer, Jorge. 1989. *Bunge & Born: Crecimiento y diversificación de un grupo económico*. Buenos Aires: CISEA/Grupo Editor Latinoamericano.

Schvarzer, Jorge and Ricardo Sidicaro. 1988. "Empresarios y estado en la reconstrucción de la democracia argentina." In Celso Garrido, ed., *Empresarios y estado en América Latina*. Pp. 231-244. Mexico City: CIDE-UAM-UNAM/Instituto de Investigaciones Sociales-Fundación Friedrich Ebert.

Schydlowsky, Daniel M. 1986. "The Tragedy of Lost Opportunity in Perú." In Jonathan Hartlyn and Samuel A. Morley, eds., *Latin American Political Economy*. Pp. 217-242. Boulder and London: Westview Press.

Scurrah, Martin J. 1987. "The Latin American State and the Politics of Austerity:

Perú, 1980-1985." La Trobe University, Institute of Latin American Studies, Occasional Papers No. 11.

Sifuentes, Pablo. 1988. "Sistema bancario Perúano: Un recuento histórico." *Actualidad Ecónomica del Perú*, No. 100 (June), pp. 46-52.

Silva Colmenares, Julio. 1983. *Tras la máscara del subdesarrollo: Dependencia y monopolios*. Bogotá: Carlos Valencia Editores.

Sistema Nacional de Apoyo a la Movilización Social-SINAMOS. 1975. "Transferencia del poder económico, participación y transformación de la estructura ideológica." 26 volumes. Sistema Nacional de Apoyo a la Mobilización Social (December), Lima.

Soberón, Luis. 1985. "Integración y diferenciación sociales en el sector empresarial." *Socialismo y Participación*, No. 32, pp. 61-75.

Sociedad de Industrias. 1977. *La revolución y la industria*. 2 volumes. Lima: Sociedad de Industrias.

Sociedad Nacional de Industrias. 1986. *Directorio industrial del Perú. 1985-1986*. Lima: Sociedad Nacional de Industrias.

_____. 1987. "La lucha contra la pobreza." *Industria Peruana*, No. 630 (June), pp. 62-67.

Soto, Hernando de. 1989. *The Other Path*. Foreword by Mario Vargas Llosa. Translated by June Abbott. New York: Harper and Row, Publishers.

Soto, Hernando de and Stephan Schmidheiny, eds. 1991. *Las nuevas reglas del juego*. Bogotá: Editorial Oveja Negra.

Spalding, Rose. 1992. "The 'Political Awakening' of the Nicaraguan Bourgeoisie: From Elite Quiescence to Elite Confrontation in Pre-Revolutionary Nicaragua." Paper presented at the 88th Annual Meeting of the American Political Science Association, Chicago, Illinois, September 3-6.

Stallings, Barbara. 1983. "International Capitalism and the Peruvian Military Government." In Abraham Lowenthal and Cynthia McClintock, eds., *The Peruvian Experiment Reconsidered*. Pp. 144-180. Princeton: Princeton University Press.

Stallings, Barbara and Robert Kauffman, eds. 1989. *Debt and Democracy in Latin America*. Boulder and San Francisco: Westview Press.

Stanworth, Philip and Anthony Giddens, eds. 1975. *Elites and Power in British Society*. 2nd. Edition. Cambridge: Cambridge University Press.

Stepan, Albert. 1978. *The State and Society*. Princeton: Princeton University Press.

Stepan, Alfred, ed. 1989. *Democratizing Brazil*. New York: Oxford University Press.

Stolovich, Luis, Juan Manuel Rodríguez and Luis Bértola. 1988. 4th Edition. *El poder económico en el Uruguay actual*. Montevideo: Centro Uruguay Independiente.

Story, Dale. 1978. "Industrialization and Political Change: The Political Role of Industrial Entrepreneurs in Five Latin American Countries." Doctoral Dissertation, Department of Political Science, Indiana University.

Strachan, Harry W. 1976. *Family and Other Business Groups in Economic Development: The Case of Nicaragua*. New York: Praeger Publishers.

Strassman, Paul. 1964. "The Industrialist." In John J. Johnson, ed., *Continuity and Change in Latin America*. Pp. 161-185. Stanford: Stanford University Press.

Sulmont, Denis. 1977. *El movimiento obrero peruano, 1890-1977*. Lima: Editorial Tarea.

Thompson, Andrés. 1987. "Los partidos políticos en América Latina." CEDES-CLACSO, Grupo de Trabajo de Estudios Políticos, Buenos Aires.

Thompson, E. P. 1979. *Tradición, revuelta y conciencia de clase*. Barcelona: Editorial Crítica.

Thorne, Alfredo. 1987. *Ahorro neto y financiamiento del desarrollo*. Lima: Fundación Friedrich Ebert.

Thorp, Rosemary. 1984. "Políticas de ajuste en el Perú, 1978-1985." *Economía 7*, No. 14 (December), pp. 81-115.

_____. 1986. "The APRA Alternative in Perú." *The Perú Report*, No. 6 (June), Special Supplement.

Thorp, Rosemary and Geoffrey Bertram. 1978. *Perú 1890-1977: Growth and Policy in an Open Economy*. New York: Columbia University Press.

Torres Guzmán, Alejandro. 1984. "Evolución política de los empresarios." *Debate*, No. 30 (December), pp. 14-20.

Touraine, Alain. 1987. *Actores sociales y sistemas políticos en América Latina*. Santiago de Chile: PREALC.

Tueros, Mario. 1983. "Autogestión y propiedad social." In Carlos Franco, coordinador, *El Perú de Velasco*. Volume 3. Pp. 843-880. Lima: Ediciones Centro de Estudios y Participación.

Tuesta Soldevilla, Fernando. 1985. *El nuevo rostro electoral del Perú: Las municipales de 1983*. Lima: Centro de Estudios y Promoción del Desarrollo-DESCO.

_____. 1986. *Perú 1985: El derrotero de una nueva elección*. Lima: Centro de Investigaciones de la Universidad del Pacífico-Fundación Friedrich Ebert.

_____. 1987. *Perú político en cifras: Elite política y elecciones*. Lima: Fundación Friedrich Ebert.

Turner, John, ed. 1984. *Businessmen and Politics*. London and Exeter: Heineman.

Ugarteche, Oscar. 1986. *El estado deudor: Economía política de la deuda, Perú y Bolivia 1968-1984*. Lima: Instituto de Estudios Perúanos.

Universidad del Pacífico. nd. "El parlamento en el Perú: Un perfil social y político de sus representantes." Centro de Investigaciones de la Universidad del Pacífico, Lima.

Useem, Michael. 1984. *The Inner Circle*. New York and Oxford: Oxford University Press.

Valderrama, Mariano. 1976. *7 años de reforma agraria peruana*. Lima: Pontificia Universidad Católica del Perú-Fondo Editorial.

Valderrama, Mariano and Patricia Ludmann. 1979. *La oligarquía terrateniente ayer y hoy*. Lima: Departamento de Ciencias Sociales-Pontificia Universidad Católica del Perú.

Vargas Llosa, Alvaro. 1991. *El diablo en campaña*. Madrid: El País/Aguilar.

Vargas Llosa, Mario. 1987. "Hacia el Perú totalitario." *El Comercio* (August 2).

_____. 1991. "A Fish Out of Water." *Granta* (London), 36,(Summer), pp. 15-75.

Velasco E. Cruz, Sebastiao C. 1988. "Doce años después: El antiestatismo en el discurso empresarial brasileño." In Celso Garrido, ed., *Empresarios y estado en América Latina*. Pp. 287-306. Mexico City: CIDE-UAM-UNAM/Instituto de Investigaciones Sociales-Fundación Friedrich Ebert.

Velasco, Juan. 1972. *Velasco: La voz de la revolución*. 2 volumes. Lima: Sistema Nacional de Apoyo a la Mobilización Social.

Vergara, Ricardo. 1983. "Un futuro diferente...al de Haya primigenio." *Quehacer*, No. 21 (February), pp. 48-51.

Villafuerte Kanemoto, Martín, et al. 1986. *Reactivación industrial de corto y mediano plazo*. Lima: Fundación Friedrich Ebert.

Vogel, David. 1989. *Fluctuating Fortunes: The Political Power of Business in America*. New York: Basic Books, Inc., Publishers.

Waisman, Carlos H. 1982. *Modernization of the Working Class: The Politics of Legitimacy*. Austin: University of Texas Press.

Webb Duarte, Richard. 1981. "Perú: Economía rentista." In Instituto Libertad y Democracia, eds., *Democracia & economía de mercado*. Lima: Instituto Libertad y Democracia.

Webb Duarte, Richard and Graciela Fernández Baca. 1992. *Perú en números 1991: Anuario estadístico*. Lima: Cuanto.

Weber, Max. 1964. *Economía y sociedad*. 2 volumes. 2nd Edition in Spanish. Mexico City: Fondo de Cultura Económica.

Weeks, John. 1985. *Limits to Capitalist Development: The Industrialization of Perú, 1950-1980*. Boulder: Westview Press.

Weyland, Kurt. 1992. "The Dispersion of Business Influence in Brazil's New Democracy." Paper presented at the 88th Annual Meeting of the American Political Science Association, Chicago, Illinois, September 3-6.

Wils, Fritz. 1979. *Industrialization, Industrialists and the Nation-State in Perú*. Berkeley: Institute of International Studies.

Windmuller, John P. and Alan Gladstone. 1984. *Employers' Association and Industrial Relations.* Oxford: Oxford University Press, 1984.

Wise, Carol. 1986. "The Perils of Orthodoxy: Perú's Political Economy." *NACLA Report on the Americas* 20, No. 3 (June), pp. 14-26.

_____. 1988. "Perú's Political Economy 1980-1987. Responses to the Debt Crisis: From Neoliberalism to New Orthodoxy." Paper presented at the Latin American Studies Association meetings, New Orleans, Louisiana, March.

_____. 1990. "Perú Post 1968: The Political Limits to State-Led Economic Development." Doctoral Dissertation, Department of Political Science, Columbia University.

_____. 1992. "Post-War Perú: State Policy and Social Conflict." Center for Politics and Policy Studies, The Claremont Graduate School, September 1992.

World Bank. 1981. "Perú: Principales cuestiones y recomendaciones en materia de desarrollo." Banco Mundial, Washington D.C.

_____. 1985. "Perú: Country Economic Memorandum." World Bank, Washington D.C.

_____. 1989. *World Debt Tables: External Debt of Developing Countries.* 2 volumes. Washington D.C.: World Bank.

Zeitlin, Maurice and Richard Earl Ratcliff. 1988. *Capitalists & Landlords: The Dominant Class in Chile.* Princeton: Princeton University Press.

Zuzunaga Flores, Carlos, ed. 1985. *Las empresas públicas en el Perú.* Lima: Fundación Friedrich Ebert.

Index